THE OFF-ROAD FOUR WHEEL DRIVE BOOK

by
Jack Jackson

Foulis

Haynes
®

A FOULIS Motoring Book

First published, by Gentry Books Ltd, 1982
Reprinted 1985

© Jack Jackson 1988

Published by:
Haynes Publishing Group
Sparkford, Nr. Yeovil, Somerset BA22 7JJ

Haynes Publications Inc.
861 Lawrence Drive, Newbury Park, California 91320 USA

British Library Cataloguing in Publication Data
Jackson, Jack
  The off-road four wheel drive book.
  1. Four-wheel-drive off-road cars –
  Illustrations
  I. Title
629.2'222
ISBN 0-85429-673-5

Editor: Rob Iles
Page Layout: Chris Hull

THE
OFF-ROAD
FOUR WHEEL DRIVE
BOOK

Dedication

This book is dedicated to all those who have travelled with me, sharing not only the joys of remote areas, but also the trials and tribulations of getting stuck or overturned vehicles mobile again.

Disclaimer

Because vehicles and parts change and methods of application vary the author disclaims any liability incurred in connection with the use of any or all of the data and ideas contained in this book.

Acknowledgements

The author would like to thank David Bowyer (Overlander) for the up to date list of four wheel drive clubs and Dave Shephard for some 20 photographs from his personal photographic collection. Apart from a few Dealer promotional shots, all other photographs are by the author.

Contents

Preface

As a working four wheel driver I am naturally biased towards reliable strongly built 'working' four wheel drive vehicles. However from the manufacturer's point of view 'working' vehicles are becoming less marketable, whilst despite the economic gloom, the recreational four wheel drive market is expanding and most vehicle manufacturers are once again putting at least one four wheel drive model on the market, even if it means importing a Japanese vehicle under their own trade name (eg Holden Australia and Bedford UK).

Due to lack of serious competition many top four wheel drive vehicle manufacturers have continued producing the same four wheel drive vehicles for many years ignoring modern trends and customer requirements, but now that competition is increasing these manufacturers will be forced into improving their breed if they are not to lose much of the market. Such competition is good for producing four wheel drives to suit the buying public, but due to constant changes and up dating it makes it more difficult for manufacturers to keep a good cross section of spares available worldwide. Not surprisingly it also means that any book of this nature will be out of date as soon as it goes to print due to new or re-vamped vehicles being announced all the time, however, as always only the few vehicles that suit the market and stay reliable will still be around in a few years time. So in general the same reliable manufacturers are likely to stay around with much the same vehicles for many years to come.

There is a tendency for smaller four wheel drive vehicles to be fitted with independent front suspension or independent suspension all round. This considerably improves road handling but rigid axles are better in rough country as they keep the ground clearance high, for instance: when one wheel goes over a large rock or hump the whole axle lifts and the transfer case and differentials are therefore less vulnerable; similarly soft sprung vehicles, besides throwing occupants about when off the road, can often get completely out of control if you hit an unexpected bump or dip. Firm springing means better adaptation to off-road conditions, stability and good ground clearance with consequent driver confidence that he is in full control of the vehicle.

Alongside the four wheel drive market there has developed a considerable industry in four wheel drive accessories, many of which are purely cosmetic, although some are almost essential, eg to beef up weak or road type suspensions for proper off-road use. Some accessories are essential items to particular uses, eg limited slip or locking differentials which many four wheel drive manufacturers supplied in the past but stopped doing so because most of their customers either did not require them, could not handle them, failed to understand why such things wear out, or did serious damage to the rest of the drive train by using them in the wrong conditions.

When an experienced four wheel driver reads a test report on a four wheel drive vehicle in a normal auto magazine or newspaper it is painfully obvious that most drivers, no matter how expert they are with two wheel drive vehicles, have little idea of what a four wheel drive vehicle should or should not be able to do. Therefore if you want to know about a particular four wheel drive vehicle, read only test reports in specialist four wheel drive magazines and then talk to owners of such vehicles, better still join a four wheel drive club and see the different vehicles in action.

As with most things you get what you pay for, the extra cost of a stronger item saves money in the end, so think before you buy. If you want to fit over-size tyres and wheels get the correct axle ratio and engine power in the first place, heavy duty shock absorbers and road springs are essential for off-road use and for towing. If you do not have much ground clearance you can fit underside protection plates, but it would have been better to buy a vehicle with more ground clearance and chassis protected vital parts in the first place. If your vehicle cannot be used with a high lift jack without damage then you cannot afford to get it stuck anywhere. If you must have a winch get one big enough to do the job with power in reserve.

Most people when they first buy a four wheel drive think it can go anywhere and immediately get it stuck, with consequent damage to bodywork and transmission getting it unstuck, or to wallet and pride having to get a tow from a recovery wagon. The answer is, most four wheel drives will go anywhere under the right conditions and with the right driving skill, so don't rush into things, learn slowly by trying harder and harder things a little at a time, get to know the limitations of your vehicle (for some vehicles the limit will be your own nerve) and by staying within this limit you will have a lot of fun.

Introduction
Why Four Wheel Drive?

Why, you might ask, do we need four wheel drive. In the easier sections of the Sahara Desert one often sees Volkswagen Minibuses, Peugeot 404's, Renault 4's and Citroen Deux Chevaux's; in fact two wheel drive will probably, in good conditions, get to 90% of places where four wheel drive is normally used. The answer is that for off the road transport it is that extra 10% of places plus the unexpected event which requires four wheel drive.

At Easter in 1972 the unexpected happened and it rained hard for three days in the central Sahara Desert. I was leading a five Land Rover convoy full of tourists and as we finished the expedition coming north from Djanet we found ourselves having to rescue five two wheel drive vehicles, spread over 250 miles,

Mud and snow makes four wheel drive essential. International Harvester Travelall and an early Chevrolet K20 (Afghanistan 9000 ft).

Desert transport old and new: a Land Rover meets one of the famous historical salt caravans in the Sahara's Tenéré sand sea, Niger

before reaching the paved road. Under normal conditions these vehicles would have succeeded in their proposed journeys, but the heavy rain had washed away the main tracks so these vehicles had got bogged down in soft sand and mud and were lucky that we came along and were able to rescue them. In short, wherever you are likely to encounter a lot of sand, mud or snow four wheel drive is a distinct advantage.

If you wish to drive in rough terrain there are good mechanical reasons for buying a four wheel drive rather than the average family car. A four wheel drive is designed for rough conditions. It has high ground clearance, a stronger frame suspension and transmission, a sturdy engine with filters designed to keep out dust and grit and a cooling system large enough to cope with long periods at slow speeds, steep hills and high ambient temperatures. It has low gears to tackle the steepest slopes and to edge slowly over large boulders plus obviously increased traction over loose and difficult surfaces. Even on paved road four wheel drive gives improved steering plus directional stability on snow or wet surfaces. Being higher off the ground you get better visibility and easier maintenance.

Being designed for a wide range of applications four wheel drives are offered with a wide range of optional equipment so you can tailor your vehicle to your own particular needs. One very important point is that four wheel drives are made to last and do not suffer from annual styling changes, thus after three years the value of your four wheel drive will have kept up with inflation whereas a standard family saloon, bought at the same time, will be almost worthless. Even after several Sahara crossings a Land Rover can usually be resold for a good price, or even a profit, whereas a normal car would be a write-off after one such expedition.

Chapter 1
Four Wheel Drive Evolution

Four wheel drive is not new. When automobiles were first being made in Europe it was reasoned that if you had four wheels you should drive four wheels, as it would spread the driving load. The main problem was that they were using solid axles, thus no differentials so that the torque wind-up between axles and also between wheels on the same axle tended to break up the drive rather quickly and in the 1890s the idea was abandoned.

The first working four wheel drive vehicle was by the Spijker brothers in 1902, this was also probably the first car to have a six cylinder engine. The improved traction and cornering power, especially under acceleration, was most beneficial on wet tracks and the car won a Birmingham Motor Club Hill Climb in 1906 during heavy rain. The engine was 8.8 litres, had a bore of 120 mm and stroke of 128 mm and a compression ration of 4.59 to 1.

It was intended for use on the slippery roads of the Dutch East Indies but was never put into production. The Spijker four wheel drive was designed in 1902 with six separately cast cylinders, originally 5.07 litres with bore 91 mm and stroke 130 mm producing 36/50 hp. It was enlarged in 1903 to 8.817 litres with a bore of 120 mm and stroke of 130 mm producing 60/80 hp.

Each cylinder had its own water jacket and there were two cam shafts, one on each side of the one piece cast aluminium crankcase, operating side valves in a T head. There was a single inlet manifold and carburettor but the exhaust manifolds were constructed in three pairs. Ignition was by magneto. Cooling was by two radiators set in a V shape. The cone clutch was leather faced.

Transmission was via a Cardan shaft to a separate gearbox containing two sets (high and low) of three forward and one reverse gears ie: six forward and two reverse. The prop shafts ran to the right of centre line of the vehicle to off-set differentials on the front and rear live axles. A contracting transmission brake acted on the front prop shaft. Both prop shafts had universal joints and were enclosed in torque tubes. Suspension was by semi-elliptic leaf springs all round without shock absorbers. The rear brakes were of the external contracting type operated both by pedal and hand lever.

Drive was transmitted through a cone clutch seated within the flywheel to a 3 speed and one reverse gearbox with two ratio's effectively giving the car six forward speeds. A system of gears stepped the drive to the right of the chassis with prop shafts to live axles at front and rear. The rear prop shaft was enclosed within a torque tube while the front prop shaft had a universal coupling just in front of the gearbox and was then enclosed from that point forward to the front axle.

The US Army caught on early to the four wheel drive principle as an answer to 'all terrain' vehicles. In 1911 the US Army invited a number of truck manufacturers to participate in a 1,500 mile run from Washington DC to Indianapolis, Indiana. One of the successful trucks was a four wheel drive light 'Scout Car' built by FWD Corporation of Clintonville, Wisconsin. It completed the run in 49 days at an average speed of 1·27 miles per hour which was a very good performance for that day and age.

In 1911 the Nash Motor Company produced the Quad; this had full time four wheel drive with locking differential and its rigid axles were of the step down type as used in modern day Unimogs ie: the drive at the wheel is above its centre line to give more ground clearance and there is a gear on the end of the half shaft which drives an internal gear fixed to the brake drum; 41,000 of these were made between 1914 and 1928, it had four wheel steering. In 1916 many four wheel drive cargo trucks, made by FWD Corporation and Jeffery, were used in the Mexican punitive expedition and proved very successful; in the past mules had been used. The same trucks were also used in France during the First World War.

These early four wheel drives had permanent four wheel drive which worked well enough on the rough tracks in use. Attempts to eliminate the wind-up problem between axles were made by putting a third differential at the transfer case between the front and rear axles. This worked well on hard terrain and protected the front and rear axle from trapped loads, but it had no limited slip or locking device such as on modern four wheel drives, so if one wheel lost traction everything went from four wheel drive to no wheel drive, so it was back to the drawing board.

In 1919 William Walter worked out a truly optimum four wheel drive system. In the typical bevel gear spider of a differential the problem is that the

Nash Quad under restoration (Nash later name for Jeffery).

11

Spijker.

device can run forward or backward at equal ratio, this balances the drive load between wheels and if one wheel slips it takes all the traction and spins at twice the speed but nothing goes anywhere. Walter replaced the bevel gears by a worm gear. The worm gear is essentially irreversible or can be cut to the degree of reversibility required. So then he had a differential on which a tractionless wheel could not spin; it would let an outside wheel go faster than an inside wheel, but if one wheel tried to go a lot faster than the other it could not. This is a true all wheel system without any limited slip clutches, dogs or locking mechanism. Unfortunately you cannot get this system for a recreational four wheel drive as it is only built for large commercial equipment like snowploughs, fire engines etc. So initially plans were made for part time four wheel drive until better designs came along.

After World War One the US Army played around with four wheel drive conversions of the Model T Ford and a few other things, but in 1935 the US Army took delivery of a Dodge 1½ ton truck which had selective four wheel drive. This was the first time that a driver was given the choice between two wheel drive for hard surface work and four wheel drive for cross country work. These Dodge 1½ tonners were followed in 1937 by a Marmon-Herrington ½ ton truck with the same four wheel drive system which later became known as the Grandaddy of the Jeep. The Japanese, by now, had the Kurogane 4 × 4 light scout car with a 1.320 litre air cooled V twin engine, a three speed gearbox and 79 inch wheelbase. Some 5,000 of these were eventually produced.

In 1939, with the advent of World War Two in Europe the US Army realized that the conflict would soon spread and they designed a requirement for a ¼ ton 4 × 4 light truck. Fortunately the American Bantam company, now out of business, had been looking at the problem and were able to offer quick delivery of a prototype in just three months for late September 1940. The Bantam as it

Ford Pygmy.

was known, had a Continental Motors 40 hp, four cylinder L head engine, Spicer four wheel drive components and a hand made body. At nearly 2,090 lbs it was much heavier than it was supposed to be, but on test it did everything that was expected of it and it got American Bantam an order for 69 pre-production models.

The US Army needed volume production so it invited a number of other manufacturers to come and look the Bantam over. One of these companies was Willys-Overland who set out to build their own prototype which arrived for testing in November 1940. It was heavier than the Bantam but was more powerful. It had Willys-Overland's 60 hp 4 cylinder L head 'Go-Devil' engine, so despite the increased weight it outperformanced the Bantam and was called the Quad. Ford built their own prototype weighing 2,200 lbs and powered by a modified 4 cylinder L head tractor engine. The Ford prototype had a flat bonnet which was a better design than the Willys and the Bantam because it added useable space to the body. The Ford model was named the Pygmy. All three vehicles used the Spicer four wheel drivetrain.

As all three prototypes were successful the US Army ordered 500 of each and later increased this to 1,500 of each, they stipulated the use of Ford's flat bonnet on all models. The Bantam (BRC 40) had the new flat bonnet and was the same as the prototype except for increasing the engine to 45 hp; it weighed 2,050 lbs and had a 79″ wheelbase. The Willys-Overland Quad (MA) had the flat bonnet, 60 hp engine, weighed 2,450 lbs and had an 80″ wheelbase; its more powerful engine made it the most mobile. The Ford Pygmy (GP for general purpose) was almost identical to the prototype, the engine was increased to 45

13

hp, it weighed 2,150 lbs and had an 80″ wheelbase. The US Army designated all three vehicles as 'light Command and Reconnaissance Cars ¼ ton 4 × 4'. Deliveries began from Ford in April 1941 and from Bantam and Willys a few weeks later. They were an immediate success with army personnel making the Solo and Sidecar motorcycles obsolete. The Press were soon glorifying them, which made them popular with civilians, but only a few 'excess' Bantams were sold before the end of the war.

The first combat use of these four wheel drives was by the British in North Africa in 1941 and later in the same year the Russians also received some. Action reports were exceptional, especially from the British Long Range desert patrol group. The word 'Jeep' probably originated from two unrelated circumstances: the most common model in use with the US Army in 1941 was the Ford Model GP which was the first model delivered in quantity; there was also a character called Eugene, the Jeep in the comic strip Popeye, who could do anything. Pronounce GP and use the comic strip's Jeep and you get the same thing. Willys-Overland, who became the main producer of the vehicle, adopted the name Jeep as their trademark and American Motors still owns the trademark today. Willys were not the first to use this name as it was used earlier for a Minneapolis—Moline farm tractor.

After building their first 1,500 Pygmys Ford dropped out because they were overwhelmed with other work, Bantam were not so fortunate and so continued to build Bantams. Willys-Overland completed their 1,500 quota and then took a second look at their design. The US Army obviously preferred to have only one vehicle, for spares supply reasons, and Willys' new model, the MB, won the new trials and they were given an order for 16,000 model MB Jeeps. Bantam were upset but were not really big enough to manage the volume production required. The US Army needed more production so Ford were asked to also manufacture the model MB under licence to Willys-Overland—the two vehicles were identical and all parts inter-changeable. All had the 60 hp Go-Devil engine, an 80″ wheelbase, Spicer drivetrain and weighed 2,325 lbs.

Various modifications were experimented with, including four wheel steering, six wheel drive, a lightweight model for airborne use and even an amphibious model called Seep, but none were really successful. The Russians liked the Seep for river crossings and have since copied it. In all 638,000 Jeeps were built during the war, 360,000 by Willys and 278,000 by Ford. Some 87,000 of these went to the British and 46,000 to the Russians. However by 1943 the Russians were making their own copy of the Jeep, the GAZ 67. At the end of the war the US Army had enough Jeeps and spares to keep the vehicles in working condition until after the Korean War in the 1950's. Germany also produced some 13,000 4 × 4 amphibious Kubelwagon 166's between 1942 and 1944 called the Schwimmwagens.

Into Civilian Use: at the end of the war surplus Jeeps were being snatched up by civilian buyers at high prices, so Willys realised that it was worth bringing out a model for the civilian market, designated CJ for Civilian Jeep. They were practically identical to the military model, but the buyers were willing to put up with the discomfort to get the benefit of four wheel drive, especially as it was the only 4 × 4 available. Willys then produced the Jeepster, originally two wheel drive, but later the commando four wheel drive.

Ford Jeep with trailer.

With the war now over automobile manufacturers in Britain were caught between the problem of needing to get their factories back into civilian production and the drastic shortage of sheet steel for body pressings. The British Government were forced to ration sheet steel supplies with preference being given to vehicles for export, which meant that the Rover company needed a stop gap. Rover realised that one way round the problem was to use aluminium alloy pressings for body panels, box section steel chassis members and also, if possible, produce some sort of agricultural machine. Maurice Wilks sparked off the idea of the Land Rover because he needed a versatile farm machine; he had been using an old Jeep which did much of what he asked and he realised that building such a vehicle was the stop gap Rover needed. He was wrong about the 'stop gap', production of the Land Rover from the first moment it came onto the market could never keep up with worldwide demand.

The original Land Rover was announced in April 1948, it was very much modelled around the Jeep but had to be more useful to the farmer. It had the same wheelbase of 80″ and was 1″shorter than the Jeep at 132″; its wheeltrack was 2″ wider due to using Rover's existing P3 axle; axle ratios, tyre size and suspension were the same but the gearbox was a 4 speed against the Jeep's 3 speed with ratios 1.0, 1.49, 2.04, 2.99:1. The transfer gear low range was greater at 2.52 step down than the Jeep's 1.97 step down. Like the Jeep there was synchromesh on the top two gears. The new Land Rover made use of Rover's new P3 engine unit, which was a 4-cylinder 1595 cc overhead inlet valve and side exhaust valve engine, 69.5 mm bore, 105 mm stroke producing 55 bhp gross at 4,000 rpm compared with the Jeep's 60 bhp at 3,600 rpm.

The unladen weight was 2,520 lbs. The Land Rover's greatest advantage was in its versatility with provision for centre and rear power take-offs and other fittings built into the original design for driving such things as: compressors, generators, saws, pumps etc and a front mounted capstan winch. All this plus the benefit of Birmabright alloy body panels which were almost corrosion proof. These alloy body panels are still the big advantage of Land Rovers and Range Rovers today, because all other production four wheel drives have steel body shells with their attendant corrosion problems. The Jeep at this stage had selective two wheel drive or four wheel drive, but the new Land Rover had

One of the first – No 4 (Land Rover Series I) rests at the National Motor Museum.

Series I SWB Land Rover spruced up and fitted with alloy wheels.

Kurogane (Japan).

permanent four wheel drive with a free wheel between the transfer box and the front propeller shaft thus avoiding enforced wind-up on roads.

The Land Rover was an immediate success, 8,000 were built in 1948-49 and 16,085 the following year. Things moved quickly and new versions were produced to meet the demand for more comfort; hard top models, vans with windows, truck cab derivatives and a seven seat station wagon were soon available. In 1950 the permanent four wheel drive with freewheel in the front drivetrain was dropped in favour of two wheel drive in high range, with four wheel drive if required, and four wheel drive only in low range. Around the same time as the Land Rover, Dodge came out with their Power Wagon, Datsun brought out the Nissan Patrol and Toyota their Jeep-type Land Cruiser.

By 1952 Austin finally put their long awaited Champ (FV 1800) into production; it had an 84″ wheelbase but weighed a hefty 3,500 lbs and though only 12 ft long it was bulky, expensive and heavy on fuel. It had a cruciform chassis design with all four wheel independent suspension, with the front and rear differentials mounted on the chassis. It was powered by the 4 cylinder 2.8 litre B40 Rolls Royce engine. It had a 5 speed all synchromesh gearbox with all speeds also operating in reverse. Four wheel drive was optional and was achieved by connecting the front and rear differentials by a propeller shaft running the length of the chassis inside the cruciform. The Austin Champ was originally built for the British Army but the Land Rover was proving to be a better all round performer, especially during the Korean War. However milit-

Land Rover Series 1.

Nissan Patrol pick-up.

Austin Champ.

ary orders were insufficient so some civilian changes were implemented, but demand for the Austin Champ fizzled out by the mid-1950's. In the 1950's all European manufacturers produced four wheel drives, either alone or in partnership with other companies; but most designs had only small production runs and few are still around today.

By the mid-1950's Jeeps with the CJ5s became longer, wider and more powerful and the M38 was introduced for military use. In 1952 Land Rover turned to a larger engine of 1,997cc with a bore of 69.5 mm and a stroke of 105 mm, with only 2 bhp more but much improved low speed torque. In 1954 the wheelbase was increased to 86″ and a new long wheelbase model of 107″ was introduced, both models were stretched a further 2″ to 88″ and 109″ in 1956 and have remained as such till this day. This extra 2″ was needed to accommodate the new diesel engine brought out in 1957, it was the first diesel engine made with a new all overhead valve 2,052 cc unit, bore 85.7 mm, stroke 88.9 mm, compression ratio 22.5:1, producing 51 bhp at 3,500 rpm, maximum torque 87 lbs ft at 2,000 rpm. Many parts of this engine were shared with the new 2,286 cc petrol unit which came out in 1958 together with new 'barrel' shaped body side panels, these new models being designated Series II. Also in 1957 Russia brought out the first Uaz four wheel drive. In 1961 the Land Rover diesel engine was enlarged to the same size as the petrol engine at 2,286 cc and the models were then designated series IIA. Both engines now had a bore of 90.47 mm and a stroke of 88.9 mm and all overhead valves. The diesel engine produced 62 bhp at 4,000 rpm and maximum torque 103 lb ft at 1,800 rpm. The petrol engine produced 70 bhp at 4,250 rpm and maximum torque 124 lb ft at 2,500 rpm.

Jeep M38.

Land Rover Series II A.

Fiat Campagnola (1951).

Austin Gipsy.

21

Competition was hotting up by 1958, the Willys Jeep was beginning to find substantial overseas markets, many being built under licence even in France and Japan. Fiat had brought out the Campagnola, Austin had produced the Gipsy. More American manufacturers were looking into more comfortable four wheel drives while the Japanese were just beginning to produce their own four wheel drives, and Steyr Puch had brought out their Haflinger. The Austin Gipsy also had a choice of petrol or diesel engines and a similar four wheel drive system to the Land Rover but it only had one wheelbase (90"); it also had four wheel independent suspension but pressed steel bodywork, whereas Land Rover's corrosion proof light alloy body was one of its biggest selling points.

The Gipsy's trailing link suspension used rubber in torsion instead of steel springs which meant that the front and rear differentials were mounted on the chassis and needed articulated drive shafts to each wheel. Therefore whilst the wheels pounded up and down on rough terrain the differential did not, thus making them more prone to failure. The independent suspension meant that the driver could drive faster at more comfort to himself thus increasing the wear and damage still further. The vehicle soon got a reputation for poor reliability. A long wheelbase version (111") came out in 1960 and in 1962 the suspension was changed through an independent front suspension rigid axle rear suspension to a full Land Rover type suspension with rigid axles and half-elliptic leaf springs. The vehicle never sold well and was withdrawn in 1968 when Leyland (now Rover's parent company) merged with BMC.

International Harvester Travelall on snow at 11,000 ft in Afghanistan

In the sixties International Harvester picked just about the right time to bring out their more comfortable compact four wheel drive, the Scout, and found that the most successful model was the enclosed estate car type. This led other manufacturers to believe that four wheel drive was to be a popular thing of the future and so they began to get involved: Citroen produced a twin engined 2CV, Austin produced a twin engined Mini Moke, Sinpar converted many Renaults, Cournil started limited production, Steyr Puch added the larger PinzGauer, Triumph their Pony and the Chinese made their Peking BJ212. In 1960 Toyota brought out their Land Cruiser (which was very much like the Nissan Patrol). In 1962 Land Rover brought out their 12 seater station wagon, thus avoiding the crippling British Purchase Tax levied on the 10 seater and a forward control 30 cwt model. Ford brought out the Bronco in 1965 and Chevrolet their Blazer in 1967 from a hybrid of the front end of their ½ ton pick up truck and the rear end of the Suburban. Chrysler copied suit and converted an existing pick-up as the Dodge's and Plymouth's entry into four wheel drive.

On the American market, with its cheap petrol, the accent was on more and more power proceeding through straight 6s to V8s, whilst the Japanese were close behind with big straight 6s. However Europe was suffering from high fuel costs so it was not until 1966 that Land Rover offered its 6 cylinder 2,625 cc

Toyota Land Cruiser FJ55 station wagon.

Land Rover ½ ton 'lightweight' designed for air lifting.

petrol engine for the long wheelbase and forward control models, though by American standards it was still small. The wheelbase of the forward control model was enlarged to 110″ and the wheel track increased by 4″ for increased stability.

In 1968 two new Land Rovers came out, a one ton version of the long wheelbase 109″ model with the 6 cylinder engine, lower ratio transfer box, stronger rear springs and heavier Salisbury rear and EMV front axles and a lightweight stripped ½ ton military version of the short wheelbase 88″ model, which in stripped down form could be dropped by parachute. In 1970 Land Rover changed things dramatically by bringing out the Range Rover, this embodied the advantages of a comfortable, level riding fast car with an exceptional off the road vehicle. It had a 100″ wheelbase, permanent four wheel drive with a limited slip but lockable third differential (the limited slip feature was dropped in 1971), a new four speed all synchromesh gearbox with a two speed transfer box, live axles front and rear suspended on vertical coil springs, a self levelling Boge Hydromat strut and disc brakes all round with split hydraulic circuits. Disc brakes have a distinct advantage over drum brakes for off the road use, where water crossings are frequent, because they dry out almost immediately and do not trap dust. To power all this Rover used the powerful light alloy, 3.5 litre V8 ex Buick engine from General Motors.

LWB Safari Land Rover V8.

The Range Rover had jumped the gun somewhat but the American manufacturers were soon to follow suit with disc brakes and permanent four wheel drive. In 1971 Land Rover changed to an all synchromesh gearbox on all models except the one ton and put the stronger rear Salisbury axle from the one ton model onto the long wheelbase models, these models were designated Series III. The V8 engine was 3,528 cc, bore 88.9 mm stroke 71.1 mm, compression ratio 8.5:1, producing 135 bhp at 4,750 rpm, maximum torque 205 lb ft at 3,000 rpm. The Range Rovers' axle ratios were 3.54:1, gearbox ratios were 4.16, 6.25, 10.17, 16.91 and reverse 15.23:1; low range step down ratio was 3.321:1 giving 11.76, 17.69, 28.78, 47.84 and reverse 43.07:1.

The V8 engine was tested in a 109″ estate Land Rover in the Sahara in 1971 but not put into production. Then from 1975 to 1978 a special 101″ wheelbase one ton military version of the Land Rover was produced with the 3.5 litre V8 engine and Range Rover drivetrain and live axles, but with half elliptic leaf springs, drum brakes, high floatation 9.00 × 16″ tyres, permanent four wheel drive with the third axle, axle ratio 5.57:1, gear ratios high 6.54, 9.84, 16.01, 26.55 and reverse 23.97:1, low range stop down ratio 3.321:1 giving 18.50, 27.84, 45.29, 75.11 and reverse 67.80:1. The unladen weight was 4,040 lbs and maximum payload 2,204 lb. The original model had a rear power take-off to give 6 × 6 capability with a powered trailer, but this was only ever used on a west to east trans Africa proving expedition. This vehicle faced competition from Volvo's 4,140 series.

When feedback from overseas markets showed that the Japanese competition was gaining a larger percentage of the market because of their higher paved road speeds, Rover countered with their 3.5 litre V8 engine with Range Rover type drivetrain which became available in the Series III 109″ wheelbase Land Rover with live axles on half elliptic leaf springs. The compression ratio is lowered to 8:1 producing 91 bhp at 3,500 rpm, maximum torque 166 lb ft at 2,000 rpm, axle ratios 3.54:1, high range step down ratio 1.336:1. Overall gear ratio 4.73, 7.12, 11.57, 19.24 and reverse 17.33:1, low range step down ratio 3.321:1 giving 11.75, 17.68, 28.76, 47.81 and reverse 43.05:1. Further bored out versions of this V8 engine exist in Australia and have already been used in specials in Britain so who knows what may yet come out in the 80s.

American manufacturers, still with the advantage of cheap fuel, concentrated more on larger models and driver comfort such as power steering and automatic transmission. Following the Range Rover, Jeep brought out the Wagoneer and Cherokee series, with the Borg Warner Quadra Trac permanent four wheel drive system and Chrysler's New Process gear division brought out their New Process 'permanent' four wheel drive system for their vehicles. In 1976 International Harvester's Scout became the first American built passenger car to be fitted with a diesel engine. Ford added independent front suspension to their Bronco and the M151A with independent suspension all round. All car manufacturers had now realized the demand of the four wheel drive market, and some more than others the demand for a powerful enough reliable diesel engine in Third World countries. Russia's Uaz Field Car and van versions were beginning to appear in Europe and Third World, together with a Chinese Peking Field Car. Russia's Lada and Rumania's Aro vehicles were also selling well, due to their low price, and Portugal brought out the Portaro version of the Aro with a Daihatsu diesel engine. When OPEC made their

Chinese Peking.

26

enormous increases in the price of oil the Japanese became successful with small engined four wheel drives, especially with their Suzuki and Daihatsu models. A small Scottish company, Stonefield brought out well designed 4 × 4 and 6 × 4 forward control models, but failed to heed the civilian requirements of manual gearbox and diesel engine and therefore soon fell out of the market.

In the USA and Italy various specialist companies were making four wheel drive conversions to recreational vans and in the USA particularly to Toyota and Datsun small pick-up trucks. This led Toyota and Datsun to bring out their own four wheel drive pick-up trucks. As we entered the 1980s Mercedes brought out their first civilian passenger-carrying four wheel drive and perhaps surprisingly fourwheel drive saloon cars such as Subaru 1600, Audi Quattro and AMC Eagle came onto the market. By now the ailing American car industry had finally realised that fuel was no longer plentiful and engines became lighter and more efficient and the market went back to the 'smaller' 6 cylinder engines with manual gearboxes and part time four wheel drive.

Of course, in the meantime bigger and better military and heavy commercial four wheel drives and six wheel drives have been built, probably the best of which is the Mercedes Unimog which is also available with many power take-offs and other options for agricultural and industrial use.

In 1983 Land Rover, now a separate company, brought out its 110 models, based on the coil sprung Range Rover chassis suspension; thus emulating the Range Rover's superior off-road performance and regaining its leading position as the standard by which all other off road four wheel drive vehicles are judged. The Land Rover 90 followed in 1984. By 1986 most production diesel vehicles were turbo assisted.

Most car manufacturers were sceptical when Audi and Subaru first put four wheel drive road cars on the market. Probably due to memories of the demise of the Jensen FF, but the Audi's meteoric rallying success soon made them think again. Vets, country doctors, midwives, winter sports enthusiasts and others needing occasional four wheel drive for muddy lanes or winter snow, found the Subaru a more available alternative to the Audi Quattro. By the mid 1980s, almost all manufacturers had four wheel drive road cars and light vans on the market, often relying on the already existing expertise of FF Developments or Steyr-Daimler-Puch. Even the diminutive Subaru Justy and Fiat Panda are now available with 4WD and at least one British Police force has a Fiat Panda "Panda Car", where occasional off road use is required.

Permanent Four Wheel Drive: when a vehicle in permanent four wheel drive does a turn the various wheels go through different arcs and therefore there is a wind-up of stress between the front and rear axles, this puts a strain on the drivetrain. On a loose surface the wheels will spin and release the pressure, but on a hard surface something has to give; if the vehicle is lightly loaded the tyres will spin and scuff, but if the vehicle is heavily loaded the strain causes excess wear in the drive train and such things as universal joints wear out very quickly.

Apart from the Walter system, mentioned earlier, the way around this is to put a third differential between the front and rear axle to let them travel their slightly different distances without winding up. The original Range Rover system and Jeep's Quadra Trac system (made by Borg Warner) have this third differential fitted with a limited slip system of clutch cones preloaded by springs. The spring pressure is designed such that the cones will not slip under

Fiat Panda 4x4 in use.

Land Rover 90 wading.

normal torque loads so that if one wheel slips, traction is instantly transferred to the other wheels. In the case of excessive wind-up on hard surfaces, when the torque goes beyond the pre-determining spring pressure, the cones will slip and release the wind-up. This provides the optimum performance for most on and off road uses, but for the real extreme need there is a lock-out device to give total four wheel drive with no limited slip. With the Quadra Trac system it would be very rare that you would need to use this lock-out.

Chysler's New Process system used by Dodge, Ford and Chevrolet uses an open third differential between the front and rear axles, so if one shaft slips then no traction is applied to the other shaft which means no drive at all. There is of course a lock-out system to give conventional four wheel drive, but it means that you have to use this more often with the New Process system than with the Quadra Trac system. So all in all the Quadra Trac is the better system of the two. In both systems, if you use the lock-out device, you must remember to unlock it again before returning to a hard surface or you will get wind-up damage to your transmission. The Quadra Trac does have its problems, but these only occur in high speed cornering such as is achieved in rallies and off the road racing. At these cornering speeds, with wheels momentarily changing between traction and no traction as all four wheels struggle for grip on a loose surface, the vehicle can suddenly change from understeer to oversteer to neutral steer and back again without warning. This can be very tricky.

The Range Rover which started with a limited slip system dropped it soon after the first models saying that the system made very little difference, but those who are serious about their off the road traction feel that the limited slip system is a definite advantage.

The most advanced four wheel drive system, the Ferguson FF was used in many racing cars in the 1960s winning one Grand Prix, many hill climbs and twice nearly winning the Indianapolis 500. It showed definite superiority on a wet track. It is a combined mechanical and hydrostatic system using pumps and electrical sensors to provide limited slip at each wheel, this also gave improved anti-lock braking. The system was only used in one production car in the 1960s, the Jensen FF coupé, and due mainly to its cost and complexity was not taken up elsewhere except for specialist competition cars. However its development was continued in England and it is now available as an option for Range Rover in England from Schuler Presses and in America it is made by Chrysler's New Process gear division as the model NP119 and fitted as standard to American Motors' Eagle four wheel drive car. The Ferguson FF system uses a central differential with a fluid coupling, which irons out all snatch in the transmission and is arranged to give 63% power to the rear wheels and 37% power to the front wheels. Having the dominant drive at the rear wheels ensures that a near neutral steering attitude can be maintained whilst accelerating round a corner, instead of the understeer normally caused by permanent four wheel drive.

FF Developments and Steyr-Daimler-Puch have continued to develop this system and it is now fitted to many vehicles, including the Bedford CF and Volkswagen Synchro, vans and minibuses. Its big advantage is that no extra levers have to be handled by the driver, making it almost idiot proof.

Options are a necessary compromise between what the customer wants and how broadly the manufacturers cover the market.
Above:- Standard Ford F250 Custom.
Below:- Toyota FJ40 hard top with a diesel engine, bull bar and all terrain tyres.

Chapter 2
Options

When you set out to buy a four wheel drive vehicle there are various options available from the factory which enable you to select a basic vehicle according to your prospective requirements. Obviously there will be a necessary compromise between what the buyer requires and how broadly the manufacturers cover the market. The buyer will then have to make up the difference between what he requires and what is available by selecting from various accessories and components available as 'after sales'.

Thus options are, for the four wheel driver, a necessary compromise between what the buyer wants and how broadly the manufacturers cover the market.

The Land Rover and to a lesser extent the Mercedes Unimog specialize in various options and power take-off points of special interest for agricultural and industrial use, such things as crop spraying, pumps, power for winches, saws, compressors, generators etc. Buyers with such needs also have access to cheap diesel fuel so they favour a diesel engine. These people formed most of the original four wheel drive civilian market, but vehicles for industrial and agricultural use have developed apart from and alongside the recreational four wheel drive market.

European and Japanese manufacturers tend to offer the basic vehicle in one or two wheelbases with body options of truck, soft top, hard top or estate and engine options of petrol or diesel, with perhaps a second larger petrol engine. A heavier duty suspension may be available for the largest models but most other things are standardized. American manufacturers tend to offer many more options covering different weights of suspension, manual and automatic gearboxes, petrol engine sizes (diesel engines are rare in America), power steering, cosmetic trim etc. The situation is further complicated by the various anti-pollution laws and uses of lead free petrol in different states.

The European and Japanese manufacturers design a basic vehicle which they think is best for reliability and do not give the buyer much choice over the matter, however the American manufacturer gives you the choice to buy cheaper, weaker, and more luxurious components. Further complications arise from the fact that European and Japanese manufacturers make more vehicles for export, which therefore need to be more standardized resulting in less options, and from the local rules in the manufacturing country. Obvious difficulties are lights having to be near the edge of the vehicle, which are then very vulnerable on narrow off road tracks, and American vehicles, made for lead free petrol, which have very narrow fuel tank filler pipes and so are very difficult to fill from cans off the road, unless you use a siphon. Many of the additions to the engine anti-pollution systems, required in America, tend to break up in really rough country; British Land Rover's estates have to be made with 12 very uncomfortable cramped seats becuase of the crippling car taxes for 10 and 7 seat versions. Manufacturers do not always get their product absolutely right and often ignore the feedback of customer requirements, until some other manufacturer gets it right and their sales start falling.

Obviously the man heading an expedition across deep sand is best off with a Unimog, that is if he could afford it, and his requirements are far different from the farmer's wife needing to take the children to school on snow covered tracks, she would be best off with a small Suzuki. But taxation and other problems are such that the farmer's wife will probably end up with a diesel Land Rover, taxed as a tractor, and the expedition man will buy two Land Rovers for the price of one Unimog.

Wheelbase: the shorter the wheelbase the better the performance in rough country, especially on sand dunes and across ruts, where you might bottom between the wheels. The smaller vehicle can be pulled by a smaller engine, thus being more economical on fuel, though for soft sand a bigger engine is preferable. The smaller vehicle will also be easier to handle and less likely to be damaged in confined spaces on narrow tracks, getting around awkward corners and over or around boulders etc. Such a vehicle however is very short on room and payload. Common short wheelbase four wheel drives include the short wheelbase Land Rover, Jeep CJ7, Suzuki, and Toyota Land Cruiser short wheelbase.

Long wheelbase models have more room, better load carrying capacity and are generally the best all round four wheel drive vehicle for most uses; they can get by on relatively small engines with careful use of the gearbox and do not need power steering in the rough. They are a little more difficult to handle in confined spaces and the longer wheelbase is a little more comfortable on badly corrugated tracks such as in the Sahara. Common vehicles in this category are the long wheelbase Land Rover, Range Rover and Toyota Land Cruiser Station Wagon.

The American market manufactures much longer wheelbase vehicles, such as the Chevrolet Suburban and Jeep J20/46. These very long wheelbase models are very difficult to handle in really rough country and need very large engines and power steering. This type of four wheel drive will carry heavy loads or six or more people in relative comfort over fairly rough ground, but if the going is to be really tough or on narrow tracks very long wheelbase models will be a problem.

Engine: back in the days when fuel was plentiful and cheap it was best to get the biggest engine you could for the four wheel drive of your choice, but things have changed and now it is best to use the smallest reliable engine you can obtain. Here I must stress reliability because although bigger engines use more fuel they usually last much longer and are relatively more trouble free than smaller engines, which revolve much faster. Most four wheel drives are in for a hard life so the larger engine will often work out cheaper. Obviously if most of your driving is in civilized surroundings and your off road work never far from civilization then the tiny engined Suzukis can give you a lot of fun but if your four wheel drive is to be working hard with a lot of slogging pulling heavy loads, operating power take-offs or working well away from civilization then you need a bigger engine for reliability.

Small engines with the appropriate gearing will do all that is necessary in most off road conditions, so long as you do not have power sapping ancilliaries such as power steering, automatic transmission or air conditioning and are not overloaded in deep mud, deep snow or soft sand. If you must have automatic transmission, power steering and air conditioning then you need just about the biggest engine available and in the case of soft sand the bigger engine's ability to power through will work out cheaper on fuel and your own energy and nerves than the smaller engine. If you are going to use your four wheel drive in places where air conditioning is necessary and fuel is cheap as in the Middle East then you can afford to use the biggest engine available, but most people must compromise with a middle size engine and cut out the power sapping ancilliaries.

Turbo Chargers: turbo chargers have been normal on large truck diesel engines for a long while but have only come into use on small vehicle engines in the last few years. Various add-on turbochargers are available, but you need to make sure that your engine can handle the extra power produced. I would not advise the use of these for third world work. Turbo chargers get very hot in use and for off-road work can be sprayed with very cold water whilst wading. Most four wheel drive manufacturers now offer turbocharged engines and have strengthened the engines and improved the oil flow where it matters, for reliability.

Turbocharged engines sold as standard by four wheel drive manufacturers will be reliable for third world work, so long as you use top quality engine oil and change it and the filter at the correct intervals; halve these intervals if you cannot be sure of the oil you are getting, an oil cooler is essential.

If you have a turbo, you should let the engine idle for $\frac{1}{2}$ a minute after start up, before moving off and do the same again at the end of a run, before switching off, so as to cool the turbo down.

Choice of Fuel: most four wheel drives sold have a petrol engine, usually the same engine is used in other vehicles on the manufacturer's production line, so it is cheaper to make, produces more power and is lighter in weight than an equivalent diesel engine. Petrol engines are more easily repaired by the owner or competent mechanic if they go wrong. Under normal conditions the petrol engine is the ideal choice, apart from the present high cost of petrol; with the liklihood of increasing fuel costs future vehicles will probably have to use a mixture of petrol and alcohol similar to that used in Britain during and after the last war. In the meantime in certain countries, where liquid petroleum gas is cheap, several companies make conversions to petrol engines so that they can be run on either liquid petroleum gas or petrol at the flick of a switch. Being a slower burning fuel liquid petroleum gas produces more low down torque and a 30-40% saving on fuel costs. LP gas is most popular in Holland, but the system is being enlarged in Britain and is very common in Pakistan. Multifuel engines of the diesel type are being produced for military use.

Petrol engines have several disadvantages in hot, dusty or wading conditions. In hot countries, besides the fire risk, even the best designed petrol

Land Rover 2.286 litre petrol engine.

Perkings 4,203 diesel engine in a Land Rover, note two in line fuel filters for Third World use.

engines suffer from vapour lock in the fuel system and the problem is at its worst on steep or long climbs at altitude. Dust, which often contains a lot of iron, gets into the distributors and shorts them out and if much river crossing has to be accomplished water forever gives trouble to the electrics of petrol engines. In such cases there is a distinct advantage in using diesel engines. In most of the less developed countries diesel is not only a third of the price of petrol, but also more commonly available as it is also used by trucks and tractors. Another advantage of diesel, to the long range expedition man, is that with the extra low down torque he is often in a higher gear in the rough and thus has improved fuel consumption; which in turn means that he has to carry less weight in fuel for a long section without fuel supplies and this in turn improves his fuel consumption still further. In the Sahara Desert for instance, using a 3.3 litre Perkins diesel engine in a long wheelbase Land Rover estate carrying eight people, food, water, spares and fuel on a sandy four day section I could manage on a 16 gallon tank plus four jerrycans of diesel; whereas the year before, with a 2.3 litre petrol engine, I needed the 16 gallon tank plus eight jerrycans of petrol for the same section.

Having done away with most of the electrics diesels have very few problems and require less maintenance than petrol engines. The only real problem with a diesel engine is that if the injector pump goes wrong in the outback there is very little you can do about it, but modern day injector pumps of the in-line type are very reliable. If you do decide on a diesel engine for third world or dusty country use, make sure you have a second fuel filter in the fuel line and this will prolong the life of your injector pump. A sedimenter is also useful near to the fuel tank to remove water and rust without your having to bleed the engine, but the glass must be protected from thrown up stones.

With the exception of Mercedes, Toyota and her sister company Daihatsu, most four wheel drive manufacturers do not like putting a diesel engine into their vehicles, mainly due to the extra weight and lower power. There is a modern tendency to use faster revving diesels to get more power from the weight and better on road performance, because these vehicles are usually used by farmers or industrial users who require a four wheel drive mainly because they can get the fuel more cheaply. Such a diesel engine is the opposite of what is required for expedition or outback work, where the older type of engine, revolving more slowly, is required for its extra reliability. For these reasons the 6 cylinder diesel in the Toyota Land Cruiser is becoming very popular in North Africa and several companies in Britain specialise in fitting larger 4 and 6 cylinder diesel engines into Land Rovers and 6 cylinder diesel engines into Range Rovers.

Diesels have a reputation for being hard to start in cold weather, but the real answer to this is a large battery in good condition. In really cold weather it is worth mixing one part petrol to fifteen parts of diesel to stop the diesel fuel from freezing, in extreme conditions use one to ten.

Automatic Transmission: the American market particularly likes automatic transmission, though this may be about to change now that higher fuel prices are forcing people back to smaller engines. The main advantage quoted for automatic transmission is that when you press on the accelerator to start off, particularly in an awkward traction situation, the torque converter delivers just enough power to turn the wheels without breaking traction; the only way you can do this with a manual transmission is by slipping the clutch which is not a good thing to do. However, if you fail on a hill and have to reverse back down again with an automatic you are in a very dangerous situation. On big boulders and the up and down of heavy slow going, manual transmission is again best as it will give instant engine compression and gear holdback which the automatic cannot do; and in going down steep hills engine holdback, using the gears, is more secure with the manual transmission than with the automatic.

In continuous heavy slow going the automatic gearbox oil will overheat and need an extra oil cooler and automatics use more fuel than manual transmissions. Automatics have one further problem for serious off road work and that is that you cannot push start or tow start the vehicle. If your battery fails you need another vehicle and jump leads, but if your starter motor fails even another vehicle cannot get you started. Many of the latest automatic gearboxes specially produced for four wheel drive vehicles have a manual lock in device on the lowest gears, thus alleviating most of the problems.

Full Time Four Wheel Drive: if you have a choice between full time four wheel drive and conventional part time four wheel drive then the full time four wheel drive is superior, but like all good things you have to pay the price of quality which in this case is the system's extra fuel consumption. Accessory manufacturers now make systems to convert New Process 203 transmission systems to part time four wheel drive plus freewheeling hubs.

Limited Slip Differentials: if you have a standard part time four wheel drive, or New Process system full time four wheel drive, then a limited slip differential on the rear axle is an improvement over the normal systems on a low traction surface. The Quadra Trac and Ferguson FF systems already have a limited slip system in the centre differential and will not therefore be improved on by an additional limited slip differential. Limited slip differentials are not advisable on front axles as you can get some awkward handling characteristics. On narrow tracks for instance one front wheel might grab traction and pull you right off the track before you can stop it and on a slippery road the limited slip could pull you from side to side and at worst induce a spin as the torque goes from wheel to wheel.

Differential Locks: people likely to be driving in really muddy or soft sand country, or who often need to cross awkward ridges at an angle (such that diagonally opposing wheels may be in the air at the same time) will find differential locks useful. You must however remember to unlock them again as soon as you are back on normal traction or you will damage your transmission.

Protection Plates: these are heavy metal shields that attach to the underside of the vehicle to protect the vulnerable parts. These will depend on the design (or poor design) of the vehicle and the manufacturer will usually have on offer the plates to protect the parts of his vehicle most likely to need protecting. The most vulnerable parts are usually the engine sump and fuel tank. In general you will only need these plates if you spend your time bouncing over a lot of rocks. Universal joint guards are not very effective and tend to clog up with grass in scrub country.

Suspension: outside America most manufacturers produce only one suspension for each vehicle, with a separate heavier suspension for heavier payloads. This means that the vehicle is designed to ride properly at its correct full payload and the ride will be rather hard if the vehicle is lightly loaded. Many recreational users complain about this ride but then the vehicle is designed for the working buyer who usually is operating near to capacity and using the vehicle off the road. The American market is more recreationally orientated and many American four wheel drives, which spend 95% of their life on the highway, are offered with various weights or suspension, most of which are too soft when the vehicle really gets into rough country and the occupants end up bounced from seat to roof. The long wheelbase Toyota Land Cruiser and Nissan Patrol suffer from the same problems. Many larger American four wheel drives have rather primitive suspension by today's standards.

If you have a choice it is always worth going for the heaviest suspension offered if you are really going to work in rough country; most of the time you will get a hard ride, but this is better than having to regularly replace broken springs and shock absorbers. If you are going to spend 95% of your time on the road then a softer suspension will give you a more comfortable ride. With independent suspension, when one wheel goes over an obstacle the differential remains low and stands more chance of striking obstacles, therefore rigid axles are best for off road work.

Most four wheel drives are a little tail heavy when fully loaded, many accessory manufacturers supply assistor springs or rubbers to help with this; the rubber models are best because their assistance is progressive, however if you expect to be overloaded most of the time the simplest answer is a stronger rear spring, or if you have leaf springs add an extra main leaf.

Air Conditioning: many four wheel drives are used in areas where air conditioning can be a great aid to comfort, especially where the area is hot and humid rather than just hot. The main problem is that air conditioning takes a lot of engine power, so you need an engine big enough to drive it without affecting the performance of the vehicle. Its main disadvantage is that it spoils your acclimatization to the outside air temperature and lowers your resistance to disease. Stick-on polarising sheet is available for windows and windscreens, which makes it difficult for outside people to see in and keeps internal vehicle temperature down.

Oil Coolers: oil coolers are necessary for vehicles being used stationary for power take-off use, they are also necessary in very hot countries where much high speed highway driving is expected. They are also very useful in hot countries with long steep inclines, especially at altitude such as in the mountainous areas of South America, Afghanistan, Pakistan and the Sahara Desert, oil coolers are advisable with turbocharged engines. If you have automatic transmission a separate oil cooler is necessary under these conditions.

Seat Belts: most developed countries now insist on seat belts being fitted to vehicle front seats and some insist on them being worn on the public road. For off the road driving there are extra problems with seatbelts. If the seat belt is tight most drivers will find it difficult or impossible to reach extra gear levers such as the four wheel drive and transfer box levers, if you have full time four wheel drive this problem does not occur. If you use the inertia type seat belts, which on a smooth road would allow you to stretch out for the farthest lever, you will find that in rough country, with the vehicle continually bouncing, you will not only be unable to move forward but will find that with each bounce the belt tightens up, thus making life very uncomfortable. If you use a normal lap diagonal belt and leave it loose enough to reach all the gear levers as the vehicle bounces you can get it caught awkwardly around your neck. So if you prefer to wear a seat belt off the road then you will find a full harness the most comfortable.

Power Steering: power steering is not essential, except on the largest American four wheel drive, and is another thing likely to go wrong in heavy expedition use. But for the recreational vehicle it can be useful, because if the wife is expected to drive a large four wheel drive vehicle down to the shops she would probably be glad to have it.

Servo Brakes: servo brakes are not necessary on short wheelbase four wheel drives, but make a big difference to all other models. Presently available systems are very reliable.

Tyres: are air containers, the air carries the load. The larger the quantity or pressure of air contained in a tyre the higher the load the tyre can support. Tyre load carrying capacity can be increased by increasing the air pressure (which might require changing to a higher load rating in the same size) or by providing a greater volume of air by changing to a larger size tyre. The load range or ply rating is an index of the maximum cold pressure and therefore load which the tyre can support. If you fit larger tyres you should check with the manufacturers of the vehicle that you are not overstressing the vehicles transmission.

For reasons of cost manufacturers supply their vehicle with the minimum cross country tyres they consider necessary. With so many different tyres on the market for different uses, it is impracticable for them to do otherwise and you have to select the tyre for your own needs. Basically there are four types of tyres:
1. Self cleaning mud tyres:- these are only of any use to operators working in heavy mud and have the same type of tread that would be fitted to a tractor; on the road they would give very difficult handling at anything more than 30 mph.
2. Sand tyres:- these are high floatation balloon tyres with almost no tread pattern so that they float over the sand, only compressing it and causing little disturbance to the surface because the crust is usually firmer than the sand underneath. These tyres often have flexible side walls, which means they should not be used over stony or mixed ground as the side walls will tear up easily. These tyres are excellent for their specialist use, but are not designed to be used on the road.

Michelin make one such tyre, the XS, which is a little more useable on the road as it has some pattern. It is often used in the Sahara and is okay on dry roads, but dangerous on wet roads or ice. Being of very soft and flexible construction it should not be used on stony ground as the stones tear it up very quickly. A Japanese copy is the Bridgestone V Steel Jamal.
3. Cross country mud and snow, or so called 'all terrain tyres':- these are the commonest type fitted to four wheel drives and have a large open cleated tread,

chelin XS tyre, good for sand and mixed ground but not sharp
...es.

Bridgestone V steel Jamal tyre.

which is excellent in mud and snow, but it has poor success in soft sand because it tears away the firmer crust, putting the vehicle into the softer sand underneath. The open tread also tears up very quickly on mixed ground with lots of stones or rocks.

American accessory manufacturers put much emphasis on aggressive tread all terrain tyres, but because they are poor in sand they have to make them wider, which means fitting new wide wheels or even larger wheels which may also mean raising the suspension. American vehicles usually have the option of a higher axle ratio, which enables you to fit larger tyres safely; but most other manufacturers only offer one axle ratio, so if you wish to fit larger tyres you should check with the manufacturers that they will not put too much stress on your transmission.

4. Truck type road tyres:- for the owner who spends most of his time on the road and is cost conscious these will give the longest life and best road performance in normal conditions. They are often made with enough tyre width and lugs on the outside of the tread to be good mixed country tyres, but obviously fall down in mud or soft sand, but then in heavy mud or snow a normal tyre plus chains is more effective than any cross country or all terrain tyre.

For general all round use it is best to have a tyre with a medium closed tread and small side lugs eg: Michelin XY, Goodyear Tracker AT, Goodyear High Milers, Dunlop Road Track.

Range Rover kitted out for desert use with sand tyres, air-conditioning built into the fitted roof rack and polarising film on all windows to keep internal temperatures down.

Radial or Cross Ply: radial tyres cost more but last twice as long and therefore work out cheaper. Being more flexible they also give a softer ride, which is better for you and your vehicle and having less rolling resistance they give you better fuel economy. For really heavy work, steel braced radials are preferable. With radial tyres you must have the correct tubes, preferably by the same manufacturer. Radial and cross ply tyres should not be mixed. Radial tyres 'set' in use so when changed around to even out tyre wear they should be kept on the same side of the vehicle, ie: move from front wheel to rear wheel or vice versa on the same side. For off road work amongst sharp stones, cross ply tyres are preferable, as their less flexible, stronger side walls are less likely to be cut up. Michelin have one tyre designed primarily for the 110 Land Rover, which combines the best of both worlds. The Michelin XCL is a radial tyre with extra protection ply in the side walls. It has a large block tread and deep lateral grooves on the shoulder, for mud clearance. This is Land Rover's recommended all round tyre and is used as standard on the *Camel Trophy* vehicles.

Michelin XM+S is the standard tyre for Range Rover. Some American tyres are *bias-belted,* which is a design half way between cross ply and radial.

Tubed or Tubeless: if you bought your four wheel drive to use it off the road, and not as a status symbol, tubeless tyres give too many problems, driving over stones, rocks or the kerb can break the bead seal. Plug type repair seals do not usually work properly, especially as off road punctures tend to be tears more than holes and tubeless tyres are more difficult to remove and replace than tubed tyres. The bigger tyres for most non-American four wheel drives only come as tubed for these reasons. Only use tubes with short valves, long truck

Michelin XCL tyre.

Michelin XM+S tyre.

type valves will rip off on sudden deflation making the tube useless. If you do use tubeless tyres you will need to carry a bead expander to use when pumping up a repaired tyre. Self inflating repair kits rarely work in off road conditions.

Tyres are cheaper in England than elsewhere, so carry spares with you if you are leaving England. If you spend much time in hot sunny countries you will notice that the majority of buses, truck and company four wheel drives use Michelin tyres, this is because they last better in the sun. Most other tyres form cracks in their side walls, even on the spare, when spending much time in direct sunlight. Some manufacturers make covers for the spare, but you still have to be careful about the other tyres being covered when parked in the sun.

Expedition or overland users on a long journey often have to cover several different sorts of ground, which makes it difficult when choosing just one type of tyre to cover the whole route. The Michelin XS is best if most of your journey is on sand, but if you have to cover mixed ground, with sharp stones, the best all round tyre is the Michelin XY, which in some countries has been replaced and the next best alternatives are the Michelin XZY and XZZ. These tyres can also be legally recut in Britain. Radial tyres have flexible side walls and these are very easily cut up by sharp stones. If you are driving in rocky country and cannot avoid a sharp stone it is best to drive directly over it, so that the stronger tread comes into contact with it rather than the side wall. Some American manufacturers produce tyres with some tread on the sidewall which helps combat this problem. Michelin light truck radial tyres have a 12 ply rating, which is much stronger than most of the other tyres on the market in the same sizes. For details of tyres for American four wheel drive vehicles see the chapter on the American scene. High flotation "terra" tyres are available for specialist soft mud or bog use.

Jeep fitted with dumper tyres for mud.

Toyota with Dunlop balloon sand tyres in the empty quarter.

The tyre sizing nomenclature is very confusing, being different in different countries, for different manufacturers and constantly changing. Even more confusing is that some nomenclature mixes both metric and imperial measurements. The old ply ratings no longer exist, because each ply nowadays is much stronger than the old plies, so now you get a load rating and sometimes a maximum speed rating.

Cross ply tyres are usually straight forward e.g. 7.50 x 16, this has a tread width of 7.5″ and it fits on a 16″ rim wheel. Some American and Japanese figures include the total size e.g. 31 x 10.5R 15 means that the overall diameter of the inflated tyre on a wheel is 31″, the tread width is 10.5″, the R refers to radial and the tyre is designed to fit on a 15″ rim wheel.

Norseman Radial W/Tredloc.

Terra tyre for low ground pressure.

A typical European size would be 225 SR x 15, where the tread width is 225 mm, S refers to a speed rating, R to radial, yet the 15 means a 15″ rim wheel. If the entire number starts with a letter e.g. H 78-15, then the tyre is bias-belted, in this case, designated letters A through to N are tyre width (A being the smallest). The next number, in this case 78, refers to the aspect ratio of the tyre, which means that you divide the height of the tyre by the overall width, in this case the tyre is 78% as tall as it is wide.

American off-road tyres are now imported into the UK, but many of them only fit to 15″ wheels, so 16″ wheel users have the extra expense of new wheels to fit them. Despite all the hype about all terrain tyres, when it comes to heavy mud, normal tyres with good chains will work just as well as all terrain tyres and better in heavy clay, but if you go on and off the road several times a day, you do not want to keep refitting them. As general all round tyres, with a bias towards off-road use (but not sand) General Grabber MT, Michelin XCL, Micky Thompson Baja Belted, B.F. Goodrich all terrain and Armstrong Norseman Tredloc seem to be best, with the Norseman having the advantage of carbon fibre (Kevlar), making it harder wearing in the rough. For use mainly on road Pirelli MS 26, Michelin XZY and Avon Rangemaster seem to be best, with the Michelin having the longest tread life.

Michelin XZY tyre for predominantly on-road use.

Avon Traction Mileage tyre.

45

BFGoodrich mud-terrain radial tyre.

Pirelli LR04 tyre, mainly for road use.

Chapter 3
Accessories

Winches: vehicle mounted winches are the most overrated equipment available to the four wheel drive owner. Such winches are really designed to be used by a vehicle to pull loads about, like logs and felled trees. To pull efficiently the vehicle needs to be placed in the right position relative to the load, and the vehicle needs to be very thoroughly anchored down, with two or more ground anchors, to stop it moving instead of the selected load. Vehicle mounted winches are not easily used for vehicle self rescue and when a vehicle gets stuck in eight cases out of ten either there is no suitable anchor for the winch to be attached to, or else the vehicle and its winch are facing entirely the wrong direction for the vehicle mounted winch to be used.

If you have a specific need to move loads around with a winch, then it is worth your paying the cost and carrying the extra weight, but unless you use your four wheel drive in forest country you will find very little opportunity to use a winch for self rescue. If you are stuck in sand the best way out is usually backwards — the same way you got in. Most vehicles' front mounted winches will not pull backwards and if you have a buddy behind you, still on hard ground, he can tow you out more easily than if you used a winch; if your are on your own and can go forward you will find it easier to dig the vehicle clear and use sand ladders than to bury your spare wheel or a sand anchor deep enough to be effective for a winch to pull you out. There are many hand winches on the market and a high lift jack also makes an effective if slow winch and these items can be used at any angle, not just ahead as with most vehicle mounted winches. If you are going to use a winch, trees are not normally in convenient places, so you also need an anchor to attach the winch to; for softish soil (not too soft) normally a triangular plate, known as a 'Dead Man', or else a standard 'Danforth' small boat anchor is used, but for hard ground a 4 ft length of 2″ × 2″ angle iron or alloy is best, plus a big hammer to knock it 3 ft into the ground.

If you really want the effect of a vehicle mounted winch, but not the weight or cost you could carry a pair of hub winches, which are bolted onto both hubs on a common axle, so they can be used to go both forward or backward. With these you should use high ratio, if you use low ratio you will be putting too much torque on one axle. Hub winches are easily available in America eg: the McCain, Winch Wheels, the Unstucker and Reel Wheels, but I have seen several home made versions in the Sahara and they all work. Perhaps the most common are an old pair of brake drums bolted inside out, outside the wheel, and for Land Rover a pair of old mini wheels filed and drilled out to fit work

47

Drum winch.

Strong arm electric winch, one of many small winches used mainly for launching boats or moving caravans.

High lift jack in use as a winch.
Superwinch – electric winch.

well. The rope from one hub should go through a Karabiner or shackle and back to the other hub, the shackle then being tied to the anchor; in this way any change in rope length due to one wheel slipping is self adjusting.

If you really need a vehicle mounted winch you have the choice of those driven by the engine, either direct or by hydraulic pump, or else those driven by the battery. Battery driven winches tend to be lighter in weight, but no battery could drive such a winch for more than ten minutes and your battery would not last long if it was used often in this hard way. Even if the engine is kept running to charge the battery, the electric winch motor heats up in use and must be shut off periodically to allow it to cool. Engine driven winches can be used for long periods, but you will then need an oil cooler for the engine oil. For recreational use the electric winch is the most popular and can more easily be fitted to another four wheel drive if you change your vehicle. With any winch good quality aircraft cable is essential.

Winches can be very useful for getting up short steep or loose gradients, but not the sort of ridiculously steep gradients one sees in some advertising pictures, where the angle is so steep that the engine oil would drain away from the oil pump and the battery acid pour out of the battery, or if it is a sealed battery away from the plates. If you are lucky enough to find a good anchor in the right place winches are very useful for crossing fast flowing rivers, where the river bed is moving due to the current. Winch cables attached directly to trees usually cut into the tree, so please protect the tree with some padding or better still use a wide nylon or terylene strap to attach the cable to the tree. Adding a snatch block will double the capacity of a winch and is equally effective on a towing car if an anchor point is available.

For self-recovery, most vehicles will require a winch with at least 8000 lbs pull (6000 lbs will do for a Suzuki, Isuzu Trooper or similar light vehicle). Most winch recoveries are around water or mud, so when buying a winch, make sure that the relays are well waterproofed, or else separate from the winch, high up on the bulkhead, well clear of water when wading.

If you are travelling as several vehicles together, it is worth carrying cable or non-stretch rope and a suitable snatch block, even if you do not have a winch available. For an awkward recovery angle, the snatch block on a line or strap can be attached to one stationary chocked vehicle, tree, or ground anchor and another vehicle under traction on firm ground used instead of a winch. This system on a winch used in the same way is very useful on steep sloping ground, as the rescuing vehicle can be kept on level ground.

Capstan winches have the advantage that they can be used to pull in most directions and the pull on the rope can be easily and instantaneously stopped and started, so they are much more controllable, hence their use in rescue work.

Winch safety: keep everyone at a safe distance to the side of the rope or cable when it is under load. If you have to sit in the vehicle, have the bonnet up to lessen the impact of any broken cable or attachment point. Place a heavy blanket or coat over the cable or rope and half way along its length, this will also reduce the speed of a broken cable, rope or attachment point. Always use heavy duty gloves when handling winch rope or cable and always inspect the rope or cable for any faults before using it.

Always make sure that cables are wound neatly back onto the drum after use, if this is not done the cable will be damaged if tensioned. Do not use oil or grease on the cable, wash off mud and grit.

Do not move the vehicle whilst winching or allow the load to snatch. When recovering another vehicle the winch hook should be attached to a properly fixed towing hitch or to a strap around a chassis cross member, never to a bumper or shipping/transit tie down hook.

Increase the engine revolutions on the winching vehicle to help the battery cope with the load.

Tow Ropes or Straps: tow ropes are best made of nylon or terylene because these materials do not rot when damp (a characteristic of hemp). However they will lose strength in time if exposed to a lot of direct sunlight (ultra violet light).

Using a capstan winch.

Snatch block for awkward angle winch recovery.

Straps roll up more neatly for storing and clean up more easily, they also dry more quickly after getting wet. Ropes are easier to slip through eyes, hooks or shackles, easier to knot, can be spliced or knotted if broken, are more pliable to handle and have more stretch and therefore absorb more shock than straps. Due to their stretch, nylon or terylene ropes are often used for shock (or 'Snatch') towing in an attempt to free a stuck vehicle. Persons attempting to free a vehicle by this method must be fully aware that if the rope snaps, or any component that the rope is attached to snaps, you will have a high speed catapulted projectile which is aimed directly at one or other driver — several deaths have resulted from this practice. Carrying two ton screw type shackles can be useful for towing a vehicle which does not have tow hooks.

Jacks: the jacks supplied as standard with most vehicles are not normally up to tough use and quite often are not strong enough to lift a fully loaded four wheel drive at the rear. You will almost certainly have to buy a good hydraulic jack with enough lifting power to lift your vehicle fully loaded. Many makes of hydraulic jack will not operate on their side, so keep the original screw jack, because with a four wheel drive vehicle off the road one almost always needs two jacks in a difficult situation; also if you have to repair a spring, a jack on its side is often needed to re-position the axle. Another problem is that most hydraulic jacks, at their lowest point of travel, are taller than screw jacks and may not properly site on the vehicle axle if you have a completely flat tyre. There are two ways around this. You can use low ratio 1st gear to drive the flat tyres, wheel up onto a stone about 6″ high (so that you can get your hydraulic jack in position, or start with the original manufacturers jack to get it high enough to use the hydraulic jack). If the vehicle is heavily loaded you may have to unload it first. If you are on soft ground you will need either a 1 ft square 1″ thick piece of wood (plywood or hardwood) or a 1 ft square of ¼″ thick iron for each jack, to give the jack a sensible base area.

If your four wheel drive has a sensible chassis and bumpers you would save yourself a lot of grovelling, time and energy if you bought a high lift jack. This plus your hydraulic jack will get you out of most awkward situations and can also be used as a winch and a spreader. Scissor type jacks tend to jam easily in sandy conditions. For working under your vehicle on soft ground it helps if your jack support plates can be fitted inside the rim of your wheels, thus spreading the load over a wider area. For long expeditions, where it is often necessary to work under the vehicle on soft ground, I use an axle stand which fits into the spare wheel rim; it is also worth carrying some hydraulic oil for the hydraulic jack. The high lift jack is also more easy to use, with the weight of your vehicle, to break the bead on a stubborn tyre rather than using a smaller jack or driving over the tyre.

Bull Bags: various companies make bull bags, which are strong rubber bags which are placed under the vehicle on soft sand and blown up by the exhaust, thus jacking up the vehicle. The main problem is finding space clear of the hot exhaust pipe, fuel tank and sharp projections. The vehicle tends to wobble about on the rubber bags but they can be very useful in soft sand. Some models have the valve in a silly position, so that it gets stuck under the chassis.

One way to carry a high lift jack.

High lift jack in use, note jack pad to spread the load and guides to stop the jack from slipping off. In this case these guides are positioned so that they also fit a hydraulic jack and an axle stand to give the author stability and safety in regular desert use.

Tyre Pumps: if you spend much time off the road you are bound to get punctures from thorns and sharp stones and on a long off road journey there comes a time (often many times) where you run out of spares and just have to repair it. Pumping up a 7.50 × 16″ tyre with a footpump is one hell of a job and if you're doing it on sand the pump, being on the ground, sucks in the sand and tends to pack up. Just as much a problem when you get back onto the road is putting enough air back into the four tyres you let down, for that soft stretch.

Two types of tyre pump are available. There are various models on the market of the battery operated pump, most are Japanese and are usually made for car tyres, but they will not quite manage a 7.50 × 16″ tyre. However, there is an American made Schrader model 202 12 volt pump, which just manages 42 PSI for a 7.50 × 16″ tyre. In a hot climate it will get from flat to 36 PSI in 15 minutes and then you should let it cool down again before pumping to final pressure. The pump uses quite a high current so the engine should be kept running. If you have a diesel engine, which does not have its own compressor as on military vehicles, then this is the only type of pump you can use. I have worked one of these pumps very hard for two years in the Sahara without trouble. If you have a petrol engine then all you need to carry is one of the pumps that fit in place of a spark plug, these are more simple, lighter in weight and very robust. In England you can only get the Schrader version, but other makes are also available in America. Some of these are fitted with pressure gauges but these are not very accurate and tend to break in transport so it is better to stick to standard displacement pressure gauges and always carry a spare. A valve core tool and spare valve cores are worth keeping with the pump. The electric type pump should be used from within the vehicle, not on the ground where it will pick up sand and grit easily.

Puncture, Repair Kits: I am always surprised to see garages in England repairing punctures with patches and rubber cement, whilst throughout most of the world puncture repairers use a hot vulcanising machine, which is definitely superior for hard worked off road and truck tyres. All over the Sahara and Middle East punctures are repaired in this way and even in the far outback you can find a guy using a home made version with a clamp or an electric iron and in Southern India even using a primus stove. The sensible thing to do on a long expedition is to carry at least four spare inner tubes and each time you get a puncture replace the tube and get all the punctured tubes vulcanised properly when you reach the next place where it is possible to do so. Even so there will come the odd time when you just have to mend one yourself out in the bush (most punctures seem to be caused by acacia thorns so you tend to get many at once). The best puncture repair kit is the German Rema 'Tip Top' brand but you have to be very careful with cleanliness and once opened it is difficult to stop the cleaning solvent from evaporating. Match ignited hot patches just do not work with heavier four wheel drive type inner tubes. Use a coarse file to rough up the inner tube before patching it.

Seats: you cannot win with seats, if they are made for hard work they are not comfortable and vinyl covers make you sweat in hot countries. If they are made for comfort they break up and if cotton covered they fade and soon tear in direct sunlight. Normal Land Rover seats are only any good to the farmer doing short journeys and getting in and out very often. Land Rover so called de luxe seats are much more comfortable and come up to the standard most other four wheel drives provide. Due to British car tax laws Land Rover twelve seater estates have terrible passenger seats with no leg room, this can be improved on by fitting the ten seater type bench seat after purchase.

Most seats seem to be designed so that a tall driver has to bend down to see out of the windscreen. Various specialized seats are made by companies such as Bostrum, Recaro and Scheel, which are good for dirt roads and crossing fields, but for really bad surfaces, such as the huge corrugations of the Sahara, as opposed to the unsealed roads of Australia and South Africa, the going is so rough that such an expensive seat makes very little difference. The best answer for long expeditions or bad roads seems to be to stick to the seats supplied with the vehicle and use a folded blanket or towel between you and the seat back to cut down perspiration and a foam cushion to sit on. Whatever you use should be easily washable, as a high pressure water hose is the only way to really clean all the sand, dust or mud out of a fully used four wheel drive vehicle.

Seating and European law: under the British tax laws, vehicles with 12 seats are VAT refundable, hence the minimal leg room in the Land Rover 12 seat estate. If you have claimed back VAT you cannot take any of these seats out, not even the centre seat in the front, or you will have to pay back the VAT. The customs and excise generally stick to this for 6 years from new, though this has never been tried out in court, so it could be enforced for longer if they wished. Within the EEC but outside of the UK, vehicles with more than 9 seats are now required to be fitted with a Tachograph. This is not really a problem in itself apart from cost and the room it takes up, but the accompanying laws on driving hours and enforced rest periods etc. which you also have to comply with as though you were driving a bus, are a real headache. Thus if you wish to take a 12 seat Land Rover across the channel, the Department of Transport recommend that you take the rear seats out, but they stress that this has never been tried out in court. If you have already claimed back VAT, you should really remove these seats on the ferry to remain within British Law.

Batteries: off road vehicles, especially those that go well off into the outback are well advised to fit the largest possible batteries — 95 or 105 A/H; it is not funny to get a flat battery miles from nowhere on your own. Batteries which start giving trouble should be replaced before you go off the road. If you are also running extras eg: a fridge or winch you should also have a second battery and a split charge system. Sealed batteries are now available and do not cost much more than conventional batteries, so they are well worth buying when you need a replacement; in hot countries water loss by evaporation has much to do with short battery life. Always carry a pair of heavy duty jump leads and make sure they are at least three metres long so that you will not have two vehicles too close when using them.

Extra Cooling: a fan with an extra blade or two will help with cooling in a hot climate, there will be an increase in noise and more problems in water crossings but it is worth it. Oil coolers may be necessary for some engines eg: Rover 3.5l, V8 used at speed in hot countries.

Bull Bars: Bull Bars fixed to the front of most four wheel drives are not very effective because the chassis was not designed to give a good fixing for them. If you fit Bull Bars in the UK, make sure that there are no sharp fittings and inform your insurance company that you have fitted them. A better term for these in Europe is nudge bars. They will make very little difference in a prang, but are useful in bush country. If you do fit them it is worth fitting light guards into them, thus leaving enough room behind the bull bars to clean the lights easily.

Light Guards: light guards are very useful in stony country, but you need to find a design which gives you access to clean the glass easily to clear the mud which is always a problem, in other words the lightguards need to be far enough in front of the light to enable you to get your hand and a rag in to clean the glass.

Roll Cages: an overturned vehicle is always a possibility in difficult off road country, so if you have a soft top vehicle a roll cage is very useful but beware of the many designs which are only cosmetic and have no real strength.

A bull bar with enough room behind the light guards to clean them. (Lada Niva in safari war paint).

Laminated Windscreens: laminated glass windscreens crack when stones hit them instead of completely shattering as toughened glass windscreens do. So for off road use where stones do hit windscreens regularly the laminated windscreen is a big advantage if available.

Tow Rings, Hooks, Balls and Hitches: properly fitted towing rings or hooks, front and rear, will make it easier for you to help or be helped by another vehicle and avoid vehicle damage caused by attaching tow ropes etc to parts not designed for such stress. If you regularly tow a trailer or caravan you will probably have to lower the towing plate at the rear because your four wheel drive's ground clearance sets the towing plate too high. A second towing ball or pin on the front bumper can greatly facilitate the positioning of your trailer or caravan into an awkward parking spot and should be placed off centre so that the driver can see clearly past the trailer.

Extra Fuel Tanks: if there is room for extra fuel tanks to be fitted under your chassis, and you can afford their high cost, then this is the best way to carry extra fuel. But most people have to resort to using jerrycans either on the side or roof racks, or in the vehicle. Fuel should not be carried in jerrycans on the front of the vehicle as it is a fire risk in an accident.

Fridges: fridges work for short trips of no more than two days, beyond that length of time I have never known a fridge work well enough to be cold in a really hot climate, but it can help keep film cool. Battery drain is high so a second battery is essential and the less efficient heat transfer types can also be run on gas when the vehicle is at a standstill. Solid state coolers are useful in four wheel drives, as there are no moving parts (other than a fan), to be effected by awkward vehicle angles and bumpy roads. The Koolatron series on sale in the USA, Canada and Australia are now available in the UK as Swiftchill from Swiftech. Their efficiency is greatly improved by using freezer packs.

These coolers may also be reversed to keep things hot.

Roof Racks: for expedition use you may require a roof rack and even for normal camping a roof rack is useful for carrying light bulky items. The main requirements are that the roof rack must be strongly made and strongly fitted, otherwise off the road, especially on corrugations, everything will break up. Weight for weight tubular section is stronger than box section and it should be heavily galvanized.

Several companies in Britain advertise Safari preparation and amongst the items they sell are roof racks extending beyond the front of the roof over the windscreen. The designer and manufacturer of such an item can never have driven a loaded four wheel drive on a corrugated road let alone off the track. Even an ordinary roof rack, properly loaded with most of the weight to the rear, will in such conditions cause breaks to the bulkhead or a non-reinforced windscreen frame. To put jerrycans of water or petrol over or even beyond the windscreen as some designs do is absolute lunacy. Even worse are designs which extend the roof rack to the front bumper. In the Sahara and the Middle East I have seen vehicles fitted with such roof racks causing broken front springs and bent front axles on corrugated roads. Such extended roof racks also mean that when you are going downhill you cannot see forward properly as the roof rack obstructs your vision. Such racks should be only for very lightweight awkward loads, or used as a filming platform.

Full length roof racks can be safely fitted, but remember that the weight of such a roof rack is usually on the manufacturer's limit for roof weight. A good roof rack design will have its supports positioned in line with the main body supports of the vehicle, eg: the posts between the doors; and there should be fittings along the back of the vehicle to stop the roof rack juddering forward on corrugated roads, and making holes in the roof. A roof rack can be fitted to soft top four wheel drives by using or building a roll cage to support it. You must remember that any extra weight on the roof will raise the vehicle's centre of gravity so that it will turn over more easily. If you intend to sleep on the roof rack, and many do to avoid snakes and scorpions, it is worth putting wooden slats or thin plywood along it to lie on. One manufacturer even makes a fold up tent for roof rack fitting. Sand ladders, if you need them, can be hooked along the side of the roof rack out of the way, but become quickly available when you get stuck. If a roof rack is fixed to the roof of a Land Rover, Landcruiser or Unimog it should not be further fixed to the chassis as the bodies are designed to flex on the chassis. A good strong waterproof cover will be needed in wet areas and is also useful to keep out the dust in dusty areas. If you have a full length covered roof rack you will not need a double skinned safari roof for hot countries. Nylon or terylene rope is best for tying down baggage because hemp rots quickly and also absorbs dust and grit which tears up your hands in use. Rubber tie-downs, as sold in Europe, soon rot in strong sunlight; this method is more practicable to tie down baggage: cut old Michelin inner tubes into 2″ wide strips and make your own hooks from wire tent pegs for the ends, these straps will stand up to constant harsh sunlight without breaking.

Storage of fuel and water cans: for long distance off road work you will need to carry extra fuel and water in 20 litre ex-military jerrycans, which are relatively cheap to buy compared with the high price of extra fitted tanks. The narrow necked German designed jerrycans, used by most armies, are much better than the wide necked American version. Water should be kept in the special ex military plastic water cans, which are far more useful than the civilian variety because they are completely lightproof and therefore do not get algae growing inside them. If you do not have a winch then a couple of water cans can be carried on the front bumper without overloading the front springs or axle, but other cans will need either to be in side holders or on the roof. Put a thin sheet of plywood between the roof rack and the cans because their welded seam stands proud and if in direct contact with the metal roof rack this will split with the vibration, also allow room for the cans to expand in the heat of the day.

Lockable jerrycan holders which can also be fitted with a sheet of plywood for use as a table. Military plastic watercans, being lightproof, inhibit the growth of algae in the water.

If the fuel jerrycans are completely insulated from the metal roof rack, before you try to open a can touch it against the bodywork to short out any static electricity built up due to wind. This will avoid a possible fire with petrol. It is surprising how many people still carry jerrycans upright on the roof, untie them and then lift the heavy cans down to fill the tank. I always put the fuel cans on their backs at the rear of the roof rack and tie them down permanently with the filling spout pointed towards the rear of the vehicle. I then fill the cans in situ from station fuel pumps and when I need to fill the vehicle's tank I park the vehicle facing slightly downhill so that the fuel does not pour out of the can when opened and fill the tank by plastic syphon tube. This means that each can is only filled with 18 litres instead of 20 litres, but you save a lot of work, strained muscles and bent jerrycans.

I like to keep a second plastic filling hose of the correct size to fit most water taps and use this to fill my water cans, this hose must be kept clean and never be used for fuel.

Shovels — Picks —Axes: a shovel is always useful when camping for digging latrines, digging a safe hole for a fire, or burying rubbish. If you are likely to be in soft sand or mud a shovel is essential and you can save a lot of time if you carry two shovels so that two of you can be digging the vehicle out at the same time. Avoid having a shovel with too big a blade as this can be very tiring to work with. A long handle is useful as usually you have to clear away sand from right under the axle. Expeditions travelling on mountain tracks really need a pick axe and for camping, where fire wood is available, it is worth taking a good hand axe along. Most travellers in Africa, including the Sahara, pick up wood as they find it during the days travelling for cooking in the evening.

Sand Ladders: heavyweight perforated steel plate is used by heavy trucks for crossing or getting out of soft sand, but it is surprising how many small four wheel drives I see loaded down with these. For four wheel drives of up to 1½ tons the best answer to soft sand is to carry sand ladders These are short lengths of strong metal ladder just long enough to fit between the wheelbase, one vehicle alone would carry four of these and if two or more vehicles are travelling together then each vehicle would only need to carry two. Usually digging out the rear two wheels and making a gentle slope in front of them to place the sand ladders into, will be enough to get most vehicles free, but if the sand is very soft then the same must be done for the front wheels. With ladders for the rear wheels you must be careful that they do not rip off the exhaust pipe. In really soft sand you may have to make a ramp of several ladders to get through and if your passengers are fit enough they can remove the ladders after the vehicle clears them and run forward to drop them under the front wheels before the vehicle sticks again but this is very hard work. In really soft sand the ladders will bury themselves in the sand, so it is wise to mark their position with an upright shovel before the vehicle drives off. The vehicle needs to reach firm ground before stopping for the passengers left behind and this might entail a long walk for the passengers; if in doubt always park the vehicle downhill eg: down a sand dune. Tying the sand ladders to the vehicle so that it tows them along after getting unstuck just does not work, the vehicle will usually dig in again due to the extra drag.

Tyre Chains: tyre chains are just as useful in mud and clay as they are in snow and ice. You must make sure that you buy strong chains. Chains should either be fitted to all four wheels or else the two rear wheels; fitting them only to the front two wheels can induce a spin when going downhill or if you touch the brakes. In the UK, the best chains are German made Greifsteg, as supplied to the British, Swiss and German automobile clubs and the Ministry of Defence, they are available from Rud Chains Ltd. Slightly easier to fit are Weissenfels, available from Snowchains Ltd.

Weissenfels Quick-Fit snowchains.

Steering Dampers: on rough tracks there can be quite a lot of kick back through the steering wheel if you do not have power steering and even at slow speed, hitting or sliding off a rock can give quite a violent spin of the steering wheel. If you have weak wrists it is worth fitting a steering damper which acts as a shock absorber and remember not to hook your thumbs around the steering wheel when driving off the road.

Steering Locks — Bonnet Locks — Fuel Cap Locks: modern British built four wheel drives have to be fitted with a steering lock by law and they are fitted with snap-off bolts to stop thieves removing them. Unfortunately if you use a vehicle with such locks in dusty country they often jam up, which can be disastrous in expedition use. If you have trouble getting the key in and out it is usually best to leave it in the lock permanently rather than force and break it. Only lubricate such locks with special dry graphite lock lubricant. If such a lock does jam up completely the complete unit will take a lot of removing and is best either not replaced or else replaced using normal headed bolts, so that it can be more easily removed in future.

It is also a wise precaution to have the bonnet and fuel cap and any jerrycan holders locked, this is essential in less developed countries. Again it is best to keep it simple and use better quality padlocks so that you can replace them more easily if they go wrong. Jerrycans on the roof can be locked down with a strong chain sheathed in plastic tubing, threaded through their handles.

Free Wheeling Hubs: if you have a part time four wheel drive vehicle and only use it off the road, and then not too heavily for little of its working life, you can save a little on fuel by fitting free wheeling hubs. These hubs disconnect the drive from the hub to the axle half shaft, thus saving on the rolling resistance of the front differential. The gain is usually small, but at present fuel prices it can be worth it. Full time four wheel drive vehicles such as the Range Rover, Land Rover V8 and vehicles fitted with Chrysler's New Process 203 transfer cases can also be fitted with free wheeling hubs, but the central case also has to be adapted. If you fit free wheeling hubs you must always remember to put the hubs into lock before engaging four wheel drive. If you have free wheeling hubs you should not engage four wheel drive on the move because you might damage them. Free wheeling hubs do not stand up to hard four wheel drive work in hot countries, particularly with heavy going in soft sand, if this is your main use of four wheel drive forget them. For expedition use, if you need the fuel savings on the road, take your vehicle's original hub driving members and hub caps with you and refit these for the hard work areas. Automatic free wheeling hubs were around in the late sixties but were never very successful. American Ford are making them available for their four wheel drives, fitted with the standard front axle. Some old type automatic free wheeling hubs only engage when forward traction is required, which means that they release again in an overrun situation such as when braking downhill, this can cause problems in some situations, particularly on loose ground or when towing. Newer designs overcome this. Automatic free wheeling hubs are usually disengaged by driving backwards for a few yards.

Overdrives: overdrive units are made for many four wheel drives and for those who spend 90% of their time on the road the reduction in noise and vibration at cruising speed is worth more than their saving in fuel. Like free wheeling hubs they are not for the vehicle which spends most of its time working hard off the road. Manufacturers' claims to double the number of available gears are not to be listened to. An overdrive is best used only on the top two gears in high ratio, if you use an overdrive in low gears, off the road, or pulling a heavy trailer on the road then you will soon have trouble with it. Many modern vehicles have a 5th gear, which is really an overdrive, for good road cruising. These gears are much stronger than a separate bolt on overdrive.

Wheels: for the recreational four wheel drive market various accessory wheels, mostly wider and of alloy are big business for their manufacturers, their use is usually cosmetic. Alloy wheels are useful in racing because any cut in unsprung weight is helpful. Alloy wheels do not damage quite so easily as steel wheels, but if they are damaged they cannot be knocked back into shape like steel

AVM free wheel hub (manual).

Fairey free wheel hub (manual).

Selectro free wheel hub (manual).

63

wheels can. Therefore for serious off road use, where wheels do often get bent, steel wheels are preferable. Split rim wheels are available for some of the smaller vehicles, but should be used on the long wheelbase models as they break up with heavy use.

Fire Extinguishers: off road vehicles tend to be used in fire risk situations and may be your only way of getting back to civilization, so one or more good sized fire extinguishers should always be carried and regularly checked. Keep vehicles and fuel cans well away from camp fires. Remember that empty fuel cans contain explosive mixtures and are therefore more dangerous than full ones.

Fly Screens: in hot countries, on the four wheel drive's forward facing vents, fly screens are essential, not so much against flies but against swarms of bees, wasps and hornets which one often has to drive through.

Air Horns: air horns are essential in third world countries where most pedestrians will not hear normal horns, but remember that older pedestrians may be completely deaf anyway.

Trip Meter: off road navigation is greatly simplified if you have an easily zero-able trip meter on your odometer.

Rear Windscreen Wipers and Washers: four wheel drives tend to spend much of their time on muddy roads and their body shape tends to plaster the rear windows with mud very quickly, so a rear windscreen wiper and washer kit is very useful.

Starting Handles: only a few vehicles still supply starting handles, they are equally useful for setting-up tappets etc when working on the engine.

Rear Lighting and Fluorescent Lighting: reversing in an off road situation at night can be very tricky and is the quickest way to get stuck. Having a good rear mounted spotlight mounted safely out of the way, near to or on top of the roof, can make life a lot easier, it will also be useful for pitching camp after dark. In addition it is always worth carrying a 12 volt fluorescent striplight on five metres of cable. These lights make little demand on the battery and are useful as a camp light, reading light or light for working on the vehicle. Gas and storm lanterns save on batteries, but break easily and are not safe inside the vehicle.

Vice: for serious off road work, overlanders and expeditions, a strong metal workers' vice bolted to a bumper or tailgate can be very useful.

Radio: a radio in your four wheel drive is most useful when on the road for news of road hazards and blockages. Unfortunately in Britain such warnings are usually two hours late, but the system works better in the rest of Europe and the USA. Off the road the radio is essential if you wish to know what's going on in the rest of the world. Overlanders and expeditions will find they can get the news from back home on a short wave radio.

CB radio is very practical for four wheel drivers in large outback areas such as America, Australia and Iceland where a rescue is not unusual. CB radio is now legal in Britian and has become just as popular here as elsewhere unfortunately, with the short-range FM sets currently available, one cannot get far enough off the road to make them really essential.

Unfortunately in third world countries, where CB radio would be really useful, as in the Sahara, it is always banned as the governments equate such a radio with spying.

Cassette Players: I have often had to drive a four wheel drive vehicle alone from London to Tehran, Rawalpindi, Algiers or Casablanca and in such situations have found a cassette player and several tapes almost a necessity. Such things are very much a matter of taste but most overlanders like to have one. One has to be careful not to use them in very dusty areas or damp seaside areas where the tapes tend to slip, while in hot countries long play tapes tend to stick. Speakers do not last long with the dust and damp so have to be replaced frequently. All radios and cassettes have to be well hidden in third world countries because they are highly prized by local thieves.

Compass: for off road navigation you need to be well acquainted with the use of a magnetic compass. Magnetic compasses fitted to the vehicle will be affected by the metal and electric fields within the vehicle. But you can use such a compass if you allow for the vehicle's magnetic compass deflection and stop to check frequently with a hand held compass, well away from the vehicle. For long distance desert work it is best to use a sun compass, stopping every 15 minutes to adjust it. Unlike at sea you rarely can just follow a compass course overland as you have to go around difficult terrain like mountains or soft sand, so it is wise to write down the distance which you travel on each compass bearing so that you can work out your true position accurately and be able to backtrack if things go wrong.

Those Final Items: if a four wheel drive goes wrong off the road, then inevitably you will have to lie under it in either mud, brambles, thorns or blowing soft sand. Therefore it is always wise to have a boiler suit handy and if you do not have a cover on a roof rack then you will be glad of some form of ground sheet to lie on. In an area of windblown sand you will need to build a shelter around the part of the vehicle you are working on to keep the sand out, and for working underneath it a pair of goggles can save you a lot of eye problems.

Overlanders and expeditions will be glad of a strong dustproof metal box, with good tamperproof locks, which should be securely fixed to the vehicle for carrying money, documents and other valuables. Off the road punctures should be mended on a ground sheet so that sand and grit do not get caught between inner tube and tyre when putting them back together.

A small handbrush is always useful for brushing out your vehicle and for brushing engine, wheels or bodywork clean before you work on them, and brushing wheel rims clear of sand and grit before putting tyres and tubes back on.

Notes on High Lift Jacks: high lift jacks were originally made for farm use in the 1930s from where they got their original name of Sheepherder's Jack. The fact that a high lift jack is used at many times the extension of a normal jack means that the whole unit and its load can move around much more and thus is more likely to slip; this can sometimes be used to advantage, but in general it means that you must be extra careful with its use and be sure to chock all four of the four wheel drive's wheels.

Transmission brakes, as used on true cross country vehicles, can cause trouble when jacking because wheels at opposite ends of the vehicle can contra-rotate through the differential if the wheels are not chocked. As with any jack on soft ground you need a strong 12" square jack pad to increase the ground area, but as a high lift jack is more likely to slip than a normal jack, locating dowels or strips should be added to the jack pad to stop any slipping at the base.

It is worth obtaining a couple of shackles, look for ones as large as possible to fit the holes in the jack's beam, and then they can be used to attach ropes from the jack to trees or ground anchors to enable the jack to be used for winching or lifting. One can also be placed temporarily below the jack mechanism to avoid it slipping if someone tampers with it. The reversing latch should *never* be dropped with the handle in the down position, the leverage can work back to front so the handle can fly up, injuring the operator.

On four wheel drives without proper strong bumpers, an adaptor can be made to fit into the vehicle jack socket by welding a 3½" length of tube or channel, which will fit the jack's lifting arm to a suitable length of steel rod which will fit the vehicle's jack socket. The high lift jack can also be used for spreading or clamping which is useful for bodywork damage.

When used as a winch the jack can only manage a few feet at a time so a second rope from the anchorage to the vehicle may be necessary to hold the load whilst resetting the jack between runs. For a vehicle immobilized by spinning wheels, or by being 'high centred', the vehicle is lifted until 'packing' eg: sand ladders, logs or stones can be placed under the spinning wheels. If the ground is 'safe' to one side of the vehicle then jack-up one end and then, keeping well clear yourself, push the vehicle off the jack sideways, you may have to repeat this several times until the wheels can grip again. Never jack the wheel rim or hub directly. After use in mud and sand the jack should be thoroughly washed down and oiled. If after much heavy use the holes in the beam become burred, then the beam can be reversed.

Notes on Winching: the most valuable winch accessories are a snatch block and a nylon tow strap or rope. A snatch block is a frame containing a steel wheel and with a hole attached, either one side of the frame opens out or else the hook is removable, such that your winch cable can be fitted on the wheel. If you hook a snatch block to a tree, ground anchor or load to be moved, fit your winch cable through it and then back to your vehicle, you double the mechanical advantage and hence your winche's capacity. At the same time you should cut the line speed in half, thus giving you more control in any tricky situation. You can also pull at different angles by attaching the snatch block at an intermediate point.

A nylon tow strap used in series with the winch cable, will, by virtue of its stretchability, eliminate most of the jerks on the wire cable as the loads vary on the winch. A nylon tow strap is also essential if you use a living tree as your anchor point; the nylon tow strap wrapped round the tree several times will spread the load and do little or no damage, whereas the narrow winch cable will cut deeply into the tree and may do serious damage.

When a stuck vehicle is being winched out by another vehicle, unless the winch alone fails to move the stuck vehicle, it is unwise for either vehicle to use engine power to the wheels to assist the winch. Intermittent jerking can damage both vehicles and if the stuck vehicle suddenly gets traction and overruns the cable it can snarl up the whole cable.

Do not oil winch cables as they will pick up grit, which is bad for the cable and the drum. After use winch cables should be unwound and re-reeled correctly and washed down with fresh water if they have been used in salt or glacier fed water.

Chapter 4
Exotic and Status Symbols

The fact that four wheel drive vehicles are obviously different, can be taken off the road, tend to look high and masculine and, if they have a chassis, can be fitted with any body shape, has made them an obvious choice for anyone looking for a status symbol, for the variations on the four wheel drive vehicle are infinite.

The Land Rover with its strong box chassis, bolt on bodywork and three power take-off points was designed from the very beginning to be a most versatile vehicle and various enterprising manufacturers, as well as Land Rover themselves, have made good use of it. Other four wheel drive vehicles are not quite so easy to alter, but plenty of conversions are produced on Jeep and Range Rover chassis'.

From the very beginning the Jeep was tried in many forms, including four wheel steering, and the Ford manufactured amphibious model GPA Seep; though this was too small to be a good boat and too clumsy to be a good Jeep it was useful for river crossings. Ford also made a six wheel drive version of their GP Pygmy in 1941. Both Land Rover and Jeep were produced with railway train type wheels to run on railway lines and advertising photographs were shown of them pulling railway trucks. Obviously the trucks were much too heavy a load for them, especially for braking and these conversions were really meant as personnel carriers for railway maintenance work.

The Cuthbertson Company have made tracked conversions to Land Rovers for more than twenty years; the original versions had 12" wide tracks over standard wheels and tyres, but sharp stones tended to get caught between the tracks and the tyres causing punctures, so for a period standard tyres were filled with polyurethane foam. The modern versions use 18" wide tracks and press on wheels. Power steering is a necessary addition. These vehicles can do 30 mph on the road and with a ground pressure of less than 2 PSI they are ideal for swamp and snow. Half tracks are also made by Laird of Anglesey.

True All Terrain Vehicles (ATV's), such as the Seep, exist today in smaller forms like the Swiss Croco, the Canadian Argocat and Mitsubishi's Hill Farmer. The Croco 4 × 4 rides on 31" diameter low pressure tyres, has a 32 bhp Wankel engine, drives via a belt type torque converter to a 2 speed gearbox and lockable differentials. Steering is by all four wheels, wheelbase is 64" and it has disc brakes all round. The body is 2 mm steel plate and it can carry ½ tonne; top speed is 37 mph on land and 2½ mph on water; an outboard motor can be fitted to improve its in water performance. The Croco is aimed at military users,

Royal LR.

Croco (SK1155).

69

Crayford Cargocat (Argocat type).

Argo ATV.

whereas the Argocat and Hill Farmer vehicles are aimed more at the hill farmer needing to get feed to his livestock in winter.

The Argocat is also produced by Crayford Engineering in Britain. It has a ladder type chassis, fully waterproof plastic body and comes in 6 × 6 or 8 × 8 options. It has a single cylinder 16 hp 4 stroke engine, or 30 hp two stroke engine; drive to the 2 speed gearbox is by belt, acting as a torque converter (as in Daf cars). There is an epicyclic differential and chain drive to the wheels. Steering is by skid braking on either side and tracks can be quickly fitted. These tiny vehicles have a remarkable performance and I have even seen them as far afield as Afghanistan.

Armour plated Land Rovers have been needed in many countries where there is guerrilla warfare. Rhodesian farmers usually had to make their own, complete with underfloor protection and roll cages as land mines could turn them over. However the extra weight is slightly over the limit so the need for these, tipper bodies, fast fire tenders and ambulances, has led to a spate of 6 × 6 and 6 × 4 conversions to Land Rovers, Jeeps and Range Rovers.

In America a 6 × 6 Jeep, the Trac-Too is built on a CJ6 chassis and in Britain Pilcher-Greene make the Branbridge Cherokee 6 × 4 tender on the Jeep Cherokee chassis; 6 × 4 Land Rover conversions are made by Hunt Grange,

Mitsubishi ATV ('Hill Farmer').

Safire, and Sandringham. Sandringham also make a 6 × 6. The rear axle, springs and outrigger are moved back 16″ and the additional axle mounted 35″ in front of it. A special differential, produced by FF developments, is fixed to the front of the middle axle allowing both rear axles to be driven. Drive to the rear axle is taken from the bottom of the centre axle differential casing. Sandringham also use a similar system for a 6 × 6 Range Rover and Range Rover pick-up. Sandringham also have an easily fitted track system, made by Avon, which fits over the standard rear wheels thus converting their 6 × 6 and Land Rovers into half tracks. Safire in conjunction with Baja four wheel drive make a Land Rover V8 6 × 6. Luxury custom made 6 × 6 and 6 × 4 Range Rovers are also available from Wood and Picket, Scottorn, Carmichael, Gloster Saro,

71

6 × 6 Land Rover conversion on the LWB V8 chassis by Safire in conjunction with Baja 4WD.

6 wheel Range Rover by Alvin Smith.

Reynolds Boughton, Rapport and Alvin Smith. These must be the ultimate in status symbols; one of the early Carmichael's, after being used in Africa for two years, was snapped up by a Gulf Sheikh on resale and many others have followed suit; 6 × 4 and 6 × 6 Range Rovers are popular in the Middle East and bullet proof versions are available.

Amongst the many purpose built armoured vehicles is the Glover Tuareg, made by the Southampton company of Glover, Webb and Liversedge. This 4 × 4 has a 6 cylinder 156 bhp petrol engine, 3 speed gearbox and 2 ratio transfer box, aluminium body with armour plating, a 110″ wheelbase and carries two spare wheels. Built essentially for long range desert use it carries, as standard, 100 gallons of fuel and 25 gallons of water, a front hydraulic winch and two mounted machine guns.

Glover Tuareg.

Camper conversions to four wheel drive vehicles are a common sight in tougher terrain countries. In the Sahara desert one sees many home made conversions on larger military vehicles, particularly Mercedes Unimogs, Berliet, Magirus Deutz and Saviem trucks, with a sprinkling of ex British army three ton Bedfords and two ton Austins. But when engineers, geologists, doctors, nurses etc end up in the desert they usually select more up-to-date custom made conversions on Land Rover and Range Rover chassis' such as those made by Carawagon.

In America the four wheel drive recreational market is much bigger and it is popular to have a demountable caravan unit which can be fitted to a four wheel drive pick-up, including the smaller Toyota and Datsun four wheel drive pick-ups. There used to be a British built Suntrekker demountable for Land Rover, but it is no longer available. The only camper sized four wheel drives produced as standard factory items, are the Russian Trekmaster with the larger Renault Saviem TP3 for more space and the Rumanian Tudor. Besides factory four wheel drive, conversions to the popular recreational vans, which are factory approved, have been common in the USA, Italy and Germany for many years. Now the popular Ford transit van, Colt, Mazda and Datsun pick-ups

Camper body on a forward control Land Rover chassis

Specialist expedition bus built on a stiffened Bedford chassis and powered by the 590 engine, (Afghanistan). Constant use of low range is hard on the clutch.

can be converted to four wheel drive and Bedford CF vans can be fitted with FF Developments four wheel drive system. In the USA the recreational four wheel drive vehicles are often status symbols, most being offered first in the form of a very basic vehicle, then there are the necessary options of stronger springs and suspension as well as larger engines and automatic transmissions to air conditioning. On top of this there is big business in accessories, with wider wheels and tyres etc, the end result can often be double the price of the original vehicle. By the time one has added all the luxury seating and trim, cosmetic or real, roll bars, flash wheels and chrome bumpers, which would shudder at the thought of being touched by a high lift jack, one would certainly not wish to take the high cost status symbol off the road.

In Britain, where the Land Rover is obviously most commonly available and the best buy to the man who needs a workhorse, the obvious status symbol is to have some other less common four wheel drive. In the sixties the Austin Champ was fashionable and for most of the seventies the World War Two version of the Jeep was popular and by the end of the seventies the Jeep CJ7 with the little Suzuki LJ80 or ex Army lightweight Land Rover, for the less wealthy, led the status symbol stakes. The really wealthy would concentrate on the larger Jeeps or exotic customized version of the Range Rover, including four door models and the Wood & Pickets coachbuilt Sheer Rover. But if you really want to top the bill it has to be either a 6 × 6 Range Rover Lamborghini LM001 or the Schuler Super Ranger FF Express with 3.6 or 4.4 litre V8 engine, Jaguar/Rover SD1 5 speed manual gearbox or an automatic gearbox (Borg Warner 65 or Chrysler Torqueflite A727) and the FF Developments, Ferguson four wheel drive system with viscous coupling and anti-lock braking system.

Customised SWB Land Rover special with a V8 engine

Land Rover ambulance.

Glenfrome Engineering produced a vehicle of particular interest to Middle East buyers: their Range Rover based Ashton drophead coupé with electro-hydraulically operated hood for around £33,000 and the 120″ wheelbase 'Clifton' four door with, naturally, electrically operated roof and windows, air conditioning, drinks cooler, etc for around £31,000.

By the mid eighties, oil money was not so readily available in the Middle East, so some of the specialist converters like Glenfrome have ceased trading, but Lamborghini are producing LM002, Range Rover have the electronic fuel injected Vogue and there are plenty of carbon fibre bodied Paris Dakar Rally specials.

Chapter 5
Driving Techniques

Driving techniques can be personal, proven or arguable and there may often be more than one way of solving a problem. The newcomer to four wheel drive is advised to start with caution and if two solutions to a problem exist, would be best advised to take the solution least likely to damage his vehicle, until he has gained enough experience to use more adventurous techniques. For example, a light foot and low gears will usually get one out of soft ground situations, but sometimes sheer speed may be better, but if you lose control at speed you could suffer serious damage or injury.

This is an arguable example of driving technique: many American journals advocate the use of snow chains on the front wheels only if you do not have them for all four wheels. The thinking behind this is that with an empty four wheel drive the weight of the engine means that there is more weight and therefore more traction on the front wheels. However in this situation, when braking or descending a hill the back wheels can slip sideways and put the four wheel drive into a spin. In such a situation it is safer to use the chains on the rear wheels and if you do not find enough traction put some more weight in the back. European four wheel drivers who regularly encounter conditions which necessitate chains like snow or mud, often leave a couple of hundredweight sacks of sand over the rear axle.

The driving techniques given in this chapter applicable to various situations a four wheel driver can meet, are obviously personal, but gained from practice and, not unnaturally, often learnt from mistakes.

If you have freewheeling hubs then the first thing you must always remember before leaving the paved road is to put the hubs into the lock position. It is also wise to lock your hubs for driving in snow on the paved road, then if you need four wheel drive at any time everything is ready and you only have to use the four wheel drive lever. Most part time four wheel drives can be engaged into four wheel drive in high range at any speed, but to engage low range one usually has to be at, or nearly at, a standstill. Normally, if you are going to need low range you will have stopped and inspected the situation first, so this will not be a problem, but there are occasions where it is convenient to be able to engage low range on the move.

In the days of non-synchromesh (crash) gearboxes, double declutching was the standard way to change gears but it is now a lost art, however four wheel drive transfer boxes usually have a dog clutch, instead of synchromesh, so you must practise double declutching to be able to move in and out of low range on

Perfect conditions rarely exist off the road. Mercedes-Benz Gelandewagon S.W.B. soft top with integrated roll bar.

Approach all bends with care. Tracks like this often collapse. Land Rover Series III at Chitral, Pakistan.

Low range for control – Land Rover Series III in Afghanistan.

the move. To change down into low range with the vehicle rolling at around 2-4 mph in second gear: depress the clutch pedal and shift the transfer case lever into neutral, release the clutch pedal and dip the accelerator to increase the engine speed to an amount equivalent to the low range step down ratio (usually a little more than double), then depress the clutch pedal again and shift the transfer case lever from neutral to low range, release the clutch pedal again. If you get the engine speed right the gears will go in silently and smoothly, if you were a little out they will go in with a small clunk, if you were a long way out they will not engage at all so do not force things, if you get nasty noises go back to neutral and try again. With practice you will be able to change down into low range at 10-12 mph. To shift from low range to high range is the reverse procedure, but it is much easier; to equalize the engine speed you should slow the engine down by around half speed during the pause in neutral, use 2nd or 3rd gear.

If the vehicle is very new the transfer case gear lever may be very stiff and you may have to be at a complete standstill with the main gearbox in neutral; depress the clutch and push the transfer case lever into low range with a pause in neutral, if the gears do not go in, roll the vehicle forward a couple of metres in gear and try again, it may take two or three attempts. If you have an automatic gearbox the procedure varies with different gearboxes and has to be done at a standstill, so follow the maker's instructions. With an automatic transmission it is even more important to engage low range before you need it because it cannot be done quickly.

Tyres will last longer and cut up less if they are kept at normal inflation pressures wherever possible, pressure should only be lowered for soft sand or deep snow. Similarly there is no point in using four wheel drive when you do not need it eg: hard dry tracks without large boulders.

One of the most important things to remember when off the road is to travel at a sensible speed keeping your eyes on the track some 10-20 yards ahead for obstacles which may need special action. It is important to travel only at a speed which allows you to stop comfortably within your distance of clear vision; always travel slowly to the brow of a hump or a sharp bend, there may be a large boulder or sheer drop into a river bed beyond it.

Apart from on soft sand and snow, most cases where four wheel drive is needed also require low range. Low range gives you torque and control and if you are already in low range you will not have the problem of getting into low range in a hurry when you need it. If you are not well practised in the art of double declutching and you suddenly try to engage low range you might get stuck in neutral, which can mean either getting stuck in soft ground or dangerous loss of control on steep hills. If there is a long rise ahead, or you are following a sandy river bed, or the track is very rough and rocky then the answer is always to go slowly in low range, because then you will have full control, with the torque and engine braking available when you need it. Usually 1st gear low is too low and you might spin the wheels, use 2nd or 3rd gear except over bad rocks.

Before you do any off road driving look under your vehicle and note the position of its lowest points: springs, axles, differentials and gearbox. These will often be lower than you think and the differentials are usually off centre, and it is important to remember their clearance and position when traversing obstacles which you cannot get around.

Another important point with off road driving is not to hook your thumbs around the steering wheel, the sudden twist of the steering wheel as a front wheel touches or slides off a boulder can break your thumb. Unless you know a track very well avoid driving off the road at night, one unseen pothole can do a lot of damage.

If you have part time four wheel drive and have been in four wheel drive on a hard surface, when you get back on the paved road and change into two wheel drive you might find this change and the steering a little difficult. This is due to wind up between axles (if you have freewheel hubs you would find that you cannot free them by hand). The answer is to drive backwards for about 10 yards swinging the steering wheel about as you do so, which should free things, but if the vehicle is very heavily loaded it still may not. If the hubs are still not free you must jack up each front wheel and then things will free themselves. Never force your free wheeling hubs, if you cannot turn them by hand you must free the stress so that you can.

With fulltime four wheel drive systems remember to engage lock before entering really difficult sections. Make use of the rhythm of the suspension;

touch the brakes slightly as you approach the crest of a hump and release them as you pass over it, this will stop you flying. When you come to a sharp dip or rut, cross it at an angle so that only one wheel at a time drops into it. Steer the wheels towards and over the terrain's high points to maintain maximum ground clearance. If you cannot avoid a large boulder drive the wheels on one side over it in low range rather than trying to straddle it. Do not drive on the outside edge of tracks with a steep drop, they may be undermined by rain and collapse under the weight. If you have to travel along deep ruts try and straddle one of the ruts rather than driving in them with your transmission dragging the ground in the centre. Cross narrow river beds at an angle so that you do not get stuck in a dip at 90 degrees to the river bed with no room left to manoeuvre.

Whilst you are busy watching a difficult track ahead you may have to ask your passengers to look further ahead and warn you of any oncoming traffic. Keep an eye out for changes in surface colour, especially on sand, if the surface you are driving on is relatively firm and the colour of the surface remains the

Inspect the route on foot first. Jeep CJ5 in the Karakoram mountains Pakistan.

4WD bus on Bedford chassis, passenger gives directions to help the driver negotiate a difficult passage.

same then the going is likely to be the same, but if there is a change in colour you should slow down and inspect it in case things get more difficult. Keep an eye on other people's tracks, in soft sand always make fresh tracks as previous tracks have broken through the harder crust, but in all other situations other people's tracks are worth following if they go where you want to go. If you come to an obstacle you are not sure about always stop on firm ground, get out and inspect things on foot, this can save you a lot of trouble getting unstuck later. If you are not sure of being able to see the route clearly from the driving seat (eg: the bonnet is in the way) get a passenger to stand along the route and direct you.

Sometimes you might need to build up a route by putting stones across drainage ditches, sand ladders across weak bridges, chipping away high corners and levering aside large rocks. In third world countries always inspect locally made bridges before using them, if there are signs that local vehicles cross the river instead of the bridge then that is the best way to go.

Always inspect weak or old bridges first. Jeep CJ5 on a 90 year old British Army bridge in the Karakoram mountains.

Weak bridge — minaret of Jam, Afghanistan — always check first and unload most of the weight for safety.

Rebuilding the route after rockfall Karakoram mountains Pakistan.

If you get stuck in a rut on firm ground try rocking out by quickly shifting from first to reverse gear, but do not do this in soft sand or mud as you will only dig in deeper. If you cannot rock out of the rut jack up the offending wheel or wheels and build the rut up with stones or logs. A high lift jack makes life much easier here. If a rock suddenly appears and you cannot stop in time hit it with a tyre, which is more easily repaired than your undercarriage. Over consistently rocky terrain and large boulders go slowly in low range 1st gear using the engine for both drive and braking, then you remain in control; avoid touching the brakes or slipping the clutch.

On a loose surface it is better not to change gear whilst going up a hill because the momentary hesitation followed by the sudden torque increase may break traction and spin the wheels. It is preferable to change gear before you reach a hill, if it is steep or you are travelling slowly use low range 2nd gear; if the tyres start to lose traction near the top of a hill try swinging the steering wheel from side to side, you may get a fresh bite and make the top. If you fail on a steep hill make a fast shift into reverse, make sure the centre differential is locked if you have one, and use the engine as a brake to back down. This is more difficult with an automatic transmission, always back straight down the way you came up using the engine as a brake, if you use the brakes you will lose steering, do not try to back down in neutral or try to turn on a steep hill.

Always be prepared to stop quickly on top of a steep hill, the way down the other side might be at a completely different angle, descending a steep hill should also be done in low range 2nd or 3rd gear using the engine as a brake. Avoid tackling steep hills diagonally, if you lose traction and slip sideways you might turn over or roll to the bottom. Do not travel across slopes unless absolutely necessary, if you must do so choose the least possible angle, move at a steady pace and make any turns quickly.

In dusty country do not drive too close behind another vehicle, your vision will be impaired and your vehicle and lungs will fill with dust.

Overturned Vehicles: overturned vehicles are not an unusual hazard in off road driving, usually it happens at such slow speed that no one is injured. Once completely unloaded such vehicles are usually uprighted again fairly easily by manpower (six to eight men for a long wheelbase Land Rover) but once righted again you must sort out spilt and lost battery acid, all oil levels and turn the engine over several times, without the plugs or injectors in, before running the vehicle again.

Crossing Water: wherever possible before crossing water, get out and inspect by wading through, first noting whether the current is fast, if the bottom moves in the current, and if the bottom is level or pitted with large holes made by a previous vehicle getting stuck? Observe whether there is a sensible angle into it and out of the other side of the river and if the water comes above the axles, engine fan, exhaust outlet or vehicle body floor. All these things are important. If the current is fast or the bottom moving you may have to aim upstream to go straight across; large heavy stones will give you more grip than small ones or a sandy bottom, existing holes must be driven around or filled in with stones. If the current is really fast and the crossing more than three vehicle lengths wide it may only be sensible to cross with a winch and good anchor point.

Such things do happen – Afghanistan minaret of Jam (Land Rover Series III).

Land Rover 1 ton fording in Afghanistan. Keep it slow and steady.

Land Rover Series III fording a river.

River crossing with fast cross flow and awkward drops. Reconnoitre first on foot and keep well upstream to avoid being pushed towards the edge — Pakistan — Hindu Raj mountains. It is best to cross these in the early morning when the flow is least.

Most modern four wheel drives have fairly good poppet valves over the axle breathers which will keep water out whilst the oils are hot and there is good pressure within, but if the vehicle is stuck with these under water for several hours their oils will need to be changed. If you do a lot of water crossings you should change all transmission oils more often. Some vehicles have a plug which should be screwed into the clutch housing, if much work in water is to be done, but this should be removed again as soon as possible after wards to let any oil drain out. If the water is to come above the fan then it is wise to disconnect the fan belt. Petrol engines should have plenty of sealant around the electrics, especially the distributor. If it looks like being difficult or the water is deep then the crossing is best done in low range keeping the engine speed high, so that the back pressure of the water is not strong enough to fill the exhaust pipe and stall the engine, whilst the forward speed of the vehicle is not high enough to create a bow wave and spray water over the electrics. If the water is deep enough to enter the vehicle body you should remove damageable items from the low points likely to get wet.

Diesel engines have many advantages in deep water. If you stall in the water try removing the spark plugs or injectors and drive out in low range 1st gear on the starter motor, it does work over short distances. If the crossing is not difficult you can keep your brakes dry by keeping them lightly on with your left foot whilst crossing, or once you clear the water drive a little way with your left foot lightly on the brakes to dry them out. Drum brakes fill up with water and sand so clear them out as soon as possible after your journey's end, don't forget the handbrake drum on Land Rovers. If you have to do a lot of water crossings

Land Rover 90 turbo diesel takes a soaking.

you must expect a short life for your brake shoes, disc brakes are much better as they are self cleaning.

In high mountain areas where the streams and rivers are fed by melting snow the water will be lowest and slowest just after dawn, as the snow will have stopped melting during the night, so difficult crossings are best attempted at that time. If a vehicle gets stuck in glacier fed water or sea water for more than a couple of hours all working parts will need very thorough washing and several oil changes to get rid of the silt and salt. With salt water, electrical connections are very easily damaged.

Third World Ferries: in the third world, especially Africa, there are many river ferries which are very old or very Heath Robinson such as a few planks of wood across several canoes which are rarely moored properly to the river bank; when boarding or disembarking from these ferries it is essential to be in four wheel drive. In two wheel drive you can find yourself driving the ferry away from the bank so that your vehicle just drops straight into the river.

Salt Water and Beaches: if your vehicle has been in salt water the whole vehicle should be washed down with freshwater as soon as possible afterwards. Sandy beaches are usually firm enough for a vehicle between the high tidemark and the sea itself, though sometimes there is an undertow below the sand up to four yards from the sea so it is best not to get any closer than that. Always beware of the incoming tide which comes in faster than you expect and can cut you off from your beach exit point. Where there are large puddles of water or streaming water on a sea beach you should check for quicksand.

Beach sand is usually firmest just below the highest point still wet from the receding tide — Toyota station wagons Yemen Arab Republic.

With ferries such as this one on the river Nile at Malakal in Southern Sudan it is essential to engage 4WD both to embark and disembark or the vehicle could end up in the river.

Sand: in large sandy areas you usually have room enough to manoeuvre safely without bouncing, if you do not then life can be very difficult, the key to soft sand is momentum. Use high four wheel drive and do not use a lower gear than you have to. If you do not have special sand tyres speed up as you approach the soft stretch and try to maintain an even speed and straight line as you cross it; if you find yourself sticking press down on the accelerator gently, any abrupt change in speed or direction can break through the harder crust making you sink into the soft sand below. Avoid travelling directly in another vehicle's tracks in soft sand, but by all means follow the tracks because they will indicate where the softest sand lies but do not drive directly in them. In general if you have room to gain momentum it is best to leave your tyres at their recommended pressure because then you can use speed. For a really bad situation of soft sand with no room to get up speed safely, lower your tyres to around 15 PSI, use low range four wheel drive and gain as much speed as is possible or sensible before hitting the soft stretch. Get out and walk the section first, stomp your heels hard, you will soon learn how much your feet can sink before it will be too soft for your four wheel drive. In general if you get a firm footprint then it is hard enough for your four wheel drive, but if you get a vague oval and the sand slides back into it then it is too soft. Flat wind blown sand, with wind blown corrugations, will be quite firm as will sand with small stones on top or some grass growing through. Drift sand will be very soft. If the soft section is short it might be worth putting sand ladders down first. If there are other tracks compare the width (flotation) of those tyres against your own. A dry river bed can be very tricky, especially if it has very soft sand with no bottom and no room to manoeuvre; often the way out of a river bed is steep and needs low range so it is best to engage low range before entering it. If you wish to stop voluntarily on sand find a place on top of a rise, preferably pointing slightly downhill, and roll to a stop instead of using the brakes so as not to break the crust. Many vehicles have too much weight on the rear wheels when loaded so that the rear wheels break through the crust and stick whilst the front wheels spin uselessly on top; this is a case for wider tyres on the rear wheels, a couple of passengers sitting on the bonnet can help for short bad sections.

Ultra-light dust requires enough speed to retain visibility but not too fast or an accident may occur. Do not drive too close to other vehicles. **Land Rover in the Dasht-I-Laili desert Afghanistan 15 mph.**

Sand dunes are great fun but can be very tricky, getting stuck near your local beach is one thing but stuck for days in the Empty Quarter or Teneré Desert is another. Straight groove high flotation sand tyres are best, but any wide tyre will do so long as it does not have an aggressive tread. The more rounded the tyre profile the better because a flat profile is more likely to push sand ahead of it than to ride over it. You need speed to get up a dune but must be able to stop on the top as there may be a sheer drop on the other side. Some deserts have long uphill sections and then suddenly you drop off the end, these drops can be very hard to spot in low evening sun and I have seen several accidents. All sand is always firmest in the early morning due to some amount of dew in its crust, so experienced drivers use this period to cross the softest sections and stop to camp early in the afternoon when the sand is at its softest and the light is awkward. I have often struggled into a beautiful dune camp site in the afternoon and yet driven out again with ease early the next morning. The Sahara is mostly quite high desert and in the winter months the night temperature is often below freezing. In large sand dune areas stay as high as possible, then if you start to stick you can gain momentum by pointing downhill and then try again, the bottom of the well between dunes usually has the softest sand.

Government Land Rovers in the Sahara — note quickly available sand ladders — Hoggar mountains, Algeria.

Loaded Land Rover in the Sahara desert — too much weight on rear wheels causes these to break through the surface crust whilst the front wheels remain above it. Try to keep the weight evenly on all four wheels if possible.

When travelling in convoy in deserts it is best for the vehicles to be spread out so that each has room to manoeuvre, does not get the other vehicles dust and has room to stop on safe ground if one or more vehicles is stuck. It is best to use a system whereby vehicles which are stuck put on their headlights at main beam; others can see the beams, even if they cannot see the vehicle itself and those ahead should keep an eye out for headlights in their mirrors, thus if someone is stuck other vehicles stop where it is possible and return to help, on foot if necessary. In a convoy situation the rear vehicle should have a good mechanic and a good spare wheel and tyre in case of breakdown or punctures. Drivers in convoy should keep allotted convoy order to avoid confusion and unnecessary searches.

Getting Unstuck in Sand: once you are stuck in soft sand do not spin the wheels as you will only sink in deeper, get passengers out first and try to reverse out in low range; if the wheels spin stop immediately as you will make things worse, do not try to go forward again, rocking does not work in sand and you may blow your clutch or transmission. The torque of the propeller shaft power tends to tilt front and rear axles in opposite directions relative to the chassis, so if you avoid spinning the wheels so that it won't dig in too much you can try to reverse out, thus tilting the axles in the opposite direction and getting traction on the wheels that spun before. Dig the sand clear of all the points which are touching it, this is likely to include the axles and transmission so a couple of long handled shovels are useful (folding shovels are useless). Scout the area ahead, if forward progress looks sensible then, after digging the wheels clear, dig a sloping ramp forward from the wheels to the surface for the sand ladders, otherwise dig such a ramp backwards. Lay down the sand ladders in the ramps

Time to get out and dig – Mercedes 4WD bus, Sahara Desert

94

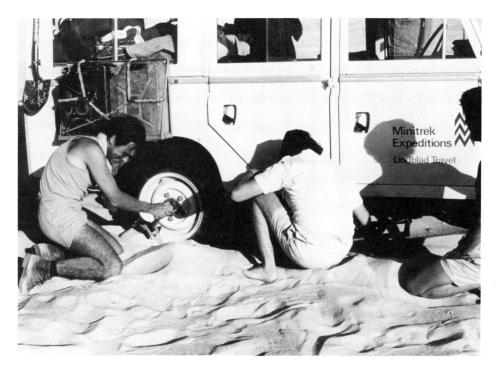

Digging it out — a regular occurrence in soft sand. Do it early before you get heavily stuck.

All hands push to free a Land Rover stuck in the Sahara's Teneré desert. Note shovels placed to mark the positions of the sand ladders to aid their recovery when buried.

you have dug, for the back wheels if you only have two ladders or for all four wheels if you have four ladders. Push the end of the ladders under the wheels as far as possible using a high lift jack, if necessary, to raise the vehicle enough to do this. Stand the shovels upright in the sand to mark the sand ladders' position if they get buried, then, with only the driver in the vehicle and all other passengers pushing, the vehicle should come free using low range. If another vehicle is on firm ground and has a long enough tow rope or winch cable it can help. Once free the driver must not stop again until he is on safe ground, so the poor pushing passengers must pick up the sand ladders and walk in a big soft sandy oven; the vehicle may stick again quite soon or the passengers may have a couple of miles to walk, it all depends on your luck. If you have come out backwards you must then try to find a way around the bad area. Sometimes, if a ladder is not properly under a wheel when the vehicle first mounts it the ladder can pitch up and rip off the exhaust pipe or a body panel. So an agile person has to keep a foot on the free end of the ladder to prevent the pitching, but must also move quickly once things are safe or else get run over. If the passengers are fit enough, once the vehicle has cleared a pair of sand ladders they can dig them up and run ahead to drop them under the wheels again but this is very hard work. With a large convoy a ramp of several ladders can be made for the vehicle.

It is very tempting when stuck to only do half of the digging out required and make an attempt at pushing out, sometimes this works but mostly it does not. If you are stuck you will save energy in the long run by doing things properly right away. Sand ladders and perforated steel plate tend to get bent in use, so when you have finished all your soft sand sections put them on hard ground with the ends on the ground and the bend in the air and straighten them out by driving over them.

Corrugations: unsurfaced tracks carrying heavy traffic and seldom scraped or graded develop parallel ridges across the road (corrugations) which in really bad areas can be 10″ deep and 20″ across. These are very rough on the vehicle and occupants, sometimes the worst of the effect can be ironed out by achieving the right speed at which the vehicle body and occupants get a relatively smoother ride, but the suspension is going through hell. This speed is generally 30-40 mph, but if you need to go faster than that it becomes too dangerous because you are only skimming across the crests of the corrugations and any sudden change of steering from hitting a stone or hump, or a burst tyre can turn the vehicle over. I have seen several serious accidents to Toyota Land Cruisers and Range Rovers caused in this fashion, because they can go much faster with relative comfort to the passengers. The only safe answer is a long tiring, slow, shake-up journey. Unfortunately there are areas in the Sahara and the Sudan where you can get 150 miles at a time of such corrugations. Travelling slowly on corrugations is usually more effective than travelling beside them. Remember that thousands of vehicles before you have tried that and given up, hence the corrugations. Travelling at speed on corrugations makes tyres hot so punctures are common; lowering the pressure keeps them cooler but lowers the speed at which you can travel without damaging them. Drivers of short wheel base vehicles should drive slowly on corrugations for safety.

Salt Flats (Sebkhas, Chotts): are like quicksand, you break through the crust into the salty bottomless mud underneath; you sink fast and if you cannot be towed out very quickly it can be for ever. In areas known for their salt flats always stick to the track, never drive at random. In remote areas where there is no track (eg: around Bilma) if you are unlucky enough to hit one it is better to try and drive back to firm ground in a wide arc than to try to stop and reverse out. It is very wise to convoy with another four wheel drive in such areas.

Tyre Pressure: only lower tyre pressure in emergencies for short periods at slow speeds and only in soft sand as rocks will cut up the side walls; the best answer is a properly designed tyre for the job, such as the Michelin XS. Always check with your tyre manufacturer but a rough guide for Michelin radials is that if you drop to 75% of the road use pressure for off road use you should not exceed 30 mph and for a real emergency dropping to 40% of road use pressure you should not exceed 15 mph. Exceeding these speeds at low pressures will break up the tyres.

If you are to spend much time in sand deserts you will find that only a small percentage of the sand is really soft so you will be best off with wide tyres at normal pressures so that you can travel at a comfortable speed on the firm sections and make full use of speed where you have room on the soft sections — only lower the pressures in an emergency. If you fit wider tyres than the makers recommend for extremely soft sand use, you should only drive at low speeds. If you drive at normal road speeds you are likely to damage the transmission.

In wide open sand seas like the Tenere in the Sahara and some areas of the Empty Quarter you can often spend a couple of hours at a comfortable 40 mph or more, so you must make an extra effort to keep wide awake to problems ahead because to hit a rock, rut or to fly off the end of a hump or sand dune at this speed can wreck the vehicle and kill occupants.

Mud: momentum is also the key to getting through mud, though speeds should not be high as there are more likely to be problems underneath than in sand. If it is not too deep the wheels may be able to dig into the harder ground underneath so you can go through in low range. If there are existing tracks and they are not so deep that you will ground your transmission in the centre then these tracks are worth using, otherwise slog through trying to keep a steady speed and direction as you would with sand. If the mud is heavy with clay even aggressive tread tyres will soon clog up, so unless you are using special mud tyres you can gain a lot by fitting tyre chains. Muddy areas are more likely to be near trees so a winch can be useful in such a situation.

If you stick badly in mud it can be very heavy work to dig out. The best way to get out of mud is to jack up the vehicle and fill in the holes with rocks, stones, logs, tree branches etc so that you can drive off again. A high lift jack can make things much easier. If there is a lot of water, try to dig a drainage channel to drain it away first. Perforated steel plate can be helpful in mud but sand ladders are usually too slippery. When you get back on the paved road clear as much mud as possible off the wheels and propeller shafts otherwise the weight of the mud will put them out of balance and cause damage; drive steadily for several miles to let your tyre treads clear of mud or you might skid.

Rocks and Tree Stumps: if you are unlucky you might get high centred on rocks or tree stumps and the only answer is to jack up the vehicle and build a ramp under the wheels. If you cannot go forward or backwards unload the

Alvin Smith blasts through mud, but you should inspect for hidden projections first.

vehicle and use a high lift jack to lever the front and rear end sideways, one end at a time. This is done by jacking up the vehicle and then pushing it sideways off the jack, but always check that it will not land in an even worse position before you do it.

Snow and Ice: snow is the most deceptive off road surface because it does not necessarily conform with the terrain it covers; if there is a track or road stay in the middle of it where possible, so as not to go into ditches on the side. Drive slowly in four wheel drive using as high a gear as possible to avoid wheel spin (lock centre differential if you have permanent four wheel drive), try to avoid touching the brakes, hard acceleration or sharp wheel movements, do everything gently. Studded snow tyres are good for icy on road driving, but for off road driving tyre chains are much better; studded snow tyres should be on all four wheels, tyre chains should either be on all four wheels or the rear wheels only. Having chains on front wheels will put you into a spin if you touch the brakes going downhill. Try to avoid using the brakes, instead use the engine for braking in four wheel drive. If you have to use the brakes use several short pumps to avoid the wheels locking.

Avoid existing tracks unless they are shallow. Coming down an icy hill use a low gear in four wheel drive. If you drive into a drift you will have to dig out and it is easiest to come out backwards. Lengths of old floor carpet can be useful as a mat under the wheels to give it some grip if you do not have chains. Off road driving will be easier at night or in the early morning when the mud beneath the snow is frozen, so you will not dig in so much. As with sand oversize tyres are good in snow, if they are to be fitted with chains they should be at correct pressures and not lowered pressures, or the chains will damage them. Carry a good sleeping bag in case you get stuck and have a long wait for help. For on road driving an extra couple of hundredweight directly over the rear axle will help your tyres get more grip, chains are good on sheet ice if you go slowly. Use only the strongest heavyweight chains, having to keep mending broken chains in freezing off road conditions is not a pleasant experience.

If you have a diesel engine and it is very cold dilute the diesel with one part petrol to 15 parts diesel to stop it freezing up (use 1 to 10 for Arctic type temperatures). If you start to spin do not touch the brakes — depress the clutch then with all four wheels rolling free you will regain steering.

Driving on Dirt Roads: when driving on dirt roads always be prepared for stones thrown up by other vehicles or in some countries, small boys, to break your windscreen. Never overtake when you cannot see through the dust of the vehicle ahead, another might be coming the other way. Use the horn to warn a person you are about to overtake. On dirt roads culverts do not always extend the full width of the road, so be careful when overtaking or you may end up in a ditch, be especially careful of this in snow.

Avoid driving at night; potholes, broken down lorries, culverts, camels, donkeys, bullock carts and people are all hard to see and many lorries drive at speed without lights, then blinding you with full beam when they see you. In some countries there are unlit chains or logs across roads as checkpoints.

Remember that careful driving in the first instance can save you a lot of time and effort in making repairs; broken half shafts, broken springs and burnt out clutches are caused by the driver, not the vehicle, and getting stuck can often be avoided by stopping to reconnoitre the difficult section first.

Typical dirt track problem, road collapses under the weight of a 1 ton Land Rover without any warning — Swat, Pakistan.

99

Offroad driving tuition: in 1987 David Bowyer set up the UK's first non-military or factory based off-road driving course, at his Overlander site in Devon. Since then others have copied the idea, but none of them come anywhere near to the quality and variety of this specially constructed course or the standard of instruction; only desert sand and salt flats are missing. The standard course is a full day, with a further half day for winching and self-recovery technique. If you wish to learn the ropes quickly without damage to your vehicle and enjoy yourself at the same time, this is the place to go.

Range Rover wading at the Overlander off-road centre.

Isuzu Trooper wading.

Towing: four wheel drive vehicles are ideal for towing trailers, boats or caravans both on and off the road because they have strong chassis, engines with high torque at low speed, strong springs and four wheel drive. For on the road driving with trailers the rules are much the same as with a two wheel drive vehicle, but you have the added advantage of four wheel drive braking in difficult downhill sections. Brake well in advance and smoothly to allow for the extra weight. Use a lower gear for engine braking downhill. Allow more room and more time to accelerate when overtaking. On hot days the extra weight can make the engine overheat on long climbs, using a lower gear will keep the engine cooler. Load the trailer carefully both side to side and front to back and have about 80 to 100 lbs weight on the trailer hitch when loaded. Remember to allow for this when calculating the loadable weight of the towing vehicle. Have your four wheel drive's tow hitch adjusted for height so that the trailer tows level and not back end down. Fit a second tow hitch on your front bumper if it is strong enough, this will make it easier to park your trailer or caravan in a tight spot or launch your boat. The front tow hitch should be off centre so that the driver can see clearly along the side of the trailer.

For off road towing there are a few more things to think about. Fit wider wheels to give the trailer more flotation, allow for the trailer's poor ground clearance on rocks and tree stumps and remember that you have a larger turning circle with a trailer. Wrap the trailer's electrical wiring into a loom and tie it safely above the trailer's chassis rails where it cannot snag. Carry spare wheel/s for the trailer. Lash down everything in the trailer very securely as it will be subjected to a lot of bumping. Fit mud flaps to the four wheel drive's rear wheels and a cover to the front of the trailer to stop it being damaged by stones, sand and brambles thrown up by the four wheel drive's rear wheels. Drive slowly and steadily and stay in four wheel drive. Be more careful not to get stuck as it is difficult to reverse with a trailer and it will be dificult to manhandle a trailer in soft sand or mud.

For expedition and military use powered trailers are available for specialist four wheel drive vehicles, but these have been known to push the towing vehicle over on occasions. In really rough country even military trailers do not work out too well. The biggest problem is keeping their contents in one piece and recognisable; they need very careful packing and padding and everything must be very securely lashed down. Such trailers have an advantage in soft sand in that they spread the load over six wheels. For expedition use the trailer should have the same wheels and high flotation tyres as the towing vehicle.

If you are buying a four wheel drive, particularly for towing, it is worth remembering that a short wheel base vehicle has the towing hitch nearest to the rear axle, thus giving a shorter combined turning circle with least pitch and roll.

A high centred Steyr-Daimler-Puch Haflinger above and a sunk in mud F.W.D. bus on a Bedford chassis. In hard off road conditions vehicles are guaranteed to get damaged.

Chapter 6
Common Problems

When normal vehicles breakdown they are taken or towed to a garage where they can be repaired or the ailing part replaced. However when a four wheel drive vehicle has problems off the road, and it may be many hundreds of miles off the road, a repair must be made at least good enough to get the vehicle and its occupants back to safety. There are also some problems that are particular to four wheel drive vehicles, either by the nature of their design or the use they are put to. Some of the more common problems are mentioned in this chapter.

Short Wheelbase Vehicles: short wheelbase vehicles by virtue of the very short distance between the front and rear wheels have a habit of breaking away, sliding sideways, or even spinning suddenly if bends are taken too fast. Things are obviously worse in slippery conditions, but the same can also happen on badly corrugated roads if travelling fast, even in a straight line. Extra care must therefore be taken with such vehicles.

Speed: Toyota Land Cruisers, Nissan Patrols and other similar fast, softly sprung vehicles are often driven at unsafe speeds on badly corrugated roads, more caution is always required off the paved road.

Punctures: if you are only off the road for a day trip you should get by without ever having to mend a puncture yourself, but the expedition man often has to mend his own in the evening to be ready for the next day, here are a few hints:-
   The advantage of Michelin radial beads is that they usually fall off their rims very easily when flat. If you cannot break the bead on a tyre try driving over it or using a jack and the weight of the vehicle. If the wheel rim is wider on one side than the other only attempt to remove the tyre over the narrowest side, starting with both beads in the well of the wheel. With a Land Rover this is the opposite side of the wheel to the valve. If the tyre is to be removed or fitted completely both sides of the tyre must be levered over this narrowest rim. Sweep out all sand and grit, file off any sharp burrs on the wheel and put everything back together on a groundsheet to stop any fresh sand or grit getting in to make future punctures.
   When refitting the tyre use liquid soap and water as a lubricant to help ease the tyre bead on the rim; use a Schrader valve tool to hold the tube valve in place whilst you refit the tyre. Pump the tyre up enough to refit the bead on the rim, then let it down again to release any twists in the inner tube and pump up

103

Overloading is normal in the Third World, Saudi Arabian-North Yemen border (Toyota Land Cruiser)

A common problem. Author repairing snow chains, Afghanistan 11,000 ft. International Harvester Travelall.

again to full rear tyre pressure. If the wheel has to be fitted to the front at a later date it is easy to let some air out.

If you are travelling in convoy with other four wheel drives it makes sense if you all use the same wheels and tyres, then you need only carry one spare wheel each and can share when punctures occur. It is important that the rear vehicle in the convoy carries a good spare wheel and tyre as he has no one behind him if he gets a puncture.

Steel braced radial tyres when punctured by sharp stones or driven on when flat often have a sharp strand of wire left pointing in towards the tube. This must be cut down as short as possible, but it will still cause another puncture. These can be gaitered for off road use using cut up truck inner tubes which are fairly thick but still flexible (there are always plenty to be found abandoned on the pistes of the Sahara). A gaitered tyre needs to be run at correct pressure, if the pressure is lowered the gaiter will move. The edges of the gaiter need to be chamfered to ease the strain on the inflated inner tube. Once back on paved road a gaitered tyre will behave like a buckled wheel so it is best changed to a good one. Michelin XY tyres can be legally recut when worn, these recuts are useful to use on sharp stone sections of piste, where tyres cut up easily, so as not to destroy an almost new tyre.

If you use tubeless tyres carry the best repair kit you can get and a bead expander, because none of the tyre pumps you can carry will have enough pressure to do this. It will also be best to carry some correct sized inner tubes to use in the tubeless tyres as a safety factor; to fit one of these you will have to pull the tubeless tyre valve out of the wheel rim first. Good quality narrow tyre levers are much easier to use than poorer quality wide ones.

It is easy to get a puncture in your rear tyre without noticing it when driving on bad or corrugated roads. Always be suspicious of any swaying about otherwise you might drive so far on a flat tyre that you destroy the tyre and tube and buckle the wheels as well. Buckled steel wheels can be hammered into good enough shape to get you home again. Wheelbraces get overworked on long off road journeys and become a loose fit, so have a good socket or ring spanner available to fit the wheel nuts as a spare.

Scissor type jacks jam regularly in sandy conditions so are best avoided.

Fuel Problems: fuel starvation is often caused by dust blocking the breather in the fuel tank filler cap, you can identify this because the fuel tank will be caved in and when you release the cap it will expand again.

If you work in extreme heat or at altitude in low gears petrol pumps may overheat and cause vapour lock. The best way to cure this if you have water to spare is to wrap the pump in rag or bandage and pour water on it. If it becomes a constant problem fit a plastic pipe from the windscreen washer tank to the bandage wrapped fuel pump and give it a squirt whenever it needs it. Electric fuel pumps are notorious for breaking down, always carry a complete spare. Carry a spare diaphragm and one way valves for mechanical fuel pumps.

Off road fuel systems often become blocked in the line from the tank to the fuel pump. This is best cleared by using a tyre pump to create back pressure from the pump, if this fails you will have to strip the whole line. The filter in the tank often breaks due to vibration. Close weave cotton will effect a repair.

Bad fuel can be a plague in third world countries. Diesel fuel often contains water and grit; using two in line filters in the fuel system helps, but water will have to be drained out if you do not have a sedimenter. Petrol can contain water, grit or worse still, old petrol stored too long so that gummy deposits form and block the lines and filters. We once filled up eight Land Rovers with such petrol in Timbuctoo and spent several days between Timbuctoo and Niamey constantly stopping to clear out the fuel lines.

Carburettors of the Stromberg and SU type need regular cleaning in dusty and hot climates as they tend to stick due to dust and/or dye from the fuel. Automatic chokes have a habit of sticking in the closed position making starting impossible in warm weather.

Pay particular attention to keeping your air inlet filters clean and if you have the oil bath type make sure that there are no holes in the rubber hose connecting the oil filter to the carburettor or inlet manifold, because any dust or grit drawn into the engine air inlet will soon destroy rings and bores. Air inlets extended to roof height tend to break off in really rough country.

Fuel problems with diesel engines are usually due to air or water in the system. You must know how to bleed the system correctly. If this fails to correct your problem check all pipes and tubing for air leaks, the fuel lift pump and the fuel line to the tank. In really cold weather the fuel may be just too thick to pump so dilute it with petrol. A sedimenter can be useful for removing water, but it needs to be well protected against stones or rocks breaking the glass. Injectors give very little trouble, but spares and spare high pressure pipes should be carried for overland and expedition work.

Electrical Problems: these are very common in off road vehicles. Always carry a spare distributor cap, rotor arm, points and condenser as these are often cracked by heat and vibration or shorted out by water or dust. Points and plugs should be checked regularly, they do not last well in hot climates. If a petrol engine in a hot climate starts losing power or missing, check the points gap. Modern high tension leads are of carbon core for suppression reasons, but they give a lot of trouble in four wheel drive vehicles. Always replace them with copper wire high tension leads and suppressed plug caps. It is worth fitting contactless electronic ignition if you do not already have it. Spray all ignition parts with ignition sealer to keep out dust and water. Keep battery terminals clean, greased and the connections tight; replace the slip-on type battery connectors with the older, better nut and bolt clamps. Keep the battery topped up so that the plates are always covered, only use distilled or deionized water for this. If your battery is giving trouble first check battery solenoid connections and check for a stuck starter pinion. If these are okay change the battery for a new one. There are no miracle cures for batteries and you do not want a flat battery off the road.

If your starter fails or your battery is dead with no spare available and you have manual transmission the vehicle can be push or tow started if you have room. If you do not have room, or are in soft sand jack up the rear wheels, put in two wheel drive high ratio second gear and have someone spin the wheels whilst you drop the clutch, it may take a few attempts but it does work. In the extreme situation, fit a hub winch hub or tyreless wheel, wind a long rope around it 10-20 times and have passengers set off at a trot pulling the rope to spin the wheels. If you have an automatic gearbox you must have the starter motor working. If your battery is flat you can use jump leads from another vehicle, but if the starter motor fails you must either repair it or fit another one. If you spend a lot of time far off the road and alone you should carry a second battery fitted with a split charge circuit and use a manual transmission.

If your vehicle is fitted with an alternator always disconnect it and the battery earth lead before having any electric welding done on the vehicle. If you use jump leads to start your vehicle or another's put on the headlights and radio to absorb some of the high surge voltage which might damage the alternator when the engine fires. Never run the engine with the battery or alternator disconnected; with a diesel this means that you must always stop the engine with the fuel cut out before switching off if a fail safe device is not already fitted in the switch. Always fit a second battery or jump leads positive to positive and negative to negative. Do not let the two vehicles touch when using jump leads.

Alternators are difficult to repair in the field and diodes impossible. If your alternator has the charging circuit diodes built in and you go a long way off the road alone it is wise to carry a complete spare alternator. On some vehicles the red charge warning light on the dashboard is part of the charging circuit so carry a spare bulb for this. Make sure you carry spare fuses.

Other Problems: Keep a spare set of keys well hidden away taped to the chassis in case yours get lost or stolen. Carry a wire brush to clean rusty and muddy threads and a soft brush to clean the engine compartment and body of dust.·

Hub bearing oil seals regularly fail in four wheel drives, usually due to sand in the brake drums; or blocked axle case breather vents; often the metal, which the seal mates against, will then have a groove worn into it so a new oil seal will not seal unless this is also replaced, or there is room to move the seal in or out about ⅛″ to mate on clean metal.

In hot countries fan belts break more often than is usual, so spares should be carried. Some vehicles have certain radiator hoses which give more problems than others and spares of these are worth carrying. Wire type hose clips are always better replaced with good Jubilee type hose clips. Always use a torque wrench for aluminium cylinder heads or other aluminium components.

If on returning to the paved road you get wheel shimmy first check for buckled wheels and loose wheel bearings. If those are not the cause then look at the swivel pins which can usually be adjusted by removing shims. If all the wheels are buckled, put the worst as spare and the next worst on the back. If a tyre has been mended locally in a Third World country, the mechanic may have fitted a gaiter which would give the same ride effect as a buckled wheel.

If you carry fuel or other heavy loads on the roof you will probably have to reinforce your windscreen frame corners, especially if you spend much time on bad corrugations.

When brake cylinder seals fail in off road driving it is usually due to sand, so fitting new seals does not usually cure the problem because the cylinder is also scored, hence the need to carry complete wheel cylinders.

Cheap spanners have a habit of breaking when you most need them, often you damage your hands at the same time, so buy good quality tools.

Never put nuts and bolts or any parts down in the sand, use a groundsheet or tarpaulin. Brush all drain and filler plugs and their surroundings clean before unscrewing to keep out sand and grit, if necessary use a brush plus petrol.

Land Rovers prior to Series III are best fitted with heavy duty half shafts in the rear axle if the driver is heavy footed.

Carry spare rubber seals for fuel jerrycan spouts, leaking fuel jerrycans can be sealed with epoxy resin. Never put petrol in polythene cans because they are porous. If you cannot get into gear check for stones jammed in the linkage.

Some Improvisations: split fuel tanks, oil sumps and radiators repair best with glass reinforced plastic kits (epoxy resin plus glass fibre). Most propriety tank sealing kits go off in hot countries. Give the epoxy plenty of time to cure, preferably overnight. Plastic and rubber low pressure fuel and water lines can be temporarily repaired with plastic tape reinforced with malleable wire. Heater water hoses can be blocked off with a spark plug.

Lengths of strong chain with long bolts can be used for emergency repairs, with various metal tools as splints for springs, chassis and axles. Leaf springs can also be splinted with 'U' bolts.

If you do not have a differential lock and need one in a bad situation, you can lock the spinning wheel by tightening its handbrake cable adjuster, if it has one, but if not, or your four wheel drive has a transmission brake, tighten up the brake shoe adjuster cams. This system should only be used for a few yards at a time.

A leaking radiator can be temporarily sealed with Radweld, raw egg or porridge. If the radiator is damaged close off as many as possible of the tubes by folding over with pliers first. I once did a Sahara crossing where the vehicle's radiator used up several pounds of porridge over four days.

If a fuel tank or line is irreparably damaged use a jerrycan set above the engine with a plastic hose direct to the carburettor or lift pump. Once you start the syphon gravity will do the rest, but you must drive slowly and carefully; having the can on the roof is best because it has more gravity and is clear of most of the dust. Do not run the can empty, keep topping up when half full.

If you are in convoy and one vehicle has a non-functioning charging system, swap that vehicle's battery every 100 kilometres.

If you are overheating you will cool the engine down quickest by going downhill in gear using the engine as a brake. If you stop with a hot engine, so long as it is not showing signs of seizure, leave it ticking over for a few minutes. This will cool it down more quickly and evenly than switching it off.

If you have a partially seized engine, a 6 cylinder engine can be run on 4 cylinders and a 4 cylinder engine can be run on 3 cylinders in a real emergency. To isolate a cylinder remove the piston and connecting rod, disconnect the spark plug and high tension lead (or if a diesel, the injector), close the valves by removing the push rods or rocker arms if overhead cam. If a diesel use a plastic pipe to feed the fuel in the disconnected fuel injector pipe away to a safe place, away from the heat of the engine. If a connecting rod has broken and gone through the block, seal the hole with any sheet metal plus glass reinforced plastic and self tapping screws to keep out dust and sand. Drive slowly.

If your big end nuts have nylon inserts instead of tab washers carry spares, if no spares are available use Locktite when refitting.

Old engine oil can be used in an oil bath type air cleaner. In an emergency you can run a diesel engine on paraffin (kerosene) or domestic heating oil by adding 1 part engine oil to 100 parts of paraffin to lubricate the injector pump. Good quality diesel engine oil is okay to use in petrol engines in warm climates, but most petrol engine oils should not be used for diesel engines.

A bent track rod should be taken off and hammered as straight as possible, if you leave it bent not only will you scrub your tyres but in soft sand it could cause you to roll.

If a four wheel drive, fitted with free wheeling hubs, breaks a front half shaft you can continue in two wheel (rear) drive just by putting the transfer into two wheel drive and the hubs into freewheel. If you do not have free wheeling hubs and you do not have far to go, you can risk driving in two wheel (rear) drive and remove the front prop shaft; but if you have a long way to go you will have to remove both front half shafts, which is complicated.

If you break a rear half shaft you can continue by withdrawing both rear half shafts (which is quick and easy) and continue by putting the vehicle into four wheel drive. If the rear differential is broken remove both half shafts and the rear prop shaft.

If a permanent four wheel drive jams in the centre differential lock position remove the front propeller shaft and drive slowly on.

An extension tube for your wheel brace can help you remove wheel nuts from a hot wheel after a puncture, but do not use it to retighten the nuts.

Temporary drain or filler plugs can be whittled from wood and sealed in with epoxy resin or Araldite.

Silicone RTV can be used for most gaskets other than cylinder head gaskets. Paper gaskets can be used again if covered in grease. Silicone RTV or PTFE tape are useful when putting together leaking fuel line connections.

If you do develop a brake line or wheel cylinder leak it is usually best to travel on slowly in low gear, using the engine as a main brake, and the hand brake for finally stopping, but go easy on using transmission type handbrakes. If things are really bad you can disconnect a metal pipe upstream of the leak, bend it over and hammer the end flat, or if a rubber hose clamp it. If you have a dual brake system the brakes will then work as normal, but if not you must be careful of the uneven braking due to braking only on three wheels.

Four wheel drive vehicles tend to be high off the ground, placing the spare wheel on the ground and standing on it can make work on the engine much easier. On some four wheel drives you can also lift the bonnet off easily or else right back against the windscreen (tie it back for safety).

If you burst an oil gauge pressure line (Smiths plastic ones go frequently) disconnect the T piece at the engine end and plug it by screwing in the electric pressure sensor which is also on the T piece, you will then still have the low pressure warning light.

If your clutch jams you can change gears without it by adjusting engine speed as you move the gear lever. Speed up the engine to change down and slow down the engine to change up. It is usually best to start the engine with the vehicle already in second gear.

Steering relays which do not have a filler point can be topped up by taking off two top cover bolts and filling up with the correct oil through one hole until oil comes out of the other hole.

Dionising water crystals are easier to carry than distilled water.

Clothes plus water and washing powder in a waterproof container make a good washing machine in the back of a four wheel drive off the road for a couple of hours.

If you do not have a starting handle, you can simplify the setting of valve tappets and static ignition timing by jacking up one rear wheel and having someone turn it with the vehicle in gear and two wheel drive, whilst you watch the valves or rotor arm. If you are alone jack up both wheels on one side, engage four wheel drive, put the vehicle in gear and you can turn the front wheel with your foot whilst watching the valves or rotor arm.

If you have a glass fibre reinforced rubber timing belt, it is not easy to check its condition for advance warning of failure, with the Land Rover. The best you can do is to remove the timing cover vent plate and gauze, push in your little finger onto the belt and feel for any fraying or grit. If you find any, then it would be wise to replace the belt.

Chapter 7
Overland and Expeditions

Apart from very rare circumstances of an expedition sponsored by a four wheel drive manufacturer, overlanders and expedition users have to make a compromise between what they can afford, what can best do the job and whether spares they need are available en route. Ignoring price, some vehicles are more useful than others in particular areas.

In 1973 I took eight Long Wheelbase Safari Land Rovers into the Hindu Kush and Karakoram Mountains of North West Pakistan before the Karakoram Highway was built. In this area of steep mountainsides and regular landslides the tracks are often built around the smallest available four wheel drive, which is the smallest open top Jeep, thus minimizing on the work necessary (all done by hand) to keep routes open where possible. The result was that in many places the Land Rovers could not get through because they were either too wide for tracks or bridges, too high to get under rock overhangs or too heavy for some of the tracks held onto mountainsides by treetrunks. I have since returned several times and made some amazing journeys, mostly following mule tracks but using small Jeeps.

When it comes to worldwide popularity and parts availability the Land Rover leads easily, except in the Americas. The second most popular four wheel drive world wide is now the Toyota Land Cruiser, but it does not have such a good parts service as the Land Rover and because its working life is less than a Land Rover you will not find many old ones around capable of being cannibalized for parts. The Land Cruiser became very popular in Islamic countries when Land Rover was blacklisted, but the Range Rover, which was not blacklisted, has since regained many of those lost markets. Many of the world's armies use Land Rovers, even in those same Islamic countries where they were blacklisted, and if you find the right military contacts, backsheesh can often find you a spare from a crashed military vehicle. But beware the electrics which are more likely to be 24 volts.

Some remote countries use the earliest designs of Jeeps, often put together locally under licence, in these countries small Jeep spares can be the easiest to get. Many countries make Land Rovers under licence so again spares can be easy to find.

For long distance work most American four wheel drives have too low a payload and too high a fuel consumption. The bigger American four wheel drives have the payload, but usually too long a wheelbase, and you would use most of the payload carrying the fuel required.

Karakoram mountains Pakistan. Track has low overhangs and is often supported on tree trunks and is thus restricted to small vehicles such as the Jeep CJ5.

Weak suspension bridge in Pakistan. The Jeep had to be manually shunted around the tight right angle turns at each end.

Trans-African group stop for a drink. This Bedford M type is equipped to carry 100 gallons of water and 200 gallons of diesel fuel.

In many parts of Africa south of the Sahara fuel is hard to find, so overlanders have to use a vehicle capable of carrying a larger payload, most of which will be its own fuel. For this use those who can afford them use the Mercedes Unimog, usually ex-military, whilst those not so well off use the Bedford 3-6 ton ex-military trucks.

Mercedes Unimog in the Nubian desert Sudan.

Mercedes Benz Unimog in the marshland of the Sudanese Sudd.

For the Americas no one vehicle stands out as the most commonly used; Land Rover spares are rare, Toyota spares are much more available, but in general in the Americas it would be best to stick to an American made vehicle.

Mercedes Unimogs have exceptional cross country ability and like the Fiat PC 65 and PC 75 have step down axles giving higher than normal ground clearance. It is very hard to get them stuck in sand though they will stick in mud, and here their extra ground clearance means that they have gone that much deeper before sticking and therefore are that much harder to dig out. Also with their higher clearance they turn over more easily due to high centre of gravity. Unimog petrol engines are relatively small so you need to use the gear box well, but fuel consumption is good. The standard 6 speed one range gearbox can be altered to a two range 4 speed gearbox, four wheel drive can be engaged very easily without double declutching at any speed. The chassis is cleverly arranged to give good weight distribution over all four wheels at most angles, but gives a bad ride on corrugations. Mechanically the Unimog is overcomplicated, it does not go wrong often but when it does it is difficult to work on and needs many special tools. The latest models have the clutch set to one side of the transmission instead of in line with it, so this makes it much easier to change.

Bedford trucks are cheap, simple and in some parts crude. They have good cross country performance if handled sensibly and slowly, but are too heavy in soft sand. Things go wrong often but repairs can usually be improvised. The 330 diesel engine is less reliable than the 550 diesel engine, but the weakest

Combining two different vehicles means doubling up on the spares to be carried. Using a larger "load carrier" only works out if you intend to have a fixed base camp. A Studebaker Rio 6 × 6 and a LWB Land Rover Series IIA station wagon.

point is usually the clutch and clutch plate. On all Bedfords the fuel tank straps regularly break, but the tank can be held in with strong nylon rope until repairs can be arranged. If you have a 550 engine and a 5 speed gearbox the vehicle will be able to manage some 50 mph plus on the road; this is too much for the front differential drive flange bearing, so it is wise to remove the front propshaft before driving at such speeds. Except in soft sand diesel engined Bedfords are very economical for their size. With much low gear and high altitude work in Afghanistan I achieved 12-14 mpg with a 550 engine powering a full 27 seat bus, plus camping equipment. The 330 produces the same in a smaller vehicle.

The ideal expedition vehicle, if cost were no problem and all spares were to be carried, would have a payload of about one ton evenly distributed between all four wheels, short wheelbase (around 100"), forward control, good ground clearance, large wheels for 9.00" × 16" radial tyres, good power to weight ratio and reasonable fuel consumption. The vehicles fitting best to this specification

Expedition uses the beach for the firmest terrain where desert meets the sea and no road exists —
Toyota Land Cruiser, Yemen Arab Republic. Similar vehicles in convoy.

are the smaller Mercedes Unimogs, Fiat PC65 and PC75 models, the now
discontinued Volvo C303 and Land Rover 101″ wheelbase military one tonne.
All these are specialist vehicles and for best cross country performance are soft
topped to keep the centre of gravity low.

By using several identical vehicles travelling in convoy you can minimize on
the weight of spares and tyres needed to be carried. The idea of using one large
vehicle to carry fuel etc accompanying several smaller more agile vehicles just
does not work. If the heavier vehicle is well bogged down smaller vehicles will
have difficulty in towing it out and the vast difference in overall journey speed,
plus extra spares, causes many problems unless you have a static base camp.

The overlander or private person in third world countries would prefer a
hard top vehicle as it is more difficult for thieves to break into. Taking into
account price, availability, spares availability, working life, fuel consumption
and resale value the most common four wheel drive bought by overlanders and
small expeditions is the Long Wheelbase hard top, or Safari Land Rover. Many
Australians and Americans complain about the Land Rover's hard ride, few
comforts and small engine which produces a low top speed, but these people
consider a well graded dirt track to be off road driving, they have never
experienced the corrugations of North and Central Africa and the Middle East.
Having spent fourteen years bouncing through roofs of Land Cruisers, Chevi's,
Dodges, Broncos and Travelalls and constantly having to pick up the bits that
fall off I am more than happy to put up with a spartan Land Rover or small Jeep
in really difficult country where they are tough and reliable. A great advantage

One of the joys of Safari travel — Mali.

Land Rovers at 9000 ft, Band-I-Amir, Afghanistan.

Lunch stop — Irans Dasht-I-Lut desert. Make your own shade — Land Rover LWB Series III.

Front mounted water jerrycans and main leaves for springs. Fuel should not be carried in front mounted cans in case of collision.

of the Land Rover is that it has an aluminium alloy body and everything bolts on, this means no rust and easy repairs in the field. Every vehicle has its faults and the Land Rover is no exception, but it still outsells all others where the going gets really tough. The new V8 Land Rover removes most user complaints so it is likely to be very successful.

When planning a long expedition or overland route in very remote areas it is wise to start off with 20% more fuel and water than you calculate to be necessary, this will give you a safety factor to allow for breakdowns, leaking fuel container, or extra fuel used in a bad soft section.

When you buy a vehicle use it for several months before setting off on an expedition with it, this will not only run any new parts in properly, but will enable you to sort out any weaknesses and so become thoroughly acquainted with its handling and maintenance. If you buy a new Land Rover it also helps to run it in a wet country before taking it to a hot dry country, this helps to rust in all the bolts holding the bodywork and roof together and can save you having to tighten up loose bolts later when the vehicle has been bouncing around on rough tracks.

If you intend to sleep in the vehicle either fit wiremesh anti-thief guards to windows you will need open, or better still fit roof vents protected by a roof rack. Mosquito netting can be fitted to vents or windows with Velcro. A closed lockable station wagon or hard top vehicle is safest against theft.

If you have a camper conversion to your four wheel drive remember that many fittings will not usually be as strong as the original fittings of the four wheel drive and often will need to be strengthened for really rough work. Fixed gas piping for cooker units will be dangerous because the connections break up and leak with the vibration, use flexible rubber gas tubing instead and remember to carry spare tubing and a spare gas regulator. Some conversions have the gas cylinders fitted under the chassis where they get plastered in mud and hit by stones. It is better to carry them inside the vehicle (turned off) when travelling, or if necessary on the roof, but well covered against the heat of the sun. Glass reinforced plastic (fibre glass) roofs break up fast in really rough country.

If a spare wheel is carried on the bonnet it is wise to supplement the standard bonnet catch with rubber, webbing or spring loaded side bonnet catches or straps. Do not carry a spare wheel on the back door for rough country work, the door will soon break; use the bonnet, roof or where possible a swing away wheel carrier. Spare wheels slung underneath the floor are bad for off road driving. There are many times when you are stuck that the spare wheel can be useful when jacking up the vehicle and if it is under the floor it will be very difficult to get out.

For accurate navigation you should know how incorrect your odometer is for the wheels and tyres you have fitted, larger tyres will have a longer rolling circumference eg: sand tyres.

Rebuilt ex-military vehicles are not a good buy for Third World use, buy the vehicle and do all the work yourself, so that you know it was done properly, and understand how to fix it if it goes wrong later.

If you have leaf springs there is no need to carry the weight of a complete spare spring. If you carry the two main leaves for each size of spring (front and rear) you should be able to achieve satisfactory repair. Fit stronger springs or an extra main leaf but you must keep an eye on the spring bushes, shackles and spring hangers. The spare leaves can be bolted to the front bumper or rear chassis using a complete set of shackles and shackle pins, then you have all these spare and can add a few spare wheelnuts as well. If you carry a complete spare spring use the same method to bolt it to the chassis, it will be too heavy for the bumper. If you have coil springs fit heavy duty models and carry a complete spare.

For overland and expedition work, springs, chassis, steering, bodywork, tyres and exhaust should be checked and bolts tightened every evening. Check engine oil, tyre pressures, cooling water and fill the fuel tank every morning when it is cool. Keep a close eye on electrical wires, corrugations can wear through the insulating covers then a shorting lead can flatten the battery or start a fire. Do not forget to check all transmission oils, steering box oils, brake and clutch fluid regularly. Keep breather vents on gearboxes and axles clear (they tend to block with dust stuck on oil and hence you blow oil seals due to pressure).

A small vice fitted to a strong bumper or convenient chassis member can aid many repairs. Locktite thread sealer will stop nuts vibrating loose.

Fuel and Oil: always keep the mesh filter in the fuel filler in place, this may be slow but it will save you a lot of time cleaning out blocked fuel lines. Start each day with a full tank and always carry spare fuel to avoid being stranded in a bad place at night. If you have a diesel engine a pair of oil resistant gloves can make

Fuelling up in Saharan conditions requires care, with additional dangers from heat fire dust and contaminated fuel. In this case, at Bilma in Niger, the fuel had to be both arranged and paid for in advance several hundred miles away at the nearest large town, Agades. The fuel was then brought in from Libya.

refuelling a less messy business and a clear plastic hose will enable you to avoid getting any in your mouth when syphoning fuel. Do not let the level of the fuel in the tank fall too low as there will always be some grit and water in it to block your fuel lines; with a diesel a low tank could mean that air gets in the system and you would then have to bleed it. When syphoning fuel from roof cans there is no need to use mouth suction for each can; start the first can by mouth and when it empties put your finger over the bottom of the tube whilst it is still full, transfer the top end to another full can and the syphon will continue.

In some countries fuel stations do not sell oil or only sell poor grade non-additive oils, so you have to go to the bazaar to buy good oil. When you buy oil make sure that it is the correct type for your engine or transmission. In many countries you will have to check the container's seal to make sure that it has not been filled with something cheaper, never buy oil that is not in a sealed container.

Many gearboxes and axles need extreme pressure gear oil, this is usually green in colour and smells strongly of sulphur. When you buy this oil make sure that EP is written on the container. Non-EP oils are the same colour but do not have the strong smell. It is very important to use the correct oil or you will damage your transmission. Some gearboxes use normal engine oil, EP oil should not be used where a non EP oil is specified.

EP oil is hard to find in remote places so always carry some with you. If you need automatic transmission fluid, power steering fluid or Girling brake fluid always carry these with you as you will not find them in remote countries. Remember to have some thin oil eg: WD 40 for hinges, door locks, latches, padlocks etc. Remember that even in hot countries you will need antifreeze in many desert and mountain areas at night.

If your axles do not have recessed drain plugs they can be battered out of shape (even turned undone and fall out) by thrown up stones in really bad country, therefore keep a check on them and carry spares.

If you have any repairs done by local mechanics in Third World countries always watch them at work. Make sure you disconnect the battery and alternator before they do any electric welding and watch that they do not replace some of your good parts or inner tubes with old ones. Make sure you retighten any nuts that were done up by young boys. If you have to reline brakes or clutch pay extra for imported western linings, cheap locally made ones will fade quickly. If you have bonded brake linings the shoes can be drilled out for riveted linings. Never let a local mechanic tighten down a cylinder head, always do it yourself and follow the correct tightening sequence closely and then tighten everything down again after 500 miles. Check that any oil they have changed has been refilled. In some countries it is wise to check any body, chassis or fuel tank repairs for evidence of false compartments filled with drugs.

Driving over large sand seas means that you end up with a sandblasted front and underside to your vehicle, which will need repainting when you return to a

Sand scours away the paint on bodywork, chassis and axles. Land Rover long wheelbase Safari in Afghanistan.

damp climate. A heavy sandstorm can scour the paint completely off your bodywork. With the Land Rover's aluminium panels it does not matter, but if you have steel bodywork it can be worth covering the front and wings with heavy grease. In some countries asphalt roads cross large sand seas, in these areas be careful not to hit a windblown sand drift across the road at speed. In a really heavy sandstorm either cover your windscreen or face it away from the wind or it will be rendered opaque. In scrub or insect country you will need to brush down your radiator regularly.

The benefits of air conditioning are questionable for really rough country, when often you have to leave the vehicle to push or dig it out, the change in temperature drains your strength and willpower. The idea that being cool conserves your water supply only works for a lightly loaded four wheel drive that never gets stuck and what you save in water has to be carried in extra fuel. Polarising plastic film on the windows will keep the interior of a hard top vehicle cooler as will aluminium cooking foil on any windows which you do not need to see out of.

Film stock is usually an important part of your journey and must be kept cool in hot countries, during the day a fridge can be used if you have a second battery. If you are one vehicle alone it is best to switch the fridge off at night or use the type which can also be run on gas at night. If you do not have a fridge some form of polystyrene insulated box will be needed.

Canvas and goatskin water bags do not work and waste a lot of precious water. Suffice to say that local desert lorry drivers now use tied up inner tubes.

Get lists of your vehicle's concessionaires and dealers along your proposed route, in many cases they will not have anything like the stock of supplies you were led to believe they held, but they will usually be able to put you in touch with a bazaar shop or garage mechanic who can help you.

In Islamic North Africa a bottle of whisky can be worth eight times what you paid for it to many local mechanics, thus cutting the cost of repairs.

Spare Parts: the spare parts to be carried will vary with the type of vehicle: how much extra weight can be carried before extra stress to the vehicle will cause further damage, the vehicle's particular weaknesses, what parts can be improvized and what if any can be easily obtained en route. You should always remember that in most third world countries spare parts for Land Rovers and Range Rovers can be sold easily and for a profit.

Vehicle Spares and Tools
Petrol Engines
3 fan belts
1 complete set of gaskets
4 oil filters (change every 3,000 miles/5,000 kilometres)
2 tubes of silicone RTV gasket compound
1 complete set of radiator hoses plus spare Jubilee clips
2 metres of spare heater hose
2 metres of spare fuel pipe hose
½ metre of spare distributor vacuum pipe hose
2 exhaust valves
1 inlet valve
2 valve springs

Fine and coarse valve grinding paste and valve grinding tool
1 valve spring compressor
1 fuel pump repair kit (if electric type take a complete spare pump)
1 water pump repair kit
1 carburettor overhaul kit
1 set of big-end nuts
2 sets of spark plugs
1 timing light or 12 volt bulb & holder with leads
3 sets of contact breaker points (preferably with hard fibre cam follower
   because plastic types wear fast & close up in the heat)
2 rotor arms
1 condenser
1 spark plug spanner
1 distributor cap
1 set of high tension leads (older copper wire type)
Starting handle if available
1 ignition coil
   Slip ring and brushes for alternator or complete spare alternator
   If you have a dynamo carry spare brushes
2 cans of spray type ignition sealer for dusty and wet conditions
2 spare air intake filters if you do not have the oil bath type
Assortment of nuts, bolts and washers of same thread as vehicle.
   Some modern engines use glass fibre reinforced timing belts. If you have
one of these (e.g. Land Rover 110 Turbo Diesel), then you should also carry
2 spare belts (stored flat, not tightly curved and in a cool place).
   3 Push rods
   3 Brass cam followers
Extras for Diesel Engines
Delete spark plugs, contact breaker points, rotor arms, distributor cap, high
   tension leads and coil from the above and substitute:-
1 spare set of injectors plus cleaning kit
2 heater plugs if fitted
1 complete set of injector pipes
1 set of injector seating washers
1 set of injector return pipe washers
1 metre plastic fuel pipe plus spare nuts and ferules
   add a second in line fuel filter
4 fuel filter elements
Brakes and Clutch
2 wheel cylinder seals kit (one right and one left)
1 flexible brake hose
1 brake bleeding kit (or fit automatic valves)
1 brake master cylinder seals kit
1 clutch master cylinder seals kit
1 clutch slave cylinder seals kit
   (it is important to keep all these away from heat)
1 clutch plate
   If you have an automatic gearbox make sure that you have plenty of the
   special fluid for this and a spare starter motor.
For power steering carry the fluid and spare hoses

General Spares
2 red warning triangles (compulsory in most countries)
1 good workshop manual (not the car handbook)
1 good torch or better still a 12 volt fluorescent light with leads to work from
vehicle battery plus spare bulbs or tubes.
1 wheel brace
1 extra tyre in addition to the spare wheel making two spares in all. Only one
spare wheel each will be necessary if two vehicles of the same type are
travelling together
1 good socket or ring spanner to fit the wheel nuts as a supplement to the
wheelbrace
4 extra inner tubes
1 large inner tube repair outfit
1 Schrader spark plug fitting tyre pump if you have a petrol engine or 1
Schrader model 202 12 volt electric tyre pump if you have a diesel engine
Plenty of good quality engine oil
2 litres of distilled water (or deionizing water crystals)
12 volt soldering iron and solder
16 metres of nylon or terylene rope strong enough to upright an overturned
vehicle
1 set of 3 tyre levers plus 2 lb sledge hammer for tyres
5 spare inner tube valve cores plus 2 valve core tools
1 good jack and wheel brace
1 (at least) metal fuel can eg: jerrycan
1 grease gun and a tin of multipurpose grease
1 gallon (4.5 litres) of correct differential and gearbox oil
1 large fire extinguisher suitable for petrol and electrical fires
1 pair heavy duty electric jump leads at least 3 metres long
10 push fit electrical connectors (of type to suit vehicle)
2 universal joints for prop shafts
Insulating tape
Malleable wire for binding
½ litre can of brake and clutch fluid
1 small can of general light oil for hinges, door locks etc
1 large can WD 40
2 complete sets of spare keys kept in different places
1 small fibre glass kit for repairing fuel tanks and body holes
2 kits of general adhesive eg: Bostik or Araldite Rapid
1 tin of hand cleaner (washing up liquid will do in an emergency)
Spare fuses and bulbs for all lights including those on dash panel *which are often
part of the charging circuit*
1 radiator cap
Antifreeze if passing through cold areas
Spare windscreen wipers for use on return journey (keep away from heat).
1 odometer drive cable
Inner and outer wheel bearings
A good tool kit containing:-
Wire brush to clean dirty threads plus large and small flat and round files
Socket set of good quality (cheap ones break)
Spark plug wrench if petrol engine

Torque wrench
Ring and open ended spanners
Hacksaw and spare blades
Selection of spare nuts, bolts and washers of same type and thread to fit vehicle
12 inch Stillson pipe wrench
1 box spanner for large wheel bearing lock nuts
Hammer
Set of taps and dies suitable for your vehicle's bolts from $\frac{1}{8}''$ to $\frac{5}{16}''$ to 'clean'
   worn threads
Small hand drill and a set of good sharp drills
Large and small cold chisels for large or stubborn nuts
Self grip wrench
Broad and thin nosed pliers
Circlip pliers
Insulating tape
10 ft electrical wire (vehicle type not mains)
1 set of feeler gauges
Small adjustable wrench
Tube of gasket cement eg: Red Hermetite, silicone RTV
Tube Locktite thread sealer
Large and small slot head and Phillips head screwdrivers
2 accurate tyre pressure gauges
1 boiler suit for working on the vehicle
Hardwood or steelplate to support the jack on soft ground
Extras for off the road use
1 pair of 5 ft sand ladders
8 wheel bearing oil seals
1 rear gearbox oil seal
1 rear differential oil seal
1 rear spring main leaf complete with bushes
1 front spring main leaf complete with bushes
   If coil springs take one complete coil spring
4 spare spring bushes
4 spring centre bolts
1 set of spring shackle plates (= 4)
1 set of spring shackle pins (= 4)
1 set of shock absorber mounting rubbers
2 spare engine mountings
1 spare gearbox mounting
2 door hinge pins
1 small vice to fit bumper or rear chassis member
1 screw jack (to use on its side when changing springs and/or bushes)
Chain and bolts for splinting broken chassis, axle and spring parts
Snow chains for rear wheels if you expect a lot of mud or snow
Paint brush to brush dust off engine before you work on it
Selection of rags
Groundsheet to lie on under vehicle or keep sand out when repairing tyres
1 pair goggles to protect eyes when working under vehicle
1 high lift jack in case you get bogged down
2 shovels for digging out, long straight handles are best

1 hand axe
2 steering ball joints
2 rear axle 'U' bolts – if you have leaf springs
1 front axle 'U' bolt – if you have leaf springs
2 spare padlocks
2 axle drain plugs if yours are not the recessed type
Radiator stop leak compound (porridge will do in emergency)
1 old truck inner tube for use as a gaiter in a damaged tyre

Tools are best kept in a strong canvas bag, in a metal tool box they will make a lot of noise and due to bouncing about will always be covered in metal filings. Fragile spares, gaskets etc should be kept in a strong protective box.

Anything affected by heat should be kept away from the bodywork of the vehicle which gets very hot when parked in the sun and also away from the engine and gearbox.

Equipment for Vehicle Camping
Good compass, maps and guidebooks
Selection of plastic bags for waste disposal etc
Clingwrap and aluminium foil for food
Large bowl for washing up and washing clothes
4 × 5 gallon water jerrycans — strong ex-military type
Fire extinguisher
Large supply of paper towel, loo paper, scotchbrites plus some J cloths and tea
    towels
Large supply of good matches in water proof box and/or disposable lighters
Supply of salt (granular), instant coffee, tea bags, powdered milk
Supply of dried and tinned meats for trip
Washing up liquid for dishes (also good for greasy hands)
Frying pan
Good vegetable cooking oil or better still ghee substitute which is solid at room
    temperature so easier to transport
Pressure cooker
Selection of strong saucepans or billies
Kettle with lid (not whistling type which are hard to fill from cans or streams)
Can opener — good heavyweight or wall type which can be fixed to vehicle
Stainless steel cutlery
Plastic screw top jars for sugar, salt, coffee, tea etc
1 large sharp bread knife
2 small sharp vegetable knives
1 large serving spoon and soup ladle
Plates and/or bowls for eating out of. Wide bottomed mugs which do not tip
    over easily
Good twin burner cooker for your gas supply otherwise petrol or kerosene twin
    burner cooker
Good sleeping bags or sleeping bag combinations for the climate expected plus
    mattresses
Combined anti-mosquito and insect spray repellant
Battery powered fluorescent light/s
Lightweight folding chairs
Supply of paper plates if you have room for them
Short handled hand axe

Thin nylon line to use as clothes line plus clothes pegs
Washing powder for clothes
6 metres of plastic tubing to fill water tank or jerrycans
2 tubes of universal glue cum sealant eg: Bostik
Chamois leather
Sponges
Water purification filters plus tablets or iodine as back-up (keep all away from heat)
Phrase book/dictionaries where necessary
Torches plus spare batteries
Scissors
Small plastic dustpan and brush
Soap, shampoo, toothpaste, towels
Medical first aid kit plus multivitamins
Sewing kit and safety pins
Mosquito nets or fitted mosquito netting if passing through areas where mosquitos are bad
Hidden strong money box or money belt
Antimalarial tablets and salt tablets where required
Anti sun cream
Personal clothing, sunglasses, medicaments and spare spectacles if you wear them

Where possible keep things carefully packed in strong boxes, these can be very adaptable as they can also be used for sitting on when camping or as a base for sleeping on inside the vehicle. Lightweight pots, pans and cutlery need careful packing or they, like your tools, will end up as a mass of metal filings due to heavy vibration.

Two extremes of four wheel drive racing: - Art Pollard and crew with the Lotus T56 at Indianapolis 1968 and a 'special' at an all wheel drive club safari speed event at Slab Common.

Chapter 8
Four Wheel Drive in Racing and Rallying

Four wheel drive's initial entry into the competition record books was in 1906 when Jackobus Spijker drove the Spijker Brothers 8.8 litre four wheel drive car to victory in a Birmingham MC Hill Climb, but the idea was not followed up until the early 1930's. For the 1932 season the Bugatti company built two T53 cars for the European Hill Climb events using a 4.8 litre twin camshaft supercharged straight eight cylinder engine. One car was crashed by Jean Bugatti at Shelsley Walsh in 1932 but the second car continued racing till 1934 when Rene Dreyfus broke the 100 kph mark for the La Turbie Hill Climb.

Around the same period Robert Waddy was sprinting his Fuzzi special, powered by two air cooled JAP engines, one driving the front wheels and the other driving the rear wheels.

Harry Miller persevered unsuccessfully with his four wheel drive racing cars at Indianapolis from 1932 until his death in 1943. Miller built two 5 litre V8 four wheel drive racers for the 1932 Indianapolis 500. One was driven by Gus Schrader who crashed into a wall in lap three and the second car was driven by Bob McDonough who retired with a broken oil line four laps later. Schrader's car was then bought by the Scully brothers, who took it to Europe for the 1933 season but found the car much too slow. Miller continued to concentrate on the Indy, coming ninth in 1934 driven by Frank Brisko and then, with Mauri Rose driving, he came twentieth in 1935 and fourth in 1936. In 1937 his car broke a crankshaft. The Indy's rules were changed for 1938 and Miller sought the sponsorship of Gulf Oil to formulate a new four wheel drive racer, but Gulf obviously wanted the publicity of running the car on their petrol which gave it a distinct disadvantage against the alcohol burning Offenhausers.

The new Gulf-Millers had a three litre two stage supercharged straight 6 cylinder engine producing around 250 bhp. The one car entered in 1938 failed to qualify and in 1939 one car driven by George Bailey retired with valve trouble after 47 laps; Bailey tried again in 1940 but was killed in practice and the remaining two cars were then used at Utah to set up 14 new Class D records whilst completing 500 miles at an average speed of 142.779 mph driven by George Barringer. In 1941 one car was destroyed in a pre-race fire and the second retired with a jammed gear lever. This was the end for Miller who died in 1943 but the car continued to race under the name of the Tucker Torpedo Special; driven by George Barringer it managed 26 laps in 1946 before retiring with gearbox trouble. After Barringer's death Al Miller drove the car in 1947, retiring after 26 laps with transmission trouble. The car, again driven by Al Miller, finally blew up whilst trying to qualify in 1948.

After the war Piero Dusio formed the Cisistalia company in Turin and in 1946 made a contract with the Porsche design team for a four wheel drive Formula 1 racing car. The car was designed with a tubular space frame, a five speed all synchromesh gearbox and a flat 12 supercharged engine; drive could be all four wheels or rear wheels only, selected by a lever in the cockpit. The whole thing was financially too much for the small company which went bankrupt, but one complete car was built with the help of a company set up by President Peron in Argentina. The car raced only once in the hands of a local driver Clemar Bucci in the 1953 Buenos Aires Grand Prix, but it suffered badly from gearbox and differential final drive ratio problems. Later Bucci tackled the South American Flying Kilometre record, but holed a piston on the return run and barely improved on the existing record, so it was forgotten until Porsche had it shipped back and placed in the Porsche Museum.

In contrast in 1948 British Hill Climbs' enthusiast, Archie Butterworth, took a Jeep chassis and axles and mated them to an air cooled Steyr V8 engine and Steyr 3 speed gearbox. This engine had individual motor cycle type barrels so by making new barrels and pistons he was able to stretch the original 3.7 litres to 4.5 litres. Individual Amal carburettors were fitted to each barrel, the engine then giving some 250 bhp. Butterworth's AJB special was very successful in hill climbs and speed trials from 1949 to 1951, when he finally up-ended it sustaining back injuries which enforced his retirement from racing.

At the end of 1960 four wheel drive racing took a great leap forward with the introduction of the Ferguson P99 Grand Prix car; built as a competition test bed for the four wheel drive ideas of Fred Dixon and Tony Rolt, with the backing of Harry Ferguson, the car was highly successful in the wet and on hill climbs. To this day developments on this system combined with fluid couplings and anti-lock braking systems are available to constructors. The early P99 had the 1.5 litre Coventry-Climax engine and a special Ferguson 5 speed gearbox developed in conjunction with the Italian gearbox specialists Colotti. Transfer gears went through a system of free wheels and a limited slip differential to drive the prop shafts, which in turn drove the front and rear axles, This 'centre differential system' made it almost impossible to spin a wheel, either all four wheels would spin or none at all. The car had servo-operated hydraulic disc brakes mounted inboard with Dunlop Maxaret anti-lock control, which could be switched on from the cockpit for wet conditions.

The early system had equal power to all four wheels which meant that the driver had to place the car accurately when he arrived at a corner, or he could not induce an oversteering slide; later models of the Ferguson system supplied 63% of the power to the rear wheels and 37% to the front wheels so that the driver could again produce a slide when required on cornering. The P99's first race was the 1961 Silverstone British Empire Trophy, driven by Jack Fairman and using a substitute 1.5 litre 4 cylinder engine. It had to retire with gearbox trouble after 3 laps. One week later, now fitted with the 1.5 litre Coventry-Climax engine it ran again in the British Grand Prix. Stirling Moss driving a Lotus retired with brake trouble and then took over Fairman's P99; the race was run in pouring rain and Moss was impressed with the P99's performance so he drove it in the Oulton Park Gold Cup and won the race easily on a wet track.

Having achieved these results Ferguson retired from competition and offered the system for sale but no-one took it up. At the end of 1962 the P99 was fitted with the 2.5 litre engine and shipped out for the Tasman series, where driven by Graham Hill and Innes Ireland it managed only a 2nd and a couple of 3rds, but in 1964 Peter Westbury borrowed the car to win the RAC Hill Climb championship, thus setting a trend towards four wheel drive on the hills which others were to follow.

Lotus Type 56 (1968), left to right, Graham Hill, Maurice Phillipe (then Lotus' Chief Designer), Dick Scammell (then Lotus' Racing Manager), Colin Chapman.

During 1964 BRM were also testing a four wheel drive car designed around the Ferguson system; the BRM P67 had a 1.5 litre BRM V8 which was set behind the driver and turned through 180 degrees with the clutch facing forward, the car had a 6 speed gearbox. The car was tested extensively, but never raced as the extra 150 lbs weight was a considerable handicap. Peter Westbury borrowed the car for the 1965 hill climb championship, but was not able to complete the full programme due to Sir Alfred Owen (the BRM's chairman) disapproving of sport on Sundays. The P67 was used by David Good for the 1967 hill climb season, but only competed in eight of the fourteen events, Tony Marsh winning the championship with another four wheel drive special using a system developed in conjunction with Hewland Engineering. Peter Lawson took over the P67 for 1968 and now using 70% power to the rear wheels and 30% power to the front wheels he won the RAC hill climb championship outright.

Four wheel drive returned to the Indianapolis 500 in 1964 when Andy Granatelli, impressed by some test runs of the Ferguson P99, asked Ferguson to develop a front engined car using a 4.4 litre Novi V8 engine, 4 speed gearbox and the Ferguson four wheel drive system, but with a variable torque split from 70/30 to 60/40. Bobby Unser finally drove the car in the race, but connected

133

with another car whilst trying to avoid the fatal accident to MacDonald and Sachs and the car could not be repaired for the restart. Unser returned with the car in 1965 but retired with an oil leak. In 1966 the Novi-Ferguson was driven by Greg Weld but he crashed attempting to qualify.

In 1967 four wheel drive returned to the Indy with Granatelli's STP Turbine, powered by a Pratt and Whitney turbine through a modified Ferguson four wheel drive system; driven by Parnelli Jones it led the field until retiring with transmission failure. Colin Chapman joined Granatelli in 1968 with his turbine powered Lotus 56's, using a lighter Canadian-built Pratt and Whitney turbine. For the first time the Ferguson's centre differential was connected to the turbine's output shaft by a Morse chain thus cutting out the transfer gears. This system was to be used later on production four wheel drive vehicles. Once again the turbines were destined not to finish — Mike Spence was killed during testing, Art Pollard and Joe Leonard went out with broken fuel pump shafts and Graham Hill spun into a wall when he lost a wheel.

The Lotus 56 used the Pratt and Whitney PT6 engine which had the gas generator turbine separate from the power output turbine. A single stage axial compressor was used with an inlet annulus of 16.999 sq inches, together with a single stage centrifugal compressor feeding air into a reverse flow annular combustion chamber. Power output was over 500 bhp and the engine weighed 325 lbs plus 44 lbs for the transmission. The engine was offset 2" to the right to accommodate the transmission running on the left side of the car. The turbine power shaft was connected to the Ferguson compound centre differential by a 3" Morse chain. From the differential solid steel torsion shafts ran fore and aft to ZF spiral bevel final drive units and power went to the wheels through Hardy Spicer constant velocity joint shafts. The chassis was full monocoque using mainly 16 SWG aluminium alloy sheet with glass reinforced fibre nose cone and upper body panels.

The four wheels had a common suspension system of double wishbones, inboard telescopic coil springs/damper units operated by rocking arms, rack and pinion steering and ventilated disc brakes 10.25" × 1.125". The Magnesium wheels had 9.5" wide rims. 70 gallons of Kerosene was carried in rupture proof bags in four bays.

Also at the Indy in 1968 was the George Bignotti Lola T150 driven by Al Unser, which had a four wheel drive system built by Hewland Engineering, but Unser spun out of the race after forty laps. In 1969 Lotus and STP were back with turbocharged Ford powered TC64 cars modelled on the T63's, but all three cars suffered hub problems and retired before the race. Lola however were more successful, using Offenhauser engines and a similar Hewland four-wheel drive transmission to the previous year. Bobby Unser came third and Mark Donohue seventh; the third car driven by Bud Tingelstad failed to finish. 1969 was to be the last year of four wheel drives at Indianapolis when the organizers banned their use.

The STP Lotus Ford Type 64 cars had the Type T63 chassis transmission and reversed engine layout but used the Ford 2.6 litre supercharged V8 engine producing 700 bhp.

Like the hill climbs and straight line sprints, the Indianapolis 500 with its gentle curves was a special case for four wheel drives. However on road circuits, with tight corners and awkward cambers, the variations on torque were greater and the extra weight, larger front tyres, and heavier steering tended to outweigh the advantages of four wheel drive. Even so, several Grand Prix teams. tried four wheel drive designs during 1969.

Keith Duckworth with designer Robin Herd used the Cosworth DFV engine turned through 180 degrees with the clutch facing forward, a 6 speed Hewland gearbox, and Hewland four wheel drive system. The main problem was still the steering problems on tight corners; limited slip differentials were tried but at that time the available designs did not really improve things.

Lotus Type 63 (1969).

The Lotus 63 also used the Cosworth DFV engine turned through 180 degrees and a Lotus/ZF 5-speed gearbox. To keep the weight evenly distributed on all four wheels the Lotus type 63 engine was reversed and drove foward to the gearbox which was in the centre of the car. The chassis was semi-monocoque using 18 SWG aluminium sheet with cavities supporting five rubberized fabric fuel cells holding 40 gallons of petrol. All suspension and steering mounting points were incorporated in two steel tube sub frames which formed the front and rear extremities of the chassis structure. The 5 speed transmission combined Lotus/Hewland/ZF design, using the Hewland engineering expertise for the change gears, and the Zahnrad Fabrik Friedrichshafen expertise for the transfer drive and the torque split differential. The main drive shafts to the axles were of solid steel and housed in light steel tubes containing intermediate steady bearings. The axles were spiral bevel, and drive from the axles to the wheels was done by plunging constant velocity universal joints inboard and non-plunging constant velocity universal joints outboard. Steering was rack and pinion and the suspension was double wishbone type all round, with Armstrong shock absorbers and concentric helical suspension springs acted on by the rocking arm top wishbones. Anti-roll bars were incorporated front and rear. The 3 litre Ford Cosworth DFV engine produced over 425 hp. The Matra MS84 again used the Cosworth engine, a 5 speed box based on Hewland gears and Ferguson four wheel drive system.

The McLaren M9A used a McLaren/Hewland 5 speed gearbox, Hewland/ZF limited slip differentials and quickly changeable torque split ratios in the centre differential. The car was only 10 lbs heavier than the two wheel drive M7A. None of the cars was successful, although Jochen Rindt won 2nd place in the Oulton Park Gold Cup with the Lotus 63; and Johnny Servoz-Gavin drove the Matra MS84 to sixth place in the Canadian Grand Prix. 1969 was the end for four wheel drive Grand Prix cars in their present form, although Lotus brought out their four wheel drive Pratt and Whitney turbine powered 56B for the 1971 Formula 1 races with little success except at Zandvort, where David Walker crashed due to adverse weather conditions; when he stood a very good chance of winning the race.

The increase in tyre sizes plus the ground effect forces from aerofoils sealed the fate of four wheel drive Grand Prix cars. As these same sophisticated Grand Prix cars invaded the hill climbs, the four wheel drive cars were ejected from there likewise.

In the rally scene, four wheel drive cars had been equally unsuccessful mainly because before 1980 no manufacturer had built a low slung four wheel

Series IIA Land Rover competing in an All Wheel Drive Club Safari event — roll cage is essential.

Roll cage for Safari events — Austin Champ.

drive car or even one with enough power to be really competitive. Four wheel drive vehicles such as the Range Rover, Land Rover and Jeep have been entered in many rallies and one might think they would have had a good chance in such runs as the London-Sydney marathon, but their lack of top speed and high centre of gravity gives them little chance against two wheel drive rally cars except in cases of soft sand or mud, and when a jeep did win a European Rally, 4WD cars were immediately banned.

When Audi came out with the competition Quattro, designed as a high performance four wheel drive on-road car, the authorities were forced to relent. The Quattro's success was spectacular, winning the 1982 and 1984 maufacturers World Rally Championships, together with the 1983 and 1984 Drivers World Rally Chamionships. Almost all manufacturers now add 4WD to their high performance on-road cars and for championship rallying this is the only way to go.

Austin Champ in an all wheel drive club speed event avoiding the worst of the mud.

In true off the road racing, four wheel drive is essential in all but the driest conditions. In the USA, Australia, Britain and France, this is a popular sport; in the main, amateur weekend drivers are involved but big events such as the Paris-Dakar, Baja 1000, the Australia Mallee Desert Rally and Europe's Rallye des Cimes, held each September in the Pyrenees, attract sponsorship.

In America, off road racing is big business but in Britain it is mostly a lot of love and sweat putting bigger engines into existing four wheel drive chassis for the least amount of money. This does not mean a lack of innovation however, and it is not uncommon to see V8 engines in battered Mark I or lightweight Land Rover bodies putting up very creditable performances. Britain's most successful off road racer in the early 1980s was Alvin Smith.

Land Rover special built for safari speed events with oversize engine placed in the centre of the chassis to place the weight more evenly on all four wheels.

Start of an All Wheel Drive Club speed event.

Suzuki LJ80 in an All Wheel Drive Club speed event.

Land Rover Series I special with a V8 engine.

V8 engined Land Rover Series I special in an All Wheel Drive Club trial event.

Keith Gott's ex-Smith Strange Rover.

After racing a chopped down short wheelbase Land Rover, a lightweight Land Rover and two modified Range Rovers, Alvin started creating his own racers. His first vehicle built in early 1979, 'Strange Rover', consisted of a Range Rover chassis and axles with a mid-engine Rover V8, SD1 5 speed gearbox, and Schuler's Ferguson FF four wheel drive system with viscous coupling centre differential. He fitted a TR7 body to this which he considers his major mistake as it was too heavy, too wide for narrow tracks, and its low seating position gave poor visibility — the vehicle was also front heavy. Learning from this vehicle Alvin sold it to Keith Gott and set about an even more innovative vehicle called the Range Rider. The Range Rider has the 4.4 litre version of the Rover V8 engine, which has been imported from Australia where it is used in the Terrapin truck. The chassis is Range Rover and the engine and transmission are mounted 18″ back from the standard position giving better weight distribution and the vehicle now lands squarely on all four wheels. The engine mountings are boxed in so that if the rubbers give way the engine will not fall out. Lumenition pointless ignition is fitted and copper high tension leads are used. Cooling was initially a problem but Alvin now uses a Range Rover radiator with a special cowling, the whole system being easily flushed clean of mud between runs. The gearbox was supplied by Schuler presses and is the Jaguar/Rover SD1 5 speed box. Drive from the gearbox to the Schuler/Ferguson FF viscous centre differential is by twin morse chains. The epicyclic centre differential splits the torque 63% to the rear wheels and 37% to the front wheels; this gives the driver more balanced handling, less understeer on corners and the ability to induce a controlled slide with the throttle.

Alvin Smith's Range Rider.

Alvin Smith at speed in his Range Rider.

The axles are standard Range Rover, suspension uses doctored Range Rover springs, but the Boge hydromat strut was removed and replaced with a Panhard rod as it caused rear end hop. Power steering is used to decrease the steering effort and to allow the steering ratio to be increased to two turns lock to lock; it also absorbs most of the kickback. Nine inches are chopped off the chassis at the front and rear, but the wheelbase remains the standard 100″. The engine compartment is sealed as far as is possible to keep out most of the mud and water, and windscreen washers and wipers are fitted inside the driver's windscreen as well as outside — this is the sort of innovation which wins races.

Other projects are on the way including a Jaguar V12 powered Range Rover for road use and a blown 3.5 Rover V8 with Jaguar limited slip rear differential for off road use. Other racers are also working on fresh machines so the future looks very competitive.

Alvin Smith retired for a while, though still making and selling his specials. He made a successful comeback at the Rallye des Cimes in 1987. In his absence, much of the top honours have gone to Pat Willis, who won the 1985 Rallye des Cimes outright, in an ex-Alvin Smith special.

Another popular weekend sport with British four wheel drive vehicle owners is the Trial. Vehicles have to attempt a series of set courses where the ability to complete the course without getting stuck, to avoid obstacles and to negotiate awkward gradients is more important than speed; more than any other motoring event this can be easily entered by the amateur with the vehicle he drove to the event in . Once more, specials made up from old parts are popular and short wheelbase Land Rovers fitted with V8 engines are the most successful, but it is good fun for all.

Rebuilt World War II Jeep for trials use.

Rebuilt World War II Jeep taking part in an All Wheel Drive Club trial.

Land Rover SWB in a speed event.

Jeep CJ6 in an all wheel drive club trial event, note steering wheel is turned by a knob for extra control in tight conditions.

Land Rover lightweight in a trial event.

Series I and lightweight Land Rovers taking part in an All Wheel Drive Club trial event.

Trying it with speed in an All Wheel Drive Club trial event.

Chapter 9
The American Scene

Whilst most four wheel drive vehicle manufacturers make predominantly working four wheel drive vehicles, with specifications as heavy as their market requires, the mainstream of the American four wheel drive market with its high volume output is mainly recreational and, in general, American four wheel drive vehicles spend 97 per cent of their life on the paved road. Thus American four wheel drive vehicles are offered as a basic package with various options of engine size, manual or automatic transmission, axle ratios and suspension weights. However, with the exception of the smallest vehicles and largest pick-up trucks, even the heavy duty suspension packages offered are not good enough for really tough off road use. Therefore a large after sales market has developed to cater for those who need a working vehicle and the needs, often predominantly cosmetic, of the recreational vehicle owners.

Enthusiasts in Britain and Australia will often radically alter their four wheel drive vehicles for competition use, for example fitting larger engines, although they need to have a good knowledge of what they are doing. The American after sales market, more than any other, offers various kits for improving the performance of American made four wheel drive vehicles and the Toyota Land Cruiser.

In addition to the options and conversions mentioned in previous chapters, here are some which are more common to the American market.

Uprated suspension kits, either heavier springs or extra leaves plus shackles to lift the body and using heavier shackles to cut down on side sway; raised suspensions are particularly important with oversize tyres.

Heavy duty shock absorbers, sometimes two on each spring.

Replace paper air filters with foam elements, only Ford and Dodge offer the oil bath air filter which is best in dusty areas.

Higher (numerical) axle ratios and larger engines for driving the extra rolling and traction resistance of larger tyres.

Wide wheels and tyres especially those designed for mud such as Gumbo Monster Mudders and various All Terrain tyres.

A wide variety of limited slip differentials with their attendant problems of clutch disc wear, lubrication and fishtailing at speed on slippery paved roads.

A variety of locking differentials which have fewer problems than limited slip differentials, although some are noisy. An Australian-made locking rear differential is now being imported into England.

Chevrolet Blazer/GMC Jimmy. The most popular American four wheel drive recreational vehicle.

Conversions from full time four wheel drive to part time four wheel drive with free-wheeling hubs.

Underside protection plates, necessary on many American four wheel drive vehicles which are adaptations of standard road vehicles, whereas four wheel drive vehicles designed as such from the beginning already have most of the vital parts protected by the chassis.

Roll bars — these have to be inspected carefully as some are barely more than cosmetic.

Swing-away spare tyre and gas can holders, very useful where interior room is at a minimum and much better than having the spare wheel under the floor where you cannot reach it when bogged down.

Running boards, useful as a step when the suspension has been raised, also useful to protect the paintwork on curved rocker panels which tend to be struck by stones flying up from the wheels.

Heavy duty electrical systems with increased charging capacity and battery capacity, including two separate alternators to cover extra current used for electric winches, very cold starting, extra lights, snow plough equipment etc.

Engine modifications: off road vehicles need an engine which produces good torque and cools itself properly at low rpm. Standard petrol engines can be improved by fitting better multi-branch exhaust manifolds (headers), low cubic feet per minute output carburettors and for the real enthusiast, quick lift camshafts. Electronic ignitions are becoming standard but some interfere with CB radio reception.

Engine oil coolers are essential for various conditions with some engines; some manufacturers do this another way by offering a bolt-on double capacity sump, but of course with these, you have to check for good ground or protection plate clearance.

Various kits are available for swapping transmissions — either manual or automatic and including automatic transmission re-programming kits to allow you to stay in low gear at higher rpm when climbing hills, towing etc.

With the exception of the smallest vehicles most American four wheel drive vehicles are larger and heavier than their European or Japanese competitors making wider tyres essential for good off road flotation.

The small Jeeps have much to offer for real off road use, being small and lightweight with plenty of accessories and adaptations available. International Harvester have virtually dropped out of the smaller four wheel drive market, but many of their Scouts and Scout Two's are still around because they were built to last and are amongst the better off road performers. International Harvester also offer a diesel engine option.

For those who want a little more room, luxury interiors and mainly on road performance there are the Chevy Blazer/GMC Jimmy, Dodge Ramcharger/Plymouth Trail Duster and Ford Bronco. These will accommodate five-six people plus luggage in comfort, but need beefed-up suspensions for hard off-road use and overlarge tyres can quickly find weaknesses in their drive trains. The Chevy Blazer is the most popular seller in its class but the Ford Bronco with its independent front suspension and slightly smaller size has the best performance and best standard suspension. The Dodge Ramcharger now has a good integral steel roof and dustproof hatchback. It is best to keep tyres down to 11 × 15.

When it comes to the station wagons, International Harvester's huge Travelall is no longer made and its place has been taken by the Chevy/GMC Suburbans which are now the largest made. There are plenty of International Harvester's Travelers still around and the diesel option is popular where diesel is cheap. The Jeep Wagoneer and Cherokee are classic four wheel drive station wagons made predominantly for heavy duty on road use handling, more like cars, but off the road it is best to avoid really tough conditions, particularly deep mud. Jeep's Quadra Trac permanent four wheel drive improves performance; it is difficult to fit over large tyres to the Wagoneer and Cherokee because the wheel wells will not handle them. The Suburbans are large and bulky and drive as such, for real rough stuff they need beefed-up suspensions and additional fuel tanks. The new lighter jeeps, with their French influence in design, have better on-road performance and fuel efficiency.

The four wheel drive pick-ups are becoming increasingly popular buys because you get more for your money. They are not much dearer than the smaller four wheel drives, but have a stronger frame, drivetrain and suspension, better body clearance, and wheel wells which are good for the largest tyres; the heavy duty models also evade the EPA emission controls so you do not need those power sapping catalytic converters. The pick-up based enclosed people carrier, such as the Toyota 4 Runner and Nissan Pathfinder, are becoming very popular.

If you like the Quadra Trac permanent four wheel drive system, you have the Jeep J10/25 and J20/46 pick-ups and the Honcho/Golden Eagle packages have plenty of luxury. The Ford pick-ups are the biggest sellers, have plenty of strength and are very capable off-road performers. The Dodge Power wagons continue to live up to their tradition and have an optional diesel engine whilst the Chevy pick-ups are steady sellers.

For those whose main need for a four wheel drive vehicle is for use in snowy climates the American four wheel drives cater well, including mains plug-in block heaters as well as heavy duty electrical charging and battery options plus plenty of snowplough options.

Most American four wheel drive vehicles are available with optional limited slip rear differentials; locking differentials are available but more difficult to obtain. Limited slip differentials have their problems, designed with slipping clutch discs they wear out and therefore need periodic rebuilding. This is made worse because they are best lubricated with a lubricant containing sperm oil with its remarkable lubricating properties, but this is now banned because it comes from whales. Another problem is fishtailing at highway speeds on slippery roads; one wheel on slipping slightly causes the differential to grab and swing the rear end out. This can be very dangerous. I have had a vehicle fitted with a limited slip rear differential swing around quite dangerously on wet roads at around 50 mph.

Limited slip differentials are also sensitive to small differences in tyre diameter, for example, a mismatched spare or soft tyre on the same axle can cause fishtailing. For these reasons very few manufacturers, other than American manufacturers and the French Cournil, now offer limited slip rear differentials, and few manufacturers offer limited slip front differentials where, as explained previously, the problems are worse. Locking differentials avoid the problems of limited slip differentials but can be noisy and can lock in suddenly and hard at low speed although this is not so dangerous as fish tailing at higher speeds. The best known locking differentials are the Detroit Locker and the Eaton. The Eaton gives the least lock-up and noise problems, but is only available on Chevrolet/GMC trucks.

In Europe and Australia various driver operated differential locks exist which simply stop the planet gears operating; these must therefore be unlocked again as soon as the difficult traction period is over. If however you spend most of your time in mud, snow or sand, some form of limited slip or locking differential on the rear end and even on the front in extreme cases can be a distinct advantage, so long as you know what you are handling and take great care on slippery paved roads. The advantage of a simple mechanical locking device is that it can be completely unlocked for normal on or off road use.

Higher flotation tyres are particularly important for most American four wheel drive vehicles which tend to be larger and heavier than their equivalent European or Japanese four wheel drive vehicles. True high flotation tyres as needed in soft sand or mud are not good for road use, so many semi-flotation tyres are on the market in an attempt to combine on and off road performance and cut down on the high noise and high wear rates associated with aggressive treads when used on the road. Radial tyres with their many advantages were a late introduction to the American market but are now readily available.

Most American tyres are tubeless, which can be a problem in true off road use (see earlier chapter on tyres). Top of the All Terrain tyres which are also

Formula Desert Dog tyre.

Goodyear Tracker A/T tyre.

quite good for road use are the Goodrichs All Terrain T/A, Dick Cepeks new Ground Hawgs and Off Roaders and Goodyears Wrangler Radial. Amongst the many tyres meant for mainly road use with reasonable off-road performance are the Armstrong Tru-Trac radial and Norsman, Formulas Desert Dogs, Goodyears Tracker A/T, Uniroyals Land-Trac, Sears cross country, Armstrongs Rhino, Firestones All Terrain T/C. For specialist mud work the best is the Gumbo Monster Mudder whilst the Goodrich Mud Terrain radial is quieter and lasts longer on the road. This and the standard Goodrich All Terrain T/A are now available in England. Another mud tyre, the Terra, has a similar tread to the tractor/dumper tyres which are usually used for mud in England. Dick Cepeks Big Boss Bruisers Ground Hawgs are also excellent. Specialist sand tyres include Armstrong's High Flotation, National Dune Command and Dick Cepeks Multi-Paddle which is more for sand drags and hill climbs. Where vehicles spend most of their life on the paved road wheel balance is particularly important.

Goodrich all terrain tyre.

Pro-track radial.

Trail Master RV Trac.

General Grabber LT.

Appendix I
List of Available Vehicles

As manufacturers strive to slow down their falling sales new or revamped four wheel drive vehicles seem to be appearing every month; many will fall by the wayside for a variety of reasons ranging from poor reliability, poor service, heavy fuel consumption or just lack of customer appeal. The bigger and older names will soldier on, but even some of these are failing to keep up with the changing market and are turning to putting their own brand names onto Japanese imports. Small specialist companies convert existing vehicles and then find themselves very quickly challenged by a Japanese equivalent; this side of the market in particular has produced a new breed, the four wheel drive version of the already popular smaller Japanese pick-up trucks, which are finding large sales worldwide. The top names are being forced by the competition to bring out better, more advanced and more economical four wheel drives, which must be to the buyer's advantage.

In compiling this list I have kept to the main four wheel drives on sale today, but have included some of the older vehicles now out of production though still available and working regularly in many countries.

Some exotics are included because they are selling, particularly in the Middle East. Omitted are some of the endless variants on basic models.

AFRICAR
Those of us who travel Third World countries regularly, curse the obvious weaknesses of our vehicles and when we discuss these with the manufacturers we are told that the numbers of us concerned are not large enough for them to consider in production. At the same time we see standard two-wheel drive vehicles, such as the Peugeot 404 & 504 in West Africa and the Toyota and Mazda pick-ups in East Africa, being used as the standard runabout or taxi despite the punishing terrain. It must be borne in mind however, that they are always overcrowded with people, so have plenty of manpower available when they get stuck.

Six years ago, one man, Anthony Howarth, decided to do something about it and design a new vehicle and engine from scratch. It says a lot for the man that he has been able to persevere against appalling odds, take three prototypes from Northern Europe to Kenya, make a Channel 4 film and book about the journey, organise a production plant in Lancaster, license production in Australia and several Third World countries and now expects to be in production in early 1988.

Prototype Africar

Basically the vehicle will be all independent suspension, with 12″ ground clearance and 12″ individual wheel movement. The track is intentionally 10 inches wider than a Land Rover, so that the wheels fit into existing truck ruts. Engines will be air-cooled, horizontally-opposed, twin-crankshaft two-strokes, made to Howarth's own design and can be made either as petrol or diesel.

The biggest surprise is that the body is made from plywood saturated in an epoxy resin. The internal sills are filled with structural foam. Steel and aluminium are used for reinforcing where required. There are separate steel sub-frames and a roll cage.

I have my doubts on this use of wood, it is highly inflammable, termites like to eat it and other insects bore into it to deposit eggs. In many parts of Africa useable wood does not exist and is more expensive to import than cheap far eastern steel. Resin for repairs would be virtually impossible, as it has a short shelf life and needs cool storage. In my own experience, resin shipped by sea from the UK, has gone off before it clears customs in the Sudan.

The Channel 4 films on his proving run were so biased, that it could in fact hold against the vehicles, to anyone who knows the terrain. All vehicles get stuck in mud holes when badly driven: badly driven overloaded vehicles will break structural parts. To those of us who know the Sahara well, there were times when the pictures shown were hundreds of miles away from the area quoted on the commentary. Filming was often carefully arranged to show difficult backgrounds, when the vehicles themselves were on easy ground. Real soft sand and some of the more difficult areas, which must have been crossed, were omitted from the film. We now know that the vehicles were in fact only using front-wheel drive for the journey, so things were excusable, but it might have been better to explain this in the film.

PROTOTYPE AFRICAR 4 & 6 WHEEL FOR 1988

Wheelbase	100″/2.54 metres 4 wheeler

	100" – 140" (2.54 - 3.56 metres) 6 wheeler
Engines	Horizontally-opposed twin-crankshaft, air-cooled, petrol or diesel (i.e. 2 opposed pistons in each cylinder)
Displacement	1300 cc & 2000 cc
Maximum power	65 bhp diesel to 120 bhp petrol
Transmission	Permanent 4-wheel drive with limited slip differentials front, back and centre. 4-speed gearbox, 2-ratio transfer box
Suspension	All independent, with leading arm at front and trailing arms at rear, hydrogas suspension
Steering	Rack & pinion
Brakes	Discs at front, drums at rear
Tyres	185 x 15
Turning circle	34 ft/10.6 metres (4 wheeler)
	36 ft/10.97 metres (6 wheeler)
Electrical	12 volt

AGROVER

Land Rover 110 pick-up based, multipurpose vehicle, featuring raised suspension on PORTAL axles, giving 14" minimum ground clearance and 66 inches of track. Dumper type self-cleaning tyres up to 10.5 x 18m 16. A 60 bhp live power take off, independently clutched to 540 rpm @ 2000 rpm engine speed; a 20 bhp, 2500 psi, 56 litres per minute hydraulic power supply and a category 1, three-point hydraulically operated linkage suitable for seed drills, spreaders, mowers etc. The pick-up body is removable.

Agrover

AMC EAGLES

Made by the same company as Jeep these are permanent four wheel drive on/off road cars using the advanced British Formula Ferguson Developments viscous coupling limited slip centre differential. AMC still call this Quadra Trac, but this name is really the name for AMC's mechanical limited slip centre differential, used since 1973 with spring loaded braking cones. The system in the Eagle car is the same as that used on Schuler Presser's Range Rover conversions in England (and raced by Alvin Smith) except that there is only a single speed transfer case; the system is made under licence as the NP119 by Chrysler's New Process Gear Division. The rear prop shaft is driven directly from the rear of the transfer case, whilst the front prop shaft is offset to the left and driven by a morse chain. The viscous liquid silicone coupling acts as a limited slip differential between the drives and there is no mechanical lock-up between the two prop shafts. This system is more effective than any other full time four wheel drive system and in addition it improves braking on slippery

AMC Eagle.

surfaces, acting as an anti-skid device by equalizing drive shaft speeds when wheels at one end or the other want to lock and slide. The system is also arranged to handle properly for power on cornering.

Models are available in 97″ and 109″ wheelbases and now have the 2.5 litre General Motors Pontiac engine as standard (as used in CJ Jeeps). The 4.2 litre straight six is still available, 4 speed manual transmission is now standard with 3 speed automatic transmission as option. There is coil sprung independent suspension in the front and a live axle on leaf springs at the rear. The front halfshafts have enclosed constant velocity joints on each end. A heavy duty suspension package is available and is necessary for anyone using the vehicle off the road or towing as should the automatic rear load levelling option. Power steering and braking are standard with disc brakes at the front and drums at the rear.

AMERICAN MOTORS JEEP CJ5

Basic, light weight, go anywhere Jeep, modern version of the World War Two Jeep, now fitted with the more fuel efficient 2.5 litre Pontiac Hurricane engine. Available as the basic soft top or the more up market Renegade, Laredo versions, part time four wheel drive or full time Quadra Trac four wheel drive.

Jeep CJ5.

Jeep CJ5 Renegade.

Wheelbase	83½″
Engine	4 cylinder
Displacement	2.5 litre
Bore	101.6 mm
Stroke	76.2 mm
Compression ratio	8.3:1
Maximum power	87 bhp @ 4200 rpm
Maximum torque	126 lb ft @ 2800 rpm
Transmission	4 speed manual gearbox, 2 speed transfer box 1.0:1 and 2.03:1. Part time four wheel drive
Gears	1st gear 6.32:1
	2nd gear 3.09:1
	3rd gear 1.69:1
	4th gear 1.00:1
Final drive	3.73:1
Suspension	Live axles on semi-elliptic leaf springs
Brakes	Split system, discs at front, drums at rear
	Handbrake on rear drums only
Steering	Recirculating ball
Turning circle	36 ft/11 metres
Tyres	6L × 15″
Electrics	12 volt negative earth
Battery	50 AH
Alternator	55 AH
Payload	1300 lb

AMERICAN MOTORS JEEP CJ6 and CJ7

Longer wheelbase versions of the CJ5 and CJ7/8 Jeeps. Available with the 4 cylinder engine and other options of the CJ5 plus 6 cylinder and V8 engine

Jeep CJ7 Golden Eagle.

options and an automatic transmission Quadra Trac option. The up market version of CJ7 is the Golden Eagle.

Wheelbase	CJ6 103"	CJ7 93"
Engine	4.2 litre 6 cylinder	
Bore	95.25 mm	
Stroke	98.9 mm	
Compression ratio	8.5:1	
Maximum power	110 bhp @ 3500 rpm	
Maximum torque	104 lb ft @ 3200 rpm	
Gears, manual	1st gear 6.32:1	
	2nd gear 3.09:1	
	3rd gear 1.69:1	
	4th gear 1.00:1	
Gears, automatic	1st gear 2.48:1	
	2nd gear 1.48:1	
	3rd gear 1.00:1	
Tyres	H78-15	
Turning circle	CJ6 38 ft/11.46 metres. CJ7 38 ft/11.46 metres	
Payload	CJ6 1373 lb/624 kg	CJ7 1400 lb/637 kg

For export only a Japanese Izuzu 2.369 l diesel engine is available

AMERICAN MOTORS JEEP CJ8 SCRAMBLER

103" wheelbase replacement for the CJ6, standard engine is the 2.5 litre Pontiac Hurricane engine but optional engines are:- 2.4 litre diesel (65 bhp @ 3800 rpm and 107 lb ft @ 2000 rpm), the 4.2 litre or the 5.9 litre V8 (175 hp @ 4000 rpm and 170 lb ft @ 3800 rpm).

Standard gearbox is 4 speed manual but automatic transmission comes as option with the 6 and 8 cylinder engines.

Part time or full time Quadra Trac four wheel drive.

Turning circle	38 ft/11.46 metres
Payload	1500 lb

AMERICAN MOTORS JEEP CHEROKEE/CHEROKEE CHIEF/WAGONEER

Heavy four wheel drive luxury estate built in the American tradition of being large and sometimes crude rather than sophisticated; on road handling is average but off road so long as it has room enough to move its performance is better than one would expect from such a vehicle, particularly good for towing a heavy trailer with an added factory fitted towing kit. Available as 2 or 4 door options, 6 or V8 cylinder engines, automatic or 4 speed manual transmission, it comes with a single speed full time Quadra Trac four wheel drive transfer box, a 2 speed box being optional. Spare wheel badly situated under the vehicle chassis

Wheelbase	108"	
Engine	6 cylinder	V8
Bore	95.25 mm	103.6 mm
Stroke	98.9 mm	87.4 mm
Compression ratio	8.5:1	8.25:1
Displacement	4.2 litre	5.9 litre
Maximum power	120 hp @ 3800 rpm	175 bhp @ 4000 rpm

Jeep Cherokee Chief.

Jeep Wagoneer.

Maximum torque	119 lb ft @ 3650 rpm 170 lb ft @ 3800 rpm
Transmission	3 speed automatic with optional 2 speed
	Transfer box with ratios of 1:1 and 2.57:1
	1st gear 2.48:1
	2nd gear 1.48:1
	3rd gear 1.00:1
Final drive	4.09:1
Suspension	Live axles on semi-elliptic leaf springs
Brakes	Split circuit, discs at front, drums at rear
Tyres	H78 × 15″
Payload	2355 lb/1070 kg
Steering	Recirculating ball, power assisted
Turning circle	40 ft/12 metres
Electrics	12 volt negative earth
Battery	60 AH
Alternator	60 amp

The Cherokee Chief is on a cut down Honcho chassis which is wider and comes with wider 10 × 15 tyres as standard.

The Wagoneer is a more luxurious version of the Cherokee.

JEEP J10/25 HONCHO GOLDEN EAGLE/HONCHO

Luxury 1 ton pick-up truck with good off road performance though limited by its large rear overhang. Available with the 4.2 litre in line 6 engine and manual gearbox or 5.9 litre V8 engine and automatic transmission. Quadra Trac permanent four wheel drive, optional 2 ratio transfer box.

Wheelbase	119″ (131″ wheelbase available)	
Engine	6 cylinder	V8
Bore	95.25 mm	103.6 mm
Stroke	98.9 mm	87.4 mm
Compression ratio	8.5:1	8.25:1
Displacement	4.2 litres	5.9 litres
Maximum power	120 hp @ 3800 rpm	175 hp @ 4000 rpm
Maximum torque	119 lb ft @ 3650 rpm	170 lb ft @ 3800 rpm
Transmission	3 speed automatic or 4 speed manual	
	3 speed automatic	
	1st gear 2.48:1	
	2nd gear 1.48:1	
	3rd gear 1.00:1	
	4 speed manual	
	1st gear 6.32:1	
	2nd gear 3.09:1	
	3rd gear 1.69:1	
	4th gear 1.00:1	
	Transfer box ratio 1:1 and 2.73:1	
Final drive ratio	3.31:1	
Suspension	Live axles on semi-elliptic leaf springs	
Brakes	Split circuit, discs at front, drums at rear	
Steering	Recirculating ball, power assisted	
Turning circle	41 ft/12.5 metres	

165

Jeep Honcho J10

Tyres	10 × 15
Electrical	12 volt negative earth
Battery	12 volt 60 AH
Alternator	60 AH
Payload	2441 lbs/1038 kg

JEEP J20/46 LONG WHEELBASE PICK-UP TRUCK, 2 TON

As for J10/25 Honcho but with a 4133 lbs/1879 kg payload and 131″ wheelbase, final drive ratio is 3.73 (with optional 4.00). Basically a 2 ton vehicle with four wheel drive, does not handle so well as the smaller vehicles and has lots of body shake.

Large rear overhang limits its off road performance. Like all heavy payload vehicles it behaves much better when loaded and is probably one of the best of the larger American four wheel drives. Turning circle 44.5 ft/13.6 metre

AMC Jeep J20.

AMC JEEP

AMC's tie up with Renault produced a new crop of jeeps. The Grand Wagoneer continues as of old jeep tradition, large in size, with fuel guzzling V8 engine. The CJ7 is replaced by the Wrangler, either as standard soft top or the Laredo hard top. The Cherokee and Wagoneer range are smaller, more modern vehicles, showing much more Renault influence, with smaller more efficient engines, modern suspension and a unitary body/chassis construction. Gearboxes are 4-speed manual as standard with 5-speed and auto options. There are two four-wheel drive options, Command-Trac, a part time system using the NP231 transfer box and Selec-Trac which has a viscous type centre differential for on-road use with four-wheel drive using the NP242 system. A unique feature with Command-Trac is that for two wheel drive a dog clutch disconnects the right-hand half shaft, giving a similar feature to free wheeling hubs. Both systems can be engaged and disengaged on the move. The diesel engine option is a version of the engine used in the Renault 18, 25 and Espace vehicles.

The front axle is now coil sprung with four trailing links, single Cardan outboard joints and live spindle hubs, the rear axle is on cart springs. Unbelievably the standard spare wheel is a compact, limited duty type; so a full sized spare must be bought as an extra for off-road use.

No more right-hand drive Jeeps are being produced.

NEW JEEP CHEROKEE, CHEROKEE PIONEER, CHEROKEE CHIEF and CHEROKEE LAREDO, 2-DOOR or 4-DOOR

Wheelbase	101.4"/2.58 metres		
Engines	2.5 litre petrol	4 litre petrol	2.1 litre turbo diesel
No of cylinders	4	6	4
Compression ratio	9.2:1	9.2:1	21.5:1
Maximum power	84 bhp @ 3600 rpm	173 bhp @ 4500 rpm	
Maximum torque	204 lbf ft @ 1800 rpm	220 lb ft @ 2500 rpm	
Transmission	4 speed manual or 5 speed manual with overdrive or 4 speed auto		
Transfer box	Command-Trac part time four-wheel drive with dis-engageable front half shaft, or Selec-Trac permanent four-wheel drive for any road surface. Both let you change on the move. 2 ratio box with low ratio of 2.6:1		
Final drive	3.55:1		
Suspension	Front coil sprung solid axle with 4 trailing arms. Single Cardan joints and live spindle hubs with half shaft disconnect system on Command-Trac. Rear solid axle, semi-floating open end, Hotchkiss design, semi-elliptic leaf springs. Trac-Lok rear differential		
Steering	Recirculating ball, servo optional		
Brakes	Discs front, drums rear, servo assisted		
Wheels	15" x 6", limited duty spare		

Turning circle	35.7 ft/11 metres
Electrical	12 volt
Alternator	61 Ah

In the usual American way, an off-road package is available, including gas shock absorbers, protective skid plates, uprated springs and a proper full size spare wheel.

NEW JEEP WAGONEER
As for the Cherokee four-door with automatic transmission as standard and luxury trim.

JEEP GRAND WAGONEER

Wheelbase	108.7"/2.76 metres
Engine	5.9 litre V8
Maximum power	144 bhp @ 3200 rpm
Maximum torque	280 lb ft @ 1500 rpm
Transmission	3 speed automatic, column shift
	1st gear 2.74:1
	2nd gear 1.55:1
	3rd gear 1.00:1
Transfer box	Selec-Trac 2wd/4wd full time system. 2 speed NP 229 2 ratio transfer box with low ratio of 2.6:1
Final drive	2.73:1
Suspension	Solid fully-floating axles on semi-elliptic leaf springs. Single Cardan outboard joints. Gas filled shock absorbers, full chassis. The front springs are mounted below the axle and the rear springs above it - Rear Trac-Lok 3.31:1 diff. optional
Steering	Servo assisted recirculating ball
Brakes	Servo assisted discs at front, drums at rear. Foot operated parking brake on rear drums
Wheels	15" x 7", limited duty spare
Tyres	Michelin Tru Seal P235/7R15, self sealing when punctured
Turning circle	37.7ft/11.5 metres
Electrical	12 volt
Alternator	61 AH

AMC JEEP WRANGLER
Replacement for CJ7, still cart sprung but otherwise with Cherokee mechanism, available in many trim options, the top of the line being the Sahara.

Powered by 4.2 litre 6 cylinder engine with optional 4.0 litre 6 cylinder, producing 173 bhp @ 4500 rpm and 220 lb ft torque @ 2500 rpm. Peugeot 5 speed manual gearbox and the NP 207 transfer box with change on the move operation; and automatic vacuum engagement of the free wheeling hubs.

In general, off-road ability is not as good as with the CJ5 and CJ7.

Wheelbase	93.4"/2.37 metres
Engine	6 cylinder petrol

Displacement	4.2 litre
Bore	95.3 mm
Stroke	99.1 mm
Compression ratio	9.2:1
Maximum power	112 bhp @ 3000 rpm
Maximum torque	210 lb ft @ 2000 rpm
Transmission	5 speed manual gearbox
	1st gear 4.03:1
	2nd gear 2.39:1
	3rd gear 1.52:1
	4th gear 1.00:1
	5th gear 0.72:1
	Reverse 3.76:1
Transfer box	NP 207, 2 ratio with low of 2.60:1. Part time 4wd with automatic free-wheeling hubs
Final drive	3.55:1
Suspension	Hotchkiss leaf springs front & rear
Steering	Recirculating ball, servo assisted
Brakes	Discs at front, drums at rear
Wheels	7″ x 15″
Tyres	P 225/75R 15
Turning circle	33.7 ft/10.3 metres

LICENCE BUILT JEEPS

It would be almost impossible to list all the licence built jeep or jeep derivatives around the world, to say nothing of the many kit cars, built to look like them and using any available mechanicals which come to hand.

Amongst the many have been those built in Japan (Mitsubishi), Australia, Bangladesh, Brazil, Canada (Ford), China (Beijing), India (Mahindra), Holland (Nekaf), Indonesia, Israel (Matmar), France (Hotchkiss, Renault), Iran, Kenya, South Africa, Korea, Mexico, Morocco, Pakistan, Phillipines, Portugal (Bravia), Spain (Viasa), Sri Lanka. Taiwan, Thailand and Venezuela.

AMERICAN MOTORS GENERAL – HUMMER

American forces 130″/3.3 metres wheelbase 4x4 featuring aluminium body panels on a steel chassis, powered by General Motors 6 litre V8 diesel producing 150 bhp of power and 260 lb ft of torque; driving through a 3 speed automatic gearbox with a 2 ratio full time 4WD transfer box with lockable centre differential. Axles have Gleason-Torsen torque biasing differentials front and rear with 2:1 reduction boxes at each wheel. Suspension is independent all round, with double "A" frames and coil springs. Brakes are servo assisted discs all round, mounted in board. Tyres are run flat 36 x 12.5 – 16.5 and the vehicle can wade 30″ of water unprepared.

AMPHI-RANGER 2800 SR

Amphibious, sea water resistant 4x4, built in West Germany by the car department of Rheinauer Maschinen and Armaturenbau GMBH (RMA), to fit the needs of pipe line engineers; who constantly have to operate in mixed off-road and in water environments. The hull is a stressed 3mm aluminium, load bearing bodyshell (4 mm where it is needed as a protective skid pan, underneath).

The propeller stays out of harm's way, tucked up behind the rear bumper on land, but is lowered for in-water use. In water, steering is by the front wheels, which is not very effective. I have suggested that a small boat, electric bow-prop would be more suitable. Wheels and propeller can be used at the same time, but seem to make steering even worse, due to eddies. This is a very specialist vehicle and the price requires big company or millionaire status, but it works well. It could be much improved in the water if it used the water jet system, which would give steering as well as propulsion and good protection from impact damage.

AMPHI – RANGER 2800 SR

Wheelbase	98.4″/2.5 m
Engine	Ford V6
Displacement	2772 cc
Bore	93 mm
Stroke	68.5 mm
Compression ratio	9.2:1
Maximum power	135 bhp @ 5200 rpm
Maximum torque	160 lb ft @ 3000 rpm
Transmission	4 speed manual with option of 5 speed
Transfer box	2 ratio part time with high ratio 1.1:1 and low ratio 3.87:1

Amphi-Ranger, Amphibious 4x4

Suspension	Fully independent all round. Double wishbone with progressive coil springs, single at front, double at rear.
Steering	Rack and pinion, servo assisted
Brakes	Discs all round, servo assisted
Wheels	5.5x16H (8″x15″ alloy optional)
Tyres	215R 16C (31x10.5x15LT optional)
Turning circle	39.4 ft/12 m
Electrical	12 volt (24 volt optional)
Battery	60 AH
Alternator	896 watt.

Amphi-Ranger with propeller lowered

ARO

Rumanian made medium wheelbase 4 × 4 available as, 240 soft top, 242 truck cab or 243 hard top with a choice of Rumanian made petrol or diesel engines or Peugeot diesel engine.

Wheelbase	2350 mm (92.5″)		
Engine	Peugeot Diesel	Rumanian Diesel	Rumanian Petrol
Type	XDP 490	D127	L25

171

Displacement	2112 cc	3119 cc	2495 cc
No of cylinders	4	4	4
Bore (mm)	90	95	97
Stroke (mm)	83	110	84.4
Compression ratio	22.4:1	17:1	8:1
Output	57 bhp	72 bhp	83 bhp
	@ 4250 rpm	@ 3200 rpm	@ 4200 rpm
Torque	96.2 lb ft	134.7 lb ft	130 lb ft
	@ 2000 rpm	@ 1600 rpm	@ 2900 rpm
Clutch	Hydraulically actuated		
Gearbox	Type UAP 240 4 forward gears 1 reverse gear all synchromesh		
Ratios	1st 4.920:1		
	2nd 2.682:1		
	3rd 1.654:1		
	4th 1.000:1		
Reverse	5.080:1		
Transfer box	Mechanical with two ratios 1:1 and 2.12:1		
Rear axle	Live axles with full floating shafts, ratio 4.714:1		
Suspension	Rear axle with leaf springs, independent at front with helical springs		
Brakes	Drum brakes all round, hand brake mechanically actuated on rear wheels		
Steering	Hour glass screw and dual roller, divided steering linkage, minimum turning circle 12 metre (39 ft)		
Electrics	12 volt negative earth 500 watt alternator		
Tyres	6.50" × 16"		
Payload	900 kg, 1980 lbs		

ARO 10 SERIES
ARO 101 (Soft Top) and
ARO 104 (Station Wagon) see
Dacia Duster and Shifter

ARO 240.

ATW CHICO

Developed by Messerschmitt Bolkow Blohm and built by ATW Auto Monatan Werke of Frankfurt, the Chico has an articulating chassis.

Wheelbase	99"/2.519 m
Engine	Deutz 2 1648 cc air-cooled diesel
No of cylinders	2
Maximum power	35 bhp @ 3000 rpm
Transmission	4 speed manual
Transfer box	2 ratio
Turning circle	33 ft/10 metres
Tyres	205Rx16
Electrical	12 volt

AUDI QUATTRO

The Audi Quattro is not an off-road car, but a high performance four-wheel drive on-road car, designed to use the advantages of permanent four-wheel drive on slippery, wet, icy and snowy roads; its phenomenal rally success in 1982, 3 & 4 forced other manufacturers to adopt four-wheel drive systems for their high performance cars.

Until recently, on all Quattro models, the centre and rear differentials were equipped with locks that could be engaged and disengaged manually. However, the Audi 80 and 90 Quattro's are now fitted with Torsen (torque sensing) centre differentials and if the rear differential lock has been used, it now automatically disengages, when road speed exceeds 15 mph.

Wheelbase	99.3"/2.524 m
Engine	Turbocharged 2144 cc
No of cylinders	5
Bore	79.5 mm
Stroke	86.4 mm
Block	Cast iron
Head	Aluminium
Compression ratio	7.0:1
Fuel system	Bosch K-Jetronic Injection
Maximum power	200 bhp @ 5500 rpm
Maximum torque	210 lb ft @ 3500 rpm
Transmission	Permanent 4WD
	5 speed manual
	1st 3.600:1
	2nd 2.125:1
	3rd 1.458:1
	4th 1.071:1
	5th 0.778:1
	Reverse 3.500:1
Final drive	3.889:1
Suspension	MacPherson struts, triangulated lower wishbones, anti roll bars
Steering	Rack and pinion servo assisted
Brakes	Dual circuit, servo assisted, disc brakes all round, ABS anti-lock system

Wheels	8Jx15
Tyres	215/50VR 15
Electrical	12 volt
Battery	63 AH
Alternator	90 A

Audi Quattro

AUTO UNION MUNGA

Light field vehicle, made for the Bundeswehr (West German forces) but also used by those of Holland and Indonesia. It became known as the Munga when released for civilian use, from German phrase 'Mehrzweck Universal Gelandewagon mit Allradentrieb' which translates as multipurpose, universal, cross-country car, with all-wheel drive. The earliest models (1955/56), had selectable two-wheel drive, but later models were permanent four-wheel drive.

Pre-1962 models had a manual premix system of oil and petrol but models after 1962 had a lubrimat system, whereby the oil was pumped into the carburettor.

Wheelbase	79"/2 metres
Engine	3 cylinder petrol
Displacement	980 cc
Bore	77 mm
Stroke	76 mm
Compression ratio	7.0:1
Maximum power	44 bhp @ 4250 rpm

Maximum torque	58 lb ft @ 3000 rpm
Transmission	4 speed manual
	1st 24.18
	2nd 15.27
	3rd 9.36
	4th 5.79
	Reverse 29.01
Transfer box	2 ratio, step down
	Ratio 1.60:1
Steering	Rack & pinion
Brakes	Drums all round
Tyres	6.00 x 16
Turning circle	41 ft/12.5 metres
Electrical	24 volt stepped down to 12 volt for ignition, separate coil, points and condenser for each cylinder

BEDFORD CF2 4x4

Bedford CF2 vans and minibuses, fitted with FF Developments viscous coupling 4WD system. The front coil spring suspension is replaced with a torsion bar system. A raised model is available with 7.50 x 16″ tyres. The two-ratio transfer box has a low of 3.333:1.

BEDFORD KB41/HOLDEN KB41 UTE/CHEVROLET LUV/ISUZU P'UP ISUZU RODEO

Japanese Isuzu built pick-up, imported into the UK as Bedford KB41, Australia as Holden KB41 and the USA as the Chevrolet Luv./Isuzu p'up. Refer to Isuzu Rodeo.

Bedford KB41

BEIJING BJ 212/PEKING PJ 212
Chinese built field car, based on the Russian UAZ 469B. In service with the armed forces of China, Pakistan and Chad. In some countries, the vehicle is available with a Perkins 4-154 diesel engine built under licence by Mazda, in Japan.

Wheelbase	78"/2.3 metres
Engine	4 cylinder petrol
Displacement	2445 cc
Bore	92 mm
Stroke	92 mm
Compression ratio	6.6:1
Maximum power	75 bhp @ 3500 rpm
Transmission	3 speed manual
Transfer box	2 ratio
Suspension	Live axles on semi-elliptic leaf springs
Brakes	Drums on all wheels
Tyres	6.50 x 16
Turning circle	40 ft/12 metres
Electrical	12 volt

Chinese Beijing/Peking BJ212

BOMBARDIER/CITROEN C44
A Volkswagen ILTIS, built under licence in Canada by Bombardier.

BUSHWAKER
A concept vehicle based on the Chevrolet K5 two-door Blazer with a 6.7 litre V8 engine, producing 175 bhp @ 3800 rpm and 275 lb ft @ 2000 rpm driving through the Blazer's standard transmission, but having a heavily strengthened suspension, with two shock absorbers to each front wheel and three shock absorbers to each rear wheel. There are separate Warn 12,000 lb winches front and rear and a 24 volt electrical system, fed by two alternators, powering various lights and five different radios.

CHEVROLET BLAZER K10/GMC JIMMY
Typical American approach to four wheel drive market with many options in engine size, transmissions and suspensions, some 15% bigger than a Range Rover and much heavier, but with less load carrying space. Offered mainly with full time four wheel drive and central locking differential, but from 1981 a part time four wheel drive system with free wheeling hubs will be available. Despite its high cruising speed, standard Hooke joints are still used on the front axle instead of constant velocity joints. The hard top is of glass reinforced plastic which cuts weight but adds problems of its own for off road use.

The vehicle handles well on the road though with some waver at speed, but off the road there is much pitching or rolling, for real off road use the vehicle needs the heaviest available suspension and wide tyres and this shows up weaknesses in the drive shafts.

Chevrolet Blazer.

Options include   4.1 litre/250 cu inch 6 cylinder engine
                         5.0 litre/305 cu inch V8 E SC engine with computerized
                         electrical ignition
                         5·74 litre/350 cu inch V8 engine
                         6.56 litre/400 cu inch V8 engine
                         3 speed manual gearbox
                         4 speed manual gearbox
                         3 speed automatic gearbox
                         Full time NPG 203 transfer box
                         Part time NPG 205 or 208 transfer box
                         Limited slip differentials
                         Final drive ratios of 3.07, 3.73, 4.11 to 1

The following specification is the only Model imported to UK

Wheelbase	106.5″	
Engine	V8	
Displacement	5.74 litres (350 cu inch)	
Bore	101.6 mm	
Stroke	88.4 mm	
Compression ratio	8.5:1	
Maximum power	165 bhp @ 3800 rpm	
Maximum torque	255 lb ft @ 2800 rpm	
Also available in:-		
Engine	6 cylinder	5.0 litre V8 ESC
Displacement	4.1 litres	5 litres
Bore	98.3 mm	95.0 mm

GMC Jimmy.

Stroke	89.7 mm	88.4 mm
Compression ratio	8.25:1	9.2:1
Maximum output	100 bhp @ 3600 rpm	165 bhp @ 3600 rpm
Maximum torque	175 lb ft @ 1800 rpm	
Transmission	Full time four wheel drive NP 203 transfer case with ratios of 1:1 and 2.01:1 with automatic transmission or part time four wheel drive NP 208 transfer case with ratios of 1:1 and 2.60:1 plus Warner automatic locking hubs with manual transmission	

Gearbox	Manual 3 speed	Manual 4 speed	Automatic
1st gear	2.85:1	6.56:1	2.52:1
2nd gear	1.68:1	3.58:1	1.52:1
3rd gear	1.00:1	1.70:1	1.00:1
4th gear		1.00:1	

Suspension	Live axles on semi-elliptic leaf springs
Steering	Power assisted, recirculating ball
Turning circle	37 ft/11.3 metres
Brakes	Servo assisted discs at front, drums at rear
Tyres	LT10 × 15/H78 × 15B
Electrics	12 volt negative earth
Battery	12 volt 55 amp
Alternator	61 amp

CHEVROLET K10/GMC K15 PICK-UP TRUCKS, K10 SUBURBAN STATION WAGON

½ ton trucks and station wagon available in various options including the new 5 litre V8 engine with electronic spark control and the New Process 208 part time four wheel drive transfer case

Wheelbase	117.5"/131.5" Trucks		129.5" for Suburban
Engine type	6 cylinder	V8	V8
Displacement	4.1 litre	5.7 litre	5.0 litre ESC
Bore	98.3 mm	101.6 mm	95.0 mm
Stroke	89.7 mm	88.4 mm	88.4 mm
Compression ratio	8.2:1	8.5:1	9.2:1
Maximum output	100 bhp @ 3600 rpm	160 bhp @ 3600 rpm	165 bhp @ 3600 rpm
Maximum torque	175 lb ft @ 1800 rpm	290 lb ft @ 2800 rpm	
Transmission	3 speed manual	4 speed manual	3 speed automatic
1st gear	2.99:1	6.56:1	2.52:1
2nd gear	1.75:1	3.58:1	1.52:1
3rd gear	1.00:1	1.70:1	1.00:1
4th gear		1.00:1	

Final drive ratios 3.08, 3.42, 3.73 and 4.11:1

Full time four wheel drive NP 203 transfer case with automatic transmission (ratios 1 and 2.01:1)

Part time four wheel drive NP 208 transfer case with manual transmission (ratios 1 and 2.60:1)

Suspension	Live axles on semi-elliptic leaf springs

Steering	Power assisted, recirculating ball
Brakes	Servo assisted, discs at front, drums at rear
Handbrake	On rear drums
Wheels	15 × 6 JJ
Tyres	L78 × 15
Turning circle	43 ft/13.1 metres
Electrical	12 volt negative earth
Alternator	60 A
Battery	60 AH
Payload	2000 lb/909 kg

CHEVROLET K20/GMC K25 PICK-UP TRUCKS/K20 SUBURBAN STATION WAGON

3/4 ton heavier duty versions of the Chevrolet K10/GMC K15 vehicles

Wheelbase	117.5"/131.5" Trucks	129.5" Suburban	
Engine type	6 cylinder	V8	
Displacement	4.8 litre	5.7 litre	
Bore	98.3 mm	101.6 mm	
Stroke	104.7 mm	88.4 mm	
Compression ratio	8.0:1	8.5:1	
Maximum output	120 bhp @ 3600 rpm	160 bhp @ 3600 rpm	
Maximum torque	215 lb ft @ 2000 rpm	290 lb ft @ 2800 rpm	
Transmission	3 speed manual	4 speed manual	3 speed automatic
1st gear	2.99:1	6.56:1	2.52:1
2nd gear	1.75:1	3.58:1	1.52:1
3rd gear	1.00:1	1.70:1	1.00:1
4th gear		1.00:1	

Full time four wheel drive NP 203 transfer case with automatic transmission (ratios 1.0 and 2.01:1)

Part time four wheel drive NP 205 transfer case with manual transmission (ratios 1.0:1 and 1.96:1)

Final drive ratios 3.23, 3.42, 3.73 and 4.10:1

Suspension	Live axles on semi-elliptic leaf springs
Steering	Power assisted, recirculating ball
Brakes	Servo assisted, discs at front, drums at rear
Handbrake	on rear drums
Wheels	16.5 × 6
Tyres	8.75 × 16.5
Turning circle	45 ft/14.4 metres
Electrical	12 volt negative earth
Alternator	60 A
Battery	60 AH
Payload	3000 lbs/1364 kg

CHEVROLET K30/GMC K35 PICK-UP TRUCKS

Heavier duty 1 ton versions of the Chevrolet K20/GMC K25, with the addition of an optional 6.55 litre V8 engine and 4.56:1 final drive ratio.

Engine	6.55 litre V8
Bore	104.8 mm

Stroke	95.3 mm
Compression ratio	8.5:1
Maximum power	175 bhp @ 3600 rpm
Maximum torque	290 lb ft @ 2800 rpm

For 1988 Chevrolet/GMC full size vehicles will have Insta-Trac shift system, which allows you to change from 2 wheel drive free wheeling to 4 wheel drive high ratio and back, at any speed.

CHEVROLET LUV PICK-UP
Refer to Isuzu Rodeo

CHEVROLET S10 BLAZER/GMC S15 JIMMY
Smaller, less thirsty versions of the older Blazers and Jimmys, with 100.5″/2.55 metres wheelbase for the 2 door hard-top and 123″/3.12 metres wheelbase for the pick-up. Optional engines are 2 litre 4 cylinder or 2.8 litre V6 petrol engines. 4 speed manual or 5 speed manual gearbox or 4 speed auto gearbox. Rear suspension is live axle on leaf springs, front suspension is independent on torsion bars. A 2.2 litre Isuzu diesel engine is also available.

Insta-Trac 4WD lets you change from free wheeling 2 wheel drive to 4 wheel drive high ratio and back at any speed.

CITROEN MEHARI
Plastic bodied light 4 × 4 using Citroen deux cheval (2CV) components normally front wheel drive with selectable four wheel drive and all round independent suspension. The gearbox is standard 2CV but to allow for the tiny 29 lb ft torque from this flat twin air cooled 425 cc 2 hp engine the transfer box has a super low reduction ratio of 2.6:1. The Mehari is only made in France. Wheelbase is 2.40 metres 94.5 inches

Citroen Mehari.

CITROEN FAF 4 × 4

Another plastic bodied Mehari, but designed to be cheaply fabricated in developing countries, this time using the 3CV flat twin air cooled 602 cc 3hp engine with 4 speed box and 2.6:1 reduction ratio transfer box.

CITROEN 2CV 4 × 4 SAHARA

First built in 1959 but many private ones have been built since. Basically front wheel drive with the 425 cc flat twin air cooled engine, but a second engine is mounted at the rear driving the rear wheels but using the same clutch, gearbox and acceleration controls.

COLT SHOGUN
Refer to Mitsubishi Pajero

COUNTY

Ford Transit 160 Van converted to 4x4 by County Tractors. Manual free-wheeling hubs fitted as standard. The transfer box is a New Process and the front axle is a Dana unit, all other parts are Ford.

Wheelbase	short 110.8"/2.81 metres		
	long 118.9"/3.02 metres		
Engines	2.5 litre petrol	3.0 litre petrol	2.5 litre diesel
Maximum power			68 bhp @ 4000 rpm
Transmission	5 speed gearbox or 4 speed plus overdrive on the diesel		
Transfer box	Part time 4WD 2 ratio with low of 2.61:1		
Final drive	5.83:1		
Suspension	Live axles on semi-elliptic leaf springs		
Brakes	Discs at front, drums at rear servo assisted		
Tyres	205 R 16		

COURNIL (TRACTEUR COURNIL), UMM TRANSCAT/ALTER/AFRICAR, DAKARY AND SIMI COURNIL

French built in quantity between 1960 and 1970, using various Hotchkiss and Renault petrol engines or Hotchkiss and Peugeot Indenor diesel engines. To a design by Bernard Cournil, these vehicles are now available again in a slightly updated form from UMM of Portugal.

A Trak-Lok type rear differential was fitted as standard, built with the farmer in mind. Cournil options included front, rear and centre power take offs, winches, hydraulics etc as per Land Rovers and Unimogs.

Refer to UMM Transcat for latest details.

The Cournil design was also taken over by Gevelot who developed the vehicle for the military and called it Samo. Gevelot were taken over by Simi who later became Autoland and called the vehicle the Tropic.

Engines	Peugeot XD2 4 cylinder 2.3 litre diesel
	Developing 67 bhp @ 4000 rpm
	Saviem 720 4 cylinder 3.6 litre diesel
	Developing 85 bhp @ 3000 rpm
	Renault 829 4 cylinder 2 litre petrol
	Developing 83 bhp @ 5000 rpm

Cournil.

CROCO
Swiss made amphibious cross country ATV, with its body constructed in two separate units (hulls), articulating around a central chassis pivot. In water it is driven either by the wheels or by a propeller from a power take-off. The engine is a 30 bhp 0.44 litre Wankel rotary engine, driving via a belt type torque converter to a 2 speed gearbox and lockable differentials. The wheelbase is 64"/1.63 metres and it has disc brakes all round. Tyres are 31" diameter 15" low pressure tyres. Steering, engine and main transmission are housed in the front unit, to give maximum room in the rear.

The engine produces 30 bhp @ 5500 rpm and 33 lb ft at 3600 rpm. Steering is by all four wheels with a turning circle of 28 ft/8.5 metres. Suspension is non-existent, relying on the soft tyres at 7 psi. Fuel tank is removable jerry cans. UK versions of the Croco will use a Norton twin rotor 0.9 litre water-cooled engine.

DACIA DUSTER/ARO 10
Not so cheap Romanian built 4x4 with mechanicals based on the Renault 12. Off-road performance is limited by low power, low gearing, soft springing and small (14") wheels. Available as soft top or hard top.

Wheelbase	94.5"/2.4 metres
Engine	4 cylinder petrol
Displacement	1.397 litre
Bore	76 mm

Stroke   77 mm
Compression ratio   9.5:1
Maximum power   65 bhp @ 5250 rpm
Maximum torque   77.5 lbf ft @ 3000 rpm
Transmission   4 speed gearbox
                      1st gear 4.376:1
                      2nd gear 2.455:1
                      3rd gear 1.514:1
                      4th gear 1.00:1
                      Reverse 3.66:1
Transfer box   2 ratio 1.076:1 @ 2.249:1
Final drive   4.571:1
Suspension   Independent front with coil springs and wishbones.
                      Rigid at rear with semi-elliptic leaf springs
Steering   Worm & roller
Brakes   Discs at front, drums at rear servo assisted
Wheels   14″
Tyres   175 x 14
Turning circle   38 ft/11.4 metres
Electrical   12 volt
Battery   45 AH
Free wheeling hubs come as standard

Dacia Duster GLX

DAIHATSU FOURTRAK

Sold as the Rocky in Australia, Taft, Wildcat or Toyota Blizzard in other countries, Daihatsu's popular, solid, working range of lightweight off-road vehicles were restyled in 1984 to bring them up to date with the current trend for all-purpose vehicles. Thorough testing in Australia before release led to improved shock absorbers. 90% of the body panels are galvanised before painting, enabling an 8 year anti-corrosion warranty to be given and this has made the vehicle popular with farmers looking for an alternative to the Land Rover. The engines are Toyota, the same as in the Toyota Hilux utilities in Australia. Manual free-wheeling hubs and gas shock absorbers come as standard. Seats are on the small side for Europeans. Also available as a pick-up.

Daihatsu Fourtrak

Wheelbase	86.8"/2.05 metre	110"/2.79 metre
Engine	3Y 4 cylinder Petrol	DL 4 cylinder Diesel
Displacement	1.998 litre	2.765 litre
Bore	86 mm	92 mm
Stroke	86 mm	104 mm
Maximum power	87 bhp @ 4600 rpm	72 bhp @ 3600 rpm

Maximum torque	116 lb ft	126 lb ft
	@ 3000 rpm	@ 2200 rpm

In turbocharged form the 4 cylinder diesel produces 87 bhp @ 3600 rpm & 155 lb ft @ 2200 rpm

Transmission	5 speed manual
Transfer box	2 ratio part time 4WD
Suspension	Semi-elliptic leaf springs with gas-charged shock absorbers and lateral stabilizer bar on the front. All shock absorbers have 3 stage control switch on centre console. Limited slip rear diff available in Australia
Steering	Ball and nut
Brakes	Servo assisted discs at front, drums at rear
Tyres	215 SR 15
Turning circle	38 ft/11.6 metres

For 1988 the seats have been improved and a turbo diesel is available producing 90 bhp @ 3400 rpm and a maximum torque of 165 lbf ft @ 2200 rpm

DANGEL
French 4x4 conversions to Peugeot and Citroen road going vehicles and the Peugeot Talbot Express van.

DELTA MINI CRUISER/EXPLORER
Phillipine built light 4x4 based on locally built Toyota parts, with either Toyota 1.6 litre petrol engines or Isuzu C190 diesel engines.

DODGE RAMCHARGER/PLYMOUTH TRAIL DUSTER STATION WAGONS
Dodge power wagon tradition, but now with an integrated all steel roof, making it more weatherproof than the bolt-on glass reinforced plastic units on its competitors, the Blazer/Jimmy and Bronco. The new hatchback is an improvement on tailgates and is well sealed against dust and water. A 440 cu inch 7.2 litre V8 is available on the Trail Duster.

Wheelbase	106"		
Engines	318 cu inch V8	360 cu inch V8	
Displacement	5.2 litres	5.9 litres	
Bore	99.3 mm	101.6 mm	
Stroke	84.1 mm	90.9 mm	
Compression ratio	8.6:1	8.4:1	
Maximum output	150 bhp @ 4000 rpm	175 bhp @ 4000 rpm	
Maximum torque	230 lb ft @ 2400 rpm	285 lb ft @ 2400 rpm	
Transmission	Full time four wheel drive NP 203 transfer case ratios 1:1 and 2.01:1, optional part time four wheel drive transfer case with Warner automatic locking hubs		
Gearbox	4 speed manual wide ratio	4 speed manual close ratio	3 speed automatic
1st gear	6.68:1	4.56:1	2.45:1
2nd gear	3.34:1	2.28:1	1.45:1
3rd gear	1.66:1	1.31:1	1:1
4th gear	1:1	1:1	

Dodge Ramcharger.

Final drive ratios	3.21 and 3.55:1
Suspension	Live axles on semi-elliptic leaf springs
Steering	Power assisted, recirculating ball
Brakes	Servo assisted discs at front, drums at rear
Handbrake	On rear drums
Turning Circle	37 ft/11.3 metres
Tyres	H78 × 15B
Payload	1000 lbs/455 kg
Electrics	12 volt negative earth
Battery	50 AH
Alternator	41 AH
Optional 440 cu inch 7.2 litre V8	
Bore	109.7 mm
Stroke	95.3 mm
Compression ratio	8.2:1
Maximum output	225 bhp @ 4000 rpm
Maximum torque	330 lb ft @ 2400 rpm

DODGE   W150/W250/W350

Pick-up trucks and crew cab pick-up trucks on 115″, 131″ and 135″ wheelbases with many engine options including a diesel by Mitsubishi and the heaviest W350 option having a payload of 5500 lb/2500 kg

Wheelbases	115″	131″	135″	
Engines	225 cu inch 6 cylinder	318 cu inch V8	360 cu inch V8	440 cu inch V8

1982 Dodge W150.

Displacement	3.7 litre	5.2 litre	5.9 litre	7.2 litre
Bore	88.4 mm	99.3 mm	101.6 mm	109.7 mm
Stroke	104.8 mm	84.1 mm	90.9 mm	95.3 mm
Compression ratio	8.4:1	8.6:1	8.4:1	8.2:1
Maximum output	105 bhp @ 3600 rpm	150 bhp @ 4000 rpm	175 bhp @ 4000 rpm	225 bhp @ 4000 rpm
Maximum torque	175 lb ft @ 2000 rpm	230 lb ft @ 2400 rpm	285 lb ft @ 2400 rpm	330 lb ft @ 2400 rpm

Also a 243 cu inch 3.98 litre diesel by Mitsubishi giving 103 bhp @ 3700 rpm and 168 lb ft @ 2200 rpm

Transmission	Full time four wheel drive NP 203 transfer case with 1:1 and 2.01:1 ratios		
Gearbox	4 speed manual wide ratio	4 speed manual close ratio	3 speed automatic
1st gear	6.68:1	4.56:1	2.45:1
2nd gear	3.34:1	2.28:1	1.45:1
3rd gear	1.66:1	1.31:1	1:1
4th gear	1:1	1:1	
Final drive ratios	3.21, 3.55 and 4.10:1 with a 4.56:1 on the W350		
Suspension	Live axles on semi-elliptic leaf springs		
Steering	Power assisted, recirculating ball		
Brakes	Servo assisted discs at front, drums at rear		

Handbrake	On rear drums		
Turning circle	45 ft/13.7 metres		
Tyres	10 × 15 LT		
Payload	W150 = 1865 lb	W250 = 3560 lb	W350 = 5500 lb
	= 848 kg	= 1618 kg	= 2500 kg

DODGE POWER RAM
Light pick-up in the mould of the Mazda, Nissan and Toyota pick-ups with 2.6 litre petrol engine, 5 speed manual gearbox, automatic free-wheeling hubs and 15″ wheels.

DONG-A KORANDO/PANTHER STAMPEDE
Isuzu Trooper clone, made by Dong-A Motorsin, South Korea, which will be imported into UK by their associate company Panther who will fit other engines and transmissions and call it the Stampede.

EAGLE
Body/chassis kit car, intended to be used with Land Rover or Range Rover running gear. The body is glass fibre and if the donor vehicle is Land Rover, then the chassis will be converted for coil springs. Suitable engines are the Rover V8 petrol, Ford V6 petrol or 4 cylinder diesels by Rover, Mercedes or Peugeot.

Eagle Kit-Car

ENGESA EE 12
Brazilian light 4x4 with 85″ wheelbase, live axles on coil springs all round and 16″ wheels. Power units are 2.5 litre petrol or alcohol engines or 1.5 litre Volkswagen diesel. The 2.5 litre engines drive through a 5 speed gearbox and single speed transfer box, whilst the diesel engine has the 5 speed gearbox and a two ratio transfer box. AVM free wheeling hubs are standard.

ENGESA EE 34
Brazilian made 94″/2.025 metres wheelbase military 4x4 with 4 speed gearbox, 2 ratio transfer box. Free wheeling hubs and a choice of either Perkins 4,236 4 cylinder diesel engine or Mercedes-Benz OM314 6 cylinder diesel engine.

ESARCO
British designed 8x8 and 6x6, cross-country trucks, built totally on Land Rover 110 components. Axles no 1 and no 3 are driven from an LT 230 transfer box, mounted in the normal way. Axles No 2 and No 4 are driven from an identical LT 230 transfer box mounted further back on the chassis but turned through 180 degrees, so that the power take-offs of each transfer box face each other and are interconnected by a drive shaft. Steering is effected both front and back, the system being linked and operated in opposition.

   The 8x8 is 2 tonne capacity, using either the Land Rover V8 petrol engine or Range Rover VM Turbo Diesel, the 6x6 is 1 tonne capacity with the Land Rover 2.5 litre Turbo Diesel as alternative engine. Amphibious and armoured models are available and American production using Ford parts is planned. On-road performance is as good as the normal Land Rover 110.

Esarco—note steering by wheels 1 & 4

FIAT CAMPAGNOLA

Land Rover type four wheel drive but more expensive, seen mainly with Italian construction companies in Africa, available since 1974.

Wheelbase	2.3 metre (62″)
Engine	4 cylinder petrol
Displacement	1995 cc
Bore	84 mm
Stroke	90 mm
Compression ratio	8.6:1
Maximum power	80 bhp @ 4600 rpm
Maximum torque	111 lb ft @ 2800 rpm

Fiat Campagnola (Current).

Gearbox	4 forward speeds, 1 reverse
	1st 3.667:1
	2nd 2.100:1
	3rd 1.361:1
	4th 1:1
	Reverse 3.444:1
Transfer box	Two ratios 1.12:1 and 3.33:1
Final drive	5.375:1

Limited slip differentials and a locking rear differential are available as optional extras

Suspension	Independent all round with torsion bars and MacPherson struts
Steering	Worm and roller
Brakes	Servo assisted drum brakes
	Handbrake only on rear drums

FIAT PC65, PC75 and PC90

These are technically advanced 4 × 4 light duty trucks aimed at the Mercedes Unimog type commercial market, with various accessory attachment facilities for specialist work.

	65PC	75PC	90PC
Wheelbase	2380 mm (94")	2750 mm (108")	2850 mm (112")
Engine	4 cylinder diesel	6 cylinder diesel	
Displacement	3.456 litre	5.184 litre	
Maximum power	81 bhp	122 bhp	
Maximum torque	159 lb ft	234 lb ft	
Gearbox	5 speed with synchromesh on top 4 gears		
	2 speed transfer box		
Brakes	Hydraulically operated drum brakes with 3 independent circuits		
	Handbrake on rear wheels only		
Steering	Recirculating ball type		

The 65 and 75PC have rigid axles, of the double reduction load bearing type, with bevel drive and spur hub reduction units to ensure high ground clearance.

The 90PC has a single reduction higher load capacity rear axle and twin wheels.

The rear axles have limited slip differentials

Payload	65PC 2500 kg, (5500 lbs)
	75PC 3250 kg, (7150 lbs)
	90PC 5000 kg, (11000 lbs)

FORD BRONCO

Slightly smaller than the Blazer/Jimmy or Ramcharger/Trailduster which gives it better off road handling. Independent front suspension gives better all round handling but means that one has to be more careful with ground clearance over obstacles.

Wheelbase	104"

Ford Bronco.

Engines	250 cu inch 6 cylinder	300 cu inch 6 cylinder	302 cu inch V8	351 cu inch V8
Displacement	4.1 litre	4.92 litre	4.95 litre	5.75 litre
Bore	93.5 mm	101.6 mm	101.6 mm	101.6 mm
Stroke	99.3 mm	101.1 mm	76.2 mm	88.9 mm
Compression ratio	9.1:1	8.3:1	8:1	8:1
Maximum output	125 bhp @ 3700 rpm	114 bhp @ 3200 rpm	125 bhp @ 2600 rpm	162 bhp @ 3800 rpm
Maximum torque	210 lb ft @ 2400 rpm	222 lb ft @ 1600 rpm	218 lb ft @ 2200 rpm	266 lb ft @ 2200 rpm
Transmission	Full time four wheel drive NP 203 transfer case with ratios 1:1 and 2.01:1 or part time four wheel drive NP 208 transfer case with ratios 1:1 and 2.6:1 with automatic locking hubs; gearboxes are 3 speed automatic, 4 speed manual or 4 speed manual with 0.71:1 overdrive top gear.			

Gearbox	3 speed automatic	4 speed manual	4 speed manual plus overdrive
1st gear	2.46:1	6.68:1	3.29:1
2nd gear	1.46:1	3.34:1	1.84:1
3rd gear	1:1	1.66:1	1:1
4th gear		1:1	0.71:1
Final drive ratios	3.00 and 3.50:1		
Suspension	Independent with coil springs on front		
	Live axle on semi-elliptic leaf springs on rear		
Brakes	Servo assisted, discs at front, drums at rear		
Handbrake	On rear drums		
Steering	Worm and roller, optional power steering		
Turning circle	31 ft/9.5 metres		
Tyres	E78 × 15B		
Payload	1040 lbs/473 kg		
Electrics	12 volt negative earth		
Alternator	40 amp		
Battery	61 AH		

FORD F150 PICK-UP TRUCK
The same as the Ford Bronco retaining the coil spring independent front suspension and on wheelbases of 117″ and 132″.

Ford F250 pick-up truck.

FORD F250 PICK-UP TRUCK
Heavy duty 132″ wheelbase truck with independent front suspension on leaf springs, full time four wheel drive NP 203 transfer case or part time four wheel drive NP 208 transfer case with automatic locking hubs. Same engine and gearbox options as on the Ford Bronco/150 and final drive ratios of 3.07:1 and 3.54:1.

Payload	2540 lbs/1155 kg

FORD F350 PICK-UP TRUCK
Same as for Ford F250 but with 351 cu inch 5.75 litre V8 or 400 cu inch 6.6 litre V8 engines and 3.54:1 or 4.10:1 final drive ratios.

Engine	351 cu inch V8	400 cu inch V8
Displacement	5.75 litre	6.6 litre
Bore	101.6 mm	101.6 mm
Stroke	88.9 mm	101.6 mm
Compression ratio	8:1	8:1
Maximum power	162 bhp @ 3800 rpm	167 bhp @ 3600 rpm
Maximum torque	266 lb ft @ 2200 rpm	302 lb ft @ 2200 rpm

FORD HILLBILLY
Ford A series 4 × 4's up to 5.7 tonnes, made by N.A.M. of Newton Abbot, available with part time or full time four wheel drive, a choice of 3 wheelbases and two engines, either 3.5 litre diesel or 3.0 litre petrol.

Ford-based Hillbilly 4WD

Wheelbase	130"
available	145"
	156"
Engines available	AO 609 Ford 3.5 litre diesel
	AO 610 Ford 3.0 litre V6
Transfer case	NP 203 full time four wheel drive with ratios 1:1 and 2.01:1
	or NP 205 part time four wheel drive with ratios 1:1 and 1.96:1
Suspension	Live axles on leaf springs
Tyres	7.50" × 16"
Brakes	Dual circuit servo assisted drums all round. Hand brake on rear drums
Electrics	12 volt negative earth Alternator 35 amp

The chassis is *flitch plated* for extra strength and heavy duty springs and shock absorbers are added.

FORD BRONCO II

Smallest of the new breed of smaller American 4 wheel drives, with an unusual independent front suspension, which they call Twin-Traction Beam. The German engine has an electronically controlled engine management system, which does not bear thinking about if it were to fail in a remote off-road situation. Parking brake is foot operated, auto free-wheeling hubs are standard and the part time 4 wheel drive can be engaged and disengaged on the move. Ground clearance is poor, limited slip diff on the front and Trac-Loc diff on the rear are optional. The twin-traction beam suspension gives good ride quality but poor handling on twisty roads.

The spare wheel is on a swing away carrier at the rear, which has to be swung open before you can open the fibreglass rear door or rear window.

Latest models have Fords "Touch-Drive" option, which allows you to go from 2 wheel drive to 4 wheel drive high ratio at any speed, by push button.

Wheelbase	94"/2.39 metres
Engine	Petrol V6 with electronic fuel injection
Displacement	2.9 litre
Compression ratio	8.7:1
Maximum power	115 bhp @ 4600 rpm
Maximum torque	150 lb ft @ 2600 rpm
Transmission	5 speed manual with 4 speed auto optional
	1st gear 3.96:1
	2nd gear 2.08:1
	3rd gear 1.39:1
	4th gear 1.00:1
	5th gear 0.84:1
Transfer box	2 ratio, part time 4WD
	Automatic free-wheeling hubs
Suspension	Independent twin-traction beam on coil springs at front, live axle underslung on semi-elliptic leaf springs at rear. Gas pressure shock absorbers

Brakes	Discs at front, drums at rear, servo assisted. Foot operated parking brake on rear wheels
Wheels	15″
Tyres	205/75 R x 15
Turning circle	38 ft/11.5 metres

FORD 4x4 MUSCLE
South African built Ford P100 pick-up with 3 litre V6 petrol engine 4 speed manual or 3 speed automatic gearbox. 2 ratio Dana transfer box, part time 4WD, 15″ wheels and WARN free-wheeling hubs.

FORD RANGER
Light pick-up in the mould of the Mazda, Nissan and Toyota pick-ups with similar regular and super cab options and Fords Twin-Traction beam front suspension. Optional Touch-Drive which allows you to switch to 4 wheel drive high ratio at any speed. Standard engine is a 2.3 litre electronic fuel injection petrol or 2.9 litre electronic fuel injection V6 optional. 5 speed manual gearbox is standard, 4 speed automatic with overdrive is optional.

FORD TRANSIT 4x4
Refer to County

FORD/AMC 151 LIGHT VEHICLE SERIES (MUTT)
Developed by Ford to replace the M38 Jeep, manufactured by Ford and later the AM General Corporation. Many are still in service around the world.

Wheelbase	85″/2.16 metres
Engine	4 cylinder petrol 2.3 litre
Maximum power	71 bhp @ 4000 rpm
Transmission	4 speed manual
Transfer box	Single speed, selectable 4WD/2WD
Suspension	Independent all round with coil springs
Steering	Worm & double roller
Tyres	7.50 x 16
Turning circle	36 ft/11 metres
Electrical	24 volt

GMC JIMMY
Refer to Chevrolet Blazer

HOLDEN DROVER
Refer to Suzuki

HOLDEN KB41 PICK-UP
Refer to Isuzu Rodeo

HOLDEN JACKAROO
Refer to Isuzu Trooper

INTERNATIONAL HARVESTER SCOUT II, TRAVELER, TERRA PICK-UP
Wheelbase	Scout II 100″	Traveler 118″

Engines	196 cu inch 6 cylinder	304 cu inch V8	345 cu inch V8	198 cu inch 6 cylinder Nissan diesel
Displacement	3.2 litre	4.98 litre	5.65 litre	3.2 litre
Bore	104.8 mm	98.4 mm	98.4 mm	83.1 mm
Stroke	92.9 mm	81.7 mm	92.9 mm	100 mm
Compression ratio	8.02:1	8.19:1	8.05:1	22:1
Maximum power	86 bhp @ 3800 rpm	144 bhp @ 3600 rpm	163 bhp @ 3600 rpm	92 bhp @ 4000 rpm
Maximum torque	157 lb ft @ 2200 rpm	247 lb ft @ 2400 rpm	292 lb ft @ 2000 rpm	137.5 lb ft @ 2000 rpm
Transmission	Single ratio or two ratio Dana 20 transfer case with 1 and 2.03:1 ratio part time four wheel drive only			
Gearbox	3 speed manual	4 speed manual wide ratio	4 speed manual close ratio	3 speed automatic
1st gear	3.71:1	6.32:1	4.02:1	2.40:1
2nd gear	1.87:1	3.09:1	2.41:1	1.47:1
3rd gear	1:1	1.69:1	1.41:1	1:1
4th gear		1:1	1:1	
Final drive ratios	3.07, 3.54 and 4.09:1			
Suspension	Live axles on semi-elliptic leaf springs			
Steering	Worm and roller, optional power steering			
Brakes	Servo assisted, discs at front, drums at rear			

International Harvester Scout 11 diesel.

International Harvester Terra pick-up.

Handbrake	On rear drums	
Turning circle	Scout II 36 ft/11 metres	Traveler 41 ft/12.5 metres
Tyres	Scout II H 78 × 15	Traveler H 78 × 15
Payload	Scout II 1950 lbs/886 kg	Traveler 1580 lbs/718 kg

International Harvesters TERRA pick-up has the same basic configuration as the Traveler and 1960 lbs/891 kg payload. It is more strongly built than its competitors.

ISUZU P'UP
Refer to Isuzu Rodeo pick-up

ISUZU RODEO PICK-UP
Imported by General Motors into the USA as the Chevy Luv, UK as the Bedford KB41 and Australia as the Holden KB41 Rodeo. The small 14″ wheels give it a distinct disadvantage against its other Japanese competitors off-road, but then this is not really the market it is aimed at. Auto free-wheeling hubs are standard. Also sometimes known in Australia as the UTE and with a 2.3 litre petrol engine in the USA as the P'Up.

Wheelbase	104″/2.65 metres	
Engine	4 cylinder petrol	4 cylinder diesel
Displacement	1.59 litre	1.95 litre
Maximum power	71 bhp @ 5200 rpm	45 bhp @ 2200 rpm
Maximum torque	82 lb ft @ 3000 rpm	73 lb ft @ 2200 rpm
Transmission	5 speed gearbox	

Transfer box	2 ratio with a low of 1.87:1
	Part time 4WD
Final drive	4.55:1
Suspension	Front independent, double wishbone on torsion bars, rear live axle on semi-elliptic leaf springs
Steering	Recirculating ball
Brakes	Discs at front drums at rear
	Servo assisted
	Hand brake on rear wheels only
Tyres	6.50 x 14
Turning circle	37 ft/11.4 metres
Electrical	12 volt
Battery	33 AH
Payload	2200 lb/1000 kg

ISUZU TROOPER/HOLDEN JACKAROO

Imported into Australia as the Holden Jackaroo and elsewhere known as the Trooper, this award winning 4x4 comes from Japan's longest established car manufacturers who have strong connections with General Motors. The Trooper is quite lightly built for its class and has been popular around the world for its lower price. Having arrived late on the UK market, it is perhaps surprisingly expensive here. My own experience of the Trooper in Kenya is that is is very light to drive, has one of the slickest gear changes around, but that the body shell is too light, having a tendency for bits to fall off on Africa's corrugated tracks. The independent front suspension plus too soft springing give it limitations in the rough. The one third/two third rear door split falls foul of EEC regulations on lights, when open, and extra rear lights have had to be fitted into the rear bumper. Fog lights are put under the rear bumper, for you to knock off when you leave the road. Automatic free-wheeling hubs are fitted for the UK market, manual free-wheeling hubs in the Third World. Limited slip rear differential is optional. The load carrying area has useful tie-down rings. For the right-hand drive market the main rear door opens the wrong way, making loading from the kerb awkward.

Wheelbase	short 90.6"/2.30 metres	long 104.3"/2.65 metres
Engines	4 cylinder petrol	4 cylinder Turbo diesel
Displacement	2.3 litre	2.3 litre
Bore	89.3 mm	88 mm
Stroke	90 mm	92 mm
Compression ratio	8.3:1	21.1
Maximum power	88 bhp @ 4600 rpm	73.7 bhp @ 4000 rpm
Maximum torque	123 lb ft @ 2600 rpm	125 lb @ 2500 rpm
Transmission	5 speed gearbox	
	1st gear 3.785:1	
	2nd gear 2.171:1	
	3rd gear 1.413:1	
	4th gear 1.00:1	
	5th gear 0.855:1	
	Reverse 3.720:1	
Transfer box	2 ratio with low of 1.870:1	
	part time 4WD	

Available Vehicles

Isuzu Trooper long wheelbase

Isuzu Trooper short wheelbase

Holden Jackaroo (Isuzu Trooper) in Australia

Final drive	4.555:1
Suspension	Front independent, double wishbone arms, torsion bar springs with stabilizer bar, rear live axle on semi-elliptic leaf springs
Steering	Recirculating ball
Brakes	Discs at front, drums at rear
	Servo assisted
Wheels	16″ (15″ optional)
Tyres	6.00 x 16
Turning circle	31.4 ft/9.6 metres 35.4 ft/10.8 metres

Early models were called Bighorn or Rodeo because they were based on the Rodeo pick-up. 2.8 litre engines will be available in 1988

JEG
A Volkswagen Beetle based buggy type 4 × 4 built in Brazil by Dacunha, uses a 2.0 metre (79″) wheelbase with the flat 4 air cooled 1600 litre Beetle engine, soft and hard top versions will be available. Brakes are drum all round with hand brake on the rear wheels only.

Jeg.

LADA NIVA (VAZ-2121)

Russian built short wheelbase estate, with advanced full time four wheel drive and lockable centre differential. Built by a factory which builds Fiat 124s under licence but most of the vehicle is of Russian design. Later models have proved a consistent workhorse, with a surprising off-road capability, though the many niggling little faults can become annoying. The small foot pedals are designed more for shoes than muddy boots. The lack of a good bumper makes the use of a high lift jack difficult. The Lada Niva Cossack has a flash paint job and seat covers, plus many bolt-on goodies arranged in England, such as front and rear nudge bars, wheel spats, alloy wheels, swing away spare wheel carrier and spotlights.

Lada Niva.

Lada Niva Cabrio

Wheelbase	86"/2.18 m
Engine	4 cylinder petrol
Displacement	1.57 litre
Bore	79.0 mm
Stroke	80.0 mm
Compression ratio	8.5:1
Maximum power	78 bhp @ 5400 rpm
Maximum torque	88 lb @ 3000 rpm
Transmission	5 speed gearbox
Transfer box	2 ratio 1.2:1 & 2.135:1
	Full time 4WD with locking centre differential
Final drive	4.3:1
Suspension	Front independent with wishbone, coil springs and anti-roll bar. Rear live axle located by four tracking arms & a Panhard Rod, coil springs
Steering	Globoid worm on ball
Brakes	Discs at front drums at rear
	Servo assisted
	Handbrake on rear wheels
Wheels	6.00 x 16
Turning circle	36 ft/11 metres
Electrical	12 volt
Battery	55 AH
Alternator	42 A

LAMBORGHINI LM 002/5000/CHEETAH/RAGING BULL

High performance, rear engined 4WD desert vehicle. Made in small numbers and used mostly as military versions, in the sands of the Middle East, where they are particularly good for high speed border patrols.

In a similar vein, some NATO countries are looking into the use of these vehicles for high speed anti-terrorist pursuit.

A winch is fitted as standard and the fuel tank holds 64 gallons. Options include an armour-plated body, bullet-proof tyres and anti-infra-red detection devices. The massive engine powers the 60 cwt fully laden vehicle to 140 mph.

Wheelbase	118"/3 metres
Engine	V12
Displacement	5.2 litre (7 litre optional)
Maximum power	450 bhp @ 6800 rpm
Maximum torque	368 lb ft @ 4500 rpm
Transmission	ZF S-24/3, 5 speed gearbox
Transfer box	2 ratio 1.428:1 and low 4.286:1
	Permanent 4WD with front diff disconnect. Limited slip differentials front, rear and centre with manual lock-up on the centre differential
Suspension	Independent all round with double wishbones and coil springs

Lamborghini LM 002

LANDMASTER/POWRFOR

Oversized old Land Rover type 4WD, with square line aluminium alloy panel body on sturdy chassis. First launched in 1982 and now keeps re-emerging in hope of finding some military contract. Standard engines are Perkins 4,236, 3.86 litre, or 6,247, 4.05 litre diesel or Chrysler 360 V8 petrol. Transmission is 4 speed New Process NP 435 manual gearbox with NP 205, 2 ratio transfer box giving part time 4WD. Axles are Spicer 60, suspension is leaf springs all round, tyres are 7.50 x 16 and wheelbase is 115"/2.92 metres.

LAND ROVER SERIES III

Still one of the best engineered, strongest built off road four wheel drive vehicles available and the standard by which all other four wheel drive vehicles are judged. The heavy chassis and aluminium alloy bolt-on body panels mean long life and virtually no corrosion, which is important to the farmer or other four wheel drive users in very wet or snowy climates, particularly where roads are salted in winter. Land Rovers over twenty years old are a common sight worldwide and the worldwide availability of spare parts, due much to few production changes, is a big deciding factor when buying a four wheel drive for Third World use. Very few four wheel drive vehicles will really accept a good bull bar successfully for warding off minor impacts and therefore the Land Rover stands out again, in that bodywork damage can be bent roughly back to shape and then ignored because the aluminium panels when damaged will not rust like damaged steel bodywork, nor is the bodywork shape part of the strength of the vehicle. Also the body panels are all bolt-on and therefore easily and cheaply replaced. Australian made differential locks are now available both in Australia and UK.

Land Rover long wheelbase Series III hard top in Arabian trim.

All four wheel drives have their faults and the Land Rover has plenty depending on what you require, most customers would prefer to see better seats and windows, and a limited slip differential option. Australian and American markets clamour for softer springing, larger engines, automatic gearboxes, power steering and generally faster on road performance, but then this is not what the Land Rover is designed for and the Range Rover is more suitable for these lighter use conditions.

The Land Rover is available in long (109″) and short (88″) wheelbase models, with hard top, soft top, truck cab pick-up and station wagon options. Short wheelbase models are available with a 4 cylinder petrol or diesel engine. Long wheelbase models are available with 4 cylinder petrol or diesel engines, 6 cylinder petrol engines or the V8 petrol engine. When the V8 engine is fitted you also get the full time four wheel drive system with centre lockable differential as fitted to the Range Rover, all other options being standard part time four wheel drive. All Land Rovers are designed from the outset with power take-off points for the many options farmers, forestry workers, construction workers etc, require of them and have sensible oil filled air filters for dusty conditions.

The fact that Land Rovers are in use with some 140 world armies and are often bought for military use by countries which blacklist them for civilian sales says much for their reliability. One African country did a five year long term test of Land Rover versus Toyota and only the Land Rover was still running after the five years.

LAND ROVER SERIES III
SHORT WHEELBASE MODELS

Wheelbase	88"	
Engine	Petrol	Diesel
No of cylinders	4	4
Displacement	2.286 litre	2.286 litre
Bore	90.47 mm	90.47 mm
Stroke	88.9 mm	88.9 mm
Compression ratio	8:1	23:1
Maximum power	70 bhp @ 4000 rpm	62 bhp @ 4000 rpm
Maximum torque	120 lb ft @ 1500 rpm	103 lb ft @ 1800 rpm
Clutch	9.5" diaphragm type hydraulically operated	
Transmission	Gearbox 4 forward 1 reverse, synchromesh on all forward gears	
	1st 3.68:1	
	2nd 2.22:1	
	3rd 1.50:1	
	4th 1:1	
	Reverse 4.02:1	
	Transfer box step down ratios 1.148:1 and 2.35:1, part time four wheel drive in high range, permanent four wheel drive in low range	
Final drive	4.7:1	
Suspension	Live front and rear axles with half elliptic leaf springs and fully floating half shafts.	
Steering	Recirculating ball	
Brakes	Drums all round	
	Transmission handbrake on rear prop shaft	
Electrics	12 volt negative earth	
	16 ACR alternator (34 amps)	
Battery	58 AH petrol	95 AH diesel
Tyres	6.00" × 16"	
Turning circle	38 ft/11.6 metres	
Payload	680 kg/1500 lbs	

LAND ROVER SERIES III
LONG WHEELBASE 109" MODELS

Have the same 4 cylinder engines, transmission and electrics as the short wheelbase models with the addition of servo assisted brakes and 7.50" × 16" tyres, a turning circle of 47 ft and a 6 cylinder engine option. For heavy expedition use, it is worth fitting one ton rear springs.

6 cylinder engine	
Displacement	2.625 litre
Bore	77.8 mm
Stroke	92.1 mm
Compression ratio	7.8:1
Maximum power	86 bhp @ 4500 rpm
Maximum torque	132 lb ft @ 1500 rpm
Payload	1114 kg, 2450 lbs

Land Rover 1 ton in Iran.

Land Rover Series III Safari Station Wagon (12 seats) in the Teneré Sand Sea, Niger.

Land Rover 1 tonne, an excellent performer but with no civilian appeal.

LAND ROVER 1 TON

This is a special long wheelbase model using the 6 cylinder engine, heavier springs, standard Salisbury rear axle, but stronger EMV front axle, 9.00″ × 16″ tyres, the series 11A gearbox which is only synchromesh on the top two gears and a different transfer box giving step down ratios of 1.53:1 and 3.27:1

Gear Ratios	1st 3.68:1
	2nd 2.22:1
	3rd 1.50:1
	4th 1:1
	Reverse 4.02:1
Payload	1296 kg, 2850 lbs

LAND ROVER
101″ WHEELBASE 1 TONNE FORWARD CONTROL LAND ROVER

This is a special Land Rover built for military use from 1975 to 1978 and designed to operate with a Rubery Owen trailer powered through a rear power take off from the rear of the Land Rover, thus giving a 6 × 6 vehicle. This option was rarely used, but by virtue of its short wheelbase and weight evenly distributed between the wheels this four wheel drive is an exceptional vehicle for really tough country.

Engine	3.528 litre V8, all aluminium
Bore	88.9 mm
Stroke	71.1 mm
Compression ratio	8.5:1
Maximum power	135 bhp @ 4750 rpm
Maximum torque	205 lb ft @ 3000 rpm
Clutch	10.5″ diaphragm type, hydraulically operated
Transmission	Permanent four wheel drive with lockable centre differential
Gearbox	4 forward 1 reverse, synchromesh on all forward gears with 2 ratio transfer box of 1.174:1 and 3.321:1.
Gear ratios	1st 4.07:1
	2nd 2.45:1
	3rd 1.50:1
	4th 1:1
	Reverse 3.66:1
Final drive	5.57:1
Suspension	Live axles front and rear on half elliptic leaf springs, fully floating half shafts
Steering	Recirculating ball
Brakes	Servo assisted drum brakes, transmission handbrake
Tyres	9.00″ × 16″
Payload	1000 kg, 2204 lbs

LAND ROVER V8 SERIES III

Land Rover's latest vehicle using the Range Rover V8 engine and drive train giving full time four wheel drive with lockable centre differential

Wheelbase	109″
Engine	3.528 litre V8, all aluminium
Bore	88.9 mm

Stroke	71.1 mm
Compression ratio	8.1:1
Maximum power	91 bhp @ 3500 rpm
Maximum torque	166 lb ft @ 2000 rpm
Clutch	10.5″ diaphragm type, hydraulically operated
Transmission	Full time four wheel drive with lockable centre differential, two range transfer box with 1.336 or 3.321:1 step down ratios
Gearbox	4 forward and 1 reverse with synchromesh on all forward gears
Gear ratios	1st 4.07:1
	2nd 2.45:1
	3rd 1.50:1
	4th 1:1
	Reverse 3.66:1
Final drive	3.54:1
Suspension	Live axles with half elliptic leaf springs, front axle is spiral bevel with enclosed constant velocity joints, rear axle is hypoid with fully floating shafts.
Brakes	Servo assisted drum brakes with transmission handbrake
Tyres	7.50″ × 16″
Electrical	12 volt negative earth
Battery	58 AH
Alternator	18 ACR 45 amp
Towing weight	Off road 1000 kg, 2200 lbs
	On road 2000 kg, 4400 lbs
Payload	1170 kg, 2580 lbs

Land Rover V8.

LAND ROVER ½ TON AIR PORTABLE/LIGHTWEIGHT

Developed to be air portable by a Westland Wessex helicopter in the mid 1960s, which could only lift 2660 lbs. To achieve this weight a redesigned simple cut-away body 6″ narrower than the standard body, was fitted to the standard 88″ wheelbase chassis. For air transportation all the top bodywork, wings, doors, windscreen and seats were removed and were transported in the next helicopter. The vehicle was fully operational in this stripped down condition. The vehicle is now obsolete, because modern helicopters can transport the standard Land Rover 90.

Technical specifications were identical to the series IIA or series III 88″ wheelbase Land Rover.

Land Rover Lightweight

LAND ROVER 90/110

In 1983 Land Rover launched their new 110, using a 110″ wheelbase on a strengthened Range Rover type chassis, with long travel coil spring suspension and permanent four wheel drive with lockable centre differential. The shorter

Camel Trophy Land Rover 90 equipped with a Warn winch and raised air intake

Land Rover 110 Turbo Diesel County

90 version followed just over a year later, becoming available with the V8 petrol engine in 1985. At the same time improvements were made to the doors; wind down windows, better soundproofing, one-piece windscreen and easily replaceable plastic spats (wheel arch extensions) were fitted. Engines were 2.5 litre 4 cylinder diesel, 2.25 litre petrol (later 2.5 litre) or V8 petrol, though in Australia they preferred to fit a 3.9 litre Isuzu diesel, because the Land Rover diesel was so sluggish. In 1986 the 2.5 diesel became available with turbocharger and was such an improvement that the normally Aspirated diesel has now been dropped altogether. New door locks and handles were also fitted.

With these vehicles Land Rover have jumped way out ahead of the field again, with off-road performance which even the Mercedes Gelandewagon cannot match. Land Rover have at last listened to their customers, though as many of these do not go fully off-road very often, some parts of the new vehicle are not so good for Third World use. The diesel has a glass fibre reinforced timing belt, which is worrying. Uprating coil springs for heavy use is difficult, as is bodging broken ones in the field. Some military vehicles have a concentric two spring system, but civilians have to make do with rubber spring helpers. The bonnet release catch being internal means that, if you have a spare wheel on the bonnet, you either need a second person to hold the catch open whilst you lift the bonnet or else need to make yourself a wooden U-piece, to do the job for you. Seatbelts catch in the new locks, much of the very useful locker space no longer exists, except on military vehicles. Unbelievably, the nearside front passenger seat on Country models does not adjust for leg room and the gear change is still terrible, when compared with the Japanese competition. The new jack supplied is aimed at the Landed Gentry and would be the first thing an off-roader would need to replace. The new aluminium roof channel cuts roofrack weight possibilities down considerably. Estate models cannot be supplied without power steering and with the diesel engine, deep wading without the wading plug fitted could be disastrous on the timing belt.

Like their predecessors Land Rover Special products come in all manner of configurations, from 127″ wheelbase crew cab to 6x6 and 6x4 vehicles and with all sorts of machinery from drilling rigs to backhoes.

Land Rovers are put together in assembly plants all around the world, from basic UK parts but with a high local input. In Australia and Spain (Santana), the basic specifications are often changed to suit local conditions. Many of these changes later filter back to the UK product.

Wheelbase	short 93″/2.36 m		long 1 110″/2.79 m
Engine	4 cylinder petrol	V8 petrol	4 cylinder diesel turbo
Displacement	2.5 litre	3.5 litre	2.5 litre
Bore	90.47 mm	88.9 mm	90.47 mm
Stroke	97.0 mm	71.1 mm	97.0 mm
Compression ratio	8.0:1	8.3:1	21:1
Maximum power	83 bhp @ 4000 rpm	134 bhp @ 5000 rpm	85 bhp @ 4000 rpm
Maximum torque	133 lb ft @ 2000 rpm	187 lb ft @ 2500 rpm	150 lb ft @ 1800 rpm
Transmission	5 speed gearbox 4 cylinder	V8	

1st gear	3.585:1	3.65:1
2nd gear	2.301:1	2.18:1
3rd gear	1.507:1	1.436:1
4th gear	1.000:1	1.00:1
5th gear	0.8314:1	0.795:1
Reverse	3.701:1	3.824:1

Transfer box:

4 cylinder 2 ratio 1.41:1 and 3.332:1		1.67:1 and 3.32 : 1
V8 1.22:1 and 3.32:1		1.41:1 and 3.32:1

Permanent 4WD with lockable centre differential

Final drive	3.538:1
Suspension	Live axles on long travel coil springs. Panhard rod on front, A frame at rear plus self-levelling Boge Hydromat strut at rear of 110
Steering	Recirculating ball, servo assisted
Brakes	Discs at front drums at rear
	Servo assisted
	Handbrake on transmission

Wheels	16	
Tyres	6.00 x 16	7.50 x 16
Turning circle	40 ft/12.3 metre	42 ft/12.8 metre
Electrical	12 volt	
Battery	95 AH	
Alternator	45 A	

Oil cooler is now standard on the Turbo Diesel.

LAND ROVER 2 TONNE
2 tonne forward control truck, on Range Rover type chassis, transmission and coil spring suspension. 110″ wheelbase with a fibreglass cab, which tilts forward to get at the engine. The central diff. lock is by electrical switch. Present engine is the Rover V8, but a diesel such as the Perkins Phazer 90 could be fitted.

LAVERDA
Italian built forward control 4x4 with 92.5″/2.35 metres wheelbase 2.5 litre Sofim diesel engine producing 72 bhp @ 4200 rpm, 5 speed gearbox, 2 ratio transfer box. Part time 4WD but with a central, lockable, differential.

MAZDA B 2600 4x4 PICK-UP
Sold in standard, SE-5 or top of the line LX form, with regular cab or cab plus form. The cab plus is a larger cab, having fold down jump seats to the rear of the main seats. The standard vehicle has 108.7″/2.76 metre wheelbase and the cab plus has 118.1″/3.0 metre wheelbase. Engine is 2.6 litre 4 cylinder petrol, producing 102 bhp @ 4500 rpm and 132 lb ft of torque @ 2500 rpm.

Standard gearbox is 5 speed manual with optional 3 speed automatic with lock-up. Front suspension is independent with double wishbones, torsion bar and anti-roll bar, rear suspension is long travel on semi-elliptic leaf springs, transfer box is 2 ratio, wheels are 15″. Manual free-wheeling hubs are standard. Brakes are discs at front, drums at rear.

MAZDA TITAN

Forward control 2 tonne pick-up, with 3.5 litre direct injection diesel, producing 105 bhp @ 3200 rpm and 180 lb ft of torque @ 2000 rpm. 5 speed manual gearbox, 2 speed transfer box, part time 4WD with free wheeling hubs, live axles on semi-elliptic leaf springs front and rear and 16″ wheels.

MERCEDES BENZ G (GELANDEWAGON)

Built in co-operation with Cross Country Vehicles specialists Steyr-Daimler Puch, makers of the Pinzgauer and the now discontinued Haflinger. These up market vehicles were designed to be everything, both on and off the road. Built with traditional Mercedes quality and standards of comfort the G Wagon has the highest specifications of any non-military vehicle available. On the road everything is very good, but in off-road conditions the G Wagon's performance does not quite come up to expectations and this together with the very high cost has limited sales.

Made in the Steyr-Daimler Puch factory at Graz in Austria, the vehicle will be sold under the Puch trade name in Austria, Switzerland, Yogoslavia and the Comecon countries. Military versions are also made under licence by Peugot in France.

Built in long and short wheelbase versions, there are 4 engines:-
300 GD (5 cylinder 88 bhp 3.0 litre diesel)
230 GE (4 cylinder 125 bhp 2.3 litre petrol)
280 GE (6 cylinder 156 bhp 2.8 litre petrol) and the
250 GD diesel which is not imported to the UK.
The petrol engines have fuel injection.

The vehicle has part time 4WD, engageable and disengageable on the move and diff. locks front and rear also engageable and disengageable on the move. Rigid live axles with Panhard rods front and rear, with coil springs, giving 10″ of axle articulation and progressive rubber assister springs on the rear. The body is independent from the chassis and is fixed to it by 8 rubber mountings. Doors are sealed against water, dust and sand.

Wheelbase	94.5″/2.4 metre	& 112″/2.85 metre	
Engine	230GE Petrol	280GE Petrol	300 GD Diesel
No of cylinders	4	6	5
Displacement	2.299 litre	2.746 litre	2.998 litre
Bore	95.5 mm	86.0 mm	90.9 mm
Stroke	80.25 mm	78.8 mm	92.4 mm
Compression ratio	9.0:1	8.0:1	21.0:1
Maximum power	125 bhp @ 5000 rpm	150 bhp @ 5250 rpm	88 bhp @ 4400 rpm
Maximum torque	141 lb ft @ 4000 rpm	165 lb ft @ 4250 rpm	127 lb ft @ 2700 rpm
Transmission	4 speed manual gearbox, 5 speed manual or 4 speed automatic optional 1st Gear 4.628:1	4 speed automatic gearbox, 5 speed manual optional	4 speed manual gearbox, 5 speed manual or 4 speed automatic optional

	2nd gear 2.462:1		
	3rd gear 1.473:1		
	4th gear 1:1		
	Reverse 4.348:1		
Transfer box	2 ratio transfer box with low ratio of 2.14:1. Part time 4WD with diff. locks front and rear, all engageable on the move		
Final drive	5.33:1	5.33:1	4.9:1
Suspension	Rigid axles located by central arms and Panhard rod, long travel coil springs with rubber helper springs, torsion bar stabilizer at front		
Steering	Servo assisted recirculating ball		
Brakes	Servo-assisted, self-adjusting, drums at rear, discs at front, automatic load-sensitive device on rear brakes, handbrake by cable to rear wheels		
Wheels	5½ JK x 16 H2		
Tyres	205R 16		
Turning circle	Long wheelbase 42 ft/12.8 metre		
	Short wheelbase 37.5 ft/11.4 metre		
Electrical	12 volt		
Battery	12 volt	12 volt	12 volt
	66 AH	66 AH	88 AH
Alternator	55 A	55 A	55 A

Mercedes-Benz GE LW base station wagon 300 G.D.

Mercedes-Benz GE SWB station wagon.

MERCEDES-BENZ UNIMOG

Without question the top four wheel drive vehicle for go anywhere capability, designed primarily as a commercial unit with various power and hydraulic take-offs and specialized trailer couplings, these vehicles would normally be beyond the price range of private individuals and expedition users but many ex-NATO units are being snapped up cheaply in Germany and finding their way all over Africa.

The chassis is designed to keep all four wheels on the ground in all situations though, because of this plus the short wheelbase, Unimogs handle very badly on corrugated tracks. The same axles are used front and rear giving good load carrying capacity and being portal axles (step down) give greater ground clearance; diff locks front and rear are standard, four wheel drive is the part time system and four wheel drive can be engaged or disengaged at any speed without using the clutch. The factory gearbox is a 6 forward speed 2 reverse box with only one range but a conversion to 4 forward speed with 2 range transfer can be arranged giving 8 forward and 4 reverse gears. Good weight distribution between axles with long spring travel (coil spring) giving good axle articulation and low centre of gravity, plus large low pressure tyres all help to give superior cross country ability. Early models have very poor cabs and seating, later models have very good cabs and seating; with the engine protruding into the cab, all models get very hot in the cab in hot countries. Later models have the

218

clutch fitted alongside the transmission thus making clutch replacement very easy.

Available in many options with wheelbases from 2.25 metres (88.5") to 3.25 metres (128") and engines from 52 hp to 168 hp. I give two examples here:-

Unimog	U900	U1100
Wheelbase	2.38 m (94")	2.90 m (114")
Engine	OM 352 diesel	OM 352 diesel
No. of cylinders	6	6
Displacement	5.675 litre	5.675 litre
Maximum power	84 hp @ 2550 rpm	110 hp @ 2800 rpm
Maximum torque	262 NM @ 1800 rpm @ 1800 rpm	316 NM @ 1700 rpm @ 1700 rpm
Gearbox	6 forward and 2 reverse (2 × 4 unit giving 8 forward 4 reverse gears available)	

Mercedes Benz Unimog has portal axles for increased ground clearance.

Axles	Portal axles, four wheel drive and differential locks in both axles can be engaged and disengaged whilst driving without operating the clutch.	
Suspension	Coil springs with extra helper springs at rear.	
Brakes	Compressed air assisted disc brakes all round, compressed air trailer brake system.	
	Handbrake mechanical on rear wheels only.	
Steering	Hydraulic power assisted	
Electrics	12 volt negative earth	
Battery	110 AH	
Alternator	12 V 490 watt	
Tyres	12.5-20	
Turning circle	10.9 m, 36 ft	12.5 m, 41 ft
Payload	2400 kg, 5280 lb	3100 kg, 6820 lb

Mercedes-Benz Unimog in ambulance form.

MINI MOKE 4 × 4 (TWINI MOKE)

As with the Citroen 2CV's many amateurs, as well as professionals, have experimented with fitting two engines in Mini Mokes, one at the front and another at the back. BMC themselves demonstrated one in the winter of 1963 and the US Army tested one in 1964 with two 1.098 litre engines and enlarged wheels (12″ instead of 10″). John Cooper nearly killed himself with a Twin Cooper engined Moke which crashed into a wall. None of these vehicles ever went into production, but since 1968 Leyland Australia has manufactured modified versions with larger 13″ wheels and either 0.998 litre or 1.275 litre engines with disc brakes on the front; there is also a 2 seat pick-up and an up market "Californian" model, they also have a single engined 4 × 4 prototype under test.

Separate twin engined vehicles have their own problems, particularly beause only half the power is available at each axle, thus if one axle loses traction only half the power is available at the other axle which might not be enough and the engine would stall. The engine driving an unloaded slipping axle could also start revving very fast, with consequent shock damage to the driveline when the wheels suddenly find traction again.

The Moke's bottom gear was too high for slow work in difficult terrain so one had to slip the clutch, but the biggest problem with Mokes for cross country work is the lack of ground clearance.

MITSUBISHI EL LAGO

Concept amphibious Pajero/Shogun with fibre glass hull. In water propulsion and steering is by twin water jet drive.

The fibre glass hull would not stay waterproof very long if it had to bounce up and down river banks instead of using purpose built slipways.

Mitsubishi EL Lago

MITSUBISHI L 200 4WD PICK-UP

The new range of Mitsubishi L 200 1 tonne pick-ups now are essentially pick-up versions of the Pajero (Shogun), with changed main gearbox ratio and 105.5″ wheelbase. The old L200 type wheel size is increased from 14″ to 16″. Known variously as the Express, Forte or SPX, the new vehicle no longer has those stupid horn buttons where you catch them by mistake on the wheel, but the handbrake is still a pull and twist type normally associated with bench seats, which are not fitted for the UK market. The foot pedals are a bit small for muddy boots and like the Shogun it fails miserably in deep mud, ruts or soft sand due to poor "real ground clearance". So far for the UK market, only the standard wheelbase petrol model is available as 4WD. Automatic free-wheeling hubs are standard. Beefed-up suspension, rear limited slip differential and power steering are optional.

Like all Japanese pick-ups, the load bed sides are single skin, so damageable by moving loads, although the tailgate is double skinned.

Mitsubishi L200 Pick-up

Wheelbase	105.5″/2.68 metres
Engine	4 cylinder petrol, silent shaft
Displacement	1.997 litre
Bore	85 mm
Stroke	88 mm
Compression ratio	8.6:1
Maximum power	87 bhp @ 5500 rpm
Maximum torque	110 lb ft @ 3500 rpm
Transmission	5 speed manual
	1st gear 4.330:1
	2nd gear 2.355:1

3rd gear 1.509:1
4th gear 1.00:1
5th gear 0.827:1
Reverse 4.142:1
All other details are the same as the Pajero/Shogun

MITSUBISHI L 300 4x4
7 seat 4 wheel drive minibus, people carrier, wth 2.3 litre petrol engine and 5-speed manual gearbox.

MITSUBISHI MONTERO
Refer to Mitsubishi Pajero

MITSUBISHI PAJERO
Imported into the USA as the Montero and the UK as the Colt Shogun because Pajero is an Argentinian word meaning prairie and the vehicle was released just after the Falklands war. This well designed and engineered vehicle gave up trying to compete with the Land Rover, instead moving up market to compete directly with the Range Rover, where it is having considerable success. The Pajero has enjoyed very high success in the Paris-Dakar rally and the UK COP Drive events, which helped its sales success, though the vehicles used in these events were specialist rally cars, having very little in common with production machines.

Mitsubishi Pajero long wheelbase

Mitsubishi (Colt) Shogun short wheelbase

Like all the bigger Japanese 4 wheel drives, the gear selection is delightfully slick and the seats are a bit small and just not substantial enough. The finish is excellent. Limited slip rear differential is optional, as is high or low roof. Vision at all four corners is a little restricted. The power steering does not have enough feel in it and horn buttons on the steering wheel are easy to catch. On the road as a luxury people carrier or when towing, the vehicle is superb and the tie down rings are useful; off the road however it is a different story. Despite the claimed 8.3″ ground clearance, it gets bogged down as soon as it looks at soft sand or deep mud. On paper the Pajero has more ground clearance than a Range Rover, but it has much more underneath to catch, and poor rear overhang on the long wheelbase. It is soon bogged down if it tries to follow the ruts made by Land Rovers or Range Rovers, often being shown up by little Lada Nivas and Suzukis. Generally very reliable, the main weakness seems to be the clutch in off-road use. Automatic free-wheeling hubs are standard. For 1987 these vehicles have a 3 year unlimited mileage warranty plus 6 year anti-corrosion warranty in the UK.

MITSUBISHI SILENT SHAFT ENGINE
Mitsubishi's unique silent shaft system consists of two contra-rotating balancer shafts, rotating at twice the engine speed. The lower one is above the top of the crankshaft, rotating in the opposite direction to the crankshaft and the upper one is half way up the engine block and rotates in the same direction as the crankshaft.
The load of each is supported by a bulkhead in the middle of the block, the result is to substantially reduce vibration.
This system was licensed to Porsche for their 944.

Wheelbase	Short 92.5″/2.350 m	Long 106.1″/2.695 m
Engine	4 cylinder petrol silent shaft	4 cylinder Turbo diesel silent shaft
Displacement	2.6 litre	2.5 litre
Bore	91.1 mm	91.1 mm
Stroke	98.0 mm	95.0 mm
Compression ratio	8.2:1	21.0:1
Maximum power	102 bhp @ 4500 rpm	84 bhp @ 4200 rpm
Maximum torque	142 lb ft @ 2500 rpm	148 lb ft @ 2000 rpm
Transmission	5 speed manual or 4 speed automatic	
1st gear	3.967:1	2.826:1
2nd gear	2.136:1	1.493:1
3rd gear	1.360:1	1.00:1
4th gear	1.000:1	0.688:1
5th gear	0.856:1	
Reverse	3.578:1	2.703:1
Transfer box	2 ratio with low of 1.944:1, part time 4WD, automatic free-wheeling hubs	
Final drive	4.625:1	
Suspension	Front independent, double wishbones & torsion bars Back live axle on semi-elliptic leaf springs. Anti sway bar front & rear	
Steering	Variable assisted power steering. Recirculating ball & nut	
Brakes	Discs at front, drums at rear. Servo assisted	
Wheels	15″ for SWB & LWB pre 1987. 16″ for LWB 1987 onwards	
Tyres	215 SR 15/205 SR 16	
Turning circle	34.2 ft/10.5 metres	
Electrical	12 volt	
Battery	60 AH	80 AH
Alternator	45 A	45 A

The automatic gearbox is only available on the Turbo Diesel High Roof 5 Door.

MITSUBISHI J24-A JEEP

Japanese built 88″ wheelbase Jeep in service with the Japanese Self Defence Force, having a 4 cylinder diesel engine developing 80 bhp @ 3700 rpm, manual 4 speed gearbox, 2 speed transfer box, part time four wheel drive and a payload of 1080 lb, some of the earlier petrol engined J54-A variants are still in service.

MONTEVERDI SAHARA

Swiss made 2 door station wagon based on the now discontinued International Harvester Scout II

Wheelbase	100″
Engine	V8
Displacement	5.653 litre
Compression ratio	8.05:1
Maximum output	165 bhp @ 3600 rpm

Maximum torque	292 lb ft @ 2000 rpm
Transmission	Chrysler 3 speed automatic
	1st gear 2.45:1
	2nd gear 1.45:1
	3rd gear 1:1
Reverse gear	2.2:1
Transfer box	2 ratios 1:1 and 2.03:1
Final drive ratio	3.07:1
Brakes	Dual circuit servo assisted disc at front, drums at rear. Handbrake on rear drums
Tyres	LR 78-15

Monteverdi Sahara.

MONTEVERDI MILITARY 230M
Swiss made military 5 seat Command car

Wheelbase	91″
Engine	4 cylinder
Displacement	3.208 litre
Bore	104.78 mm
Stroke	92.86 mm
Compression ratio	8.02:1
Maximum power	87 bhp @ 3800 rpm
Maximum torque	157 lb ft @ 2200 rpm
Transmission	4 speed manual or 3 speed automatic gearbox, part time four wheel drive with 2 speed transfer box with ratios 1:1 and 2.03:1
Final drive	Limited slip differential with 3.73:1 ratio
Suspension	Live axles on semi-elliptic leaf springs
Brakes	Dual circuit, discs at front, drums at rear, handbrake on rear drums
Tyres	H78 × 15

226

230M Monteverdi Military.

MULTICAR
East German made light 4WD pick-up, with a 2.238 litre diesel engine, 4 speed main gearbox and 2 ratio transfer box. Part time 4 wheel drive and rear axle diff. lock. UK versions are fitted with wide, low ground pressure tyres, but it suffers from having wheels which are too small. Noise and vibration in the cab are high.

Multicar

NISSAN PATROL

Nissan (Datsun) started producing Jeep type 4 wheel drives in the early 1950's and have steadily continued, being very successful with Jeep type vehicles, some of which were built under licence in India under the trade name of "JONGA". The Patrol, which is luxury car based, has always been over-shadowed by the more robust and successful Toyotas, which also have superior off-road performance. The suspension is well tuned for road use but suffers handling problems in the rough, particularly if hitting an unexpected bump or dip at speed. Some of the diesel models have 24 volt electrical systems.

Like the Pajero and the Toyota Land Cruiser and for the same reasons, the off-road performance is particularly poor in deep ruts, mud or soft sand. The spare wheel under the chassis is particularly bad for off-road use. Australian Patrols are made in Australia and European Patrols are now made in Spain. Australian Patrols are available with the P40 4 litre petrol engine as well as the standard 6 cylinder 2.8 litre petrol L28 or the SD33T Turbo Diesel 3.3 litre and limited slip differentials. The transmission is a 5-speed gearbox. For 1988 a new model will be available with all coil spring suspension, wider body and track, a new 4.2 litre 6 cylinder petrol engine and a new suspension stabilizer system.

Nissan patrol long wheelbase

228

The Patrol pick-ups were considerably strengthened in 1984. The turbo diesel is not yet available in the UK but Spanish made bolt-on kits are available.

Wheelbase	Hard top	Estate
	92.5"/2.35 m	116.9"/2.97 m
Engine	L28 petrol	SD33 diesel
Displacement	2.753 litre	3.246 litre
Bore	86 mm	83 mm
Stroke	79 mm	100 mm
Compression ratio	8.6:1	20.8:1
Maximum power	120 bhp @4800 rpm	95 bhp @3600 rpm
Maximum torque	149 lb ft @3200 rpm	216 lb ft @1800 rpm
Transmission	5 speed manual gearbox	
	1st gear 3.895:1	
	2nd gear 2.37:1	
	3rd gear 1.44:1	
	4th gear 1.00:1	
	5th gear 0.825:1	
	Reverse 4.267:1	
Transfer box	2 ratio, part time 4WD, low ratio 2.22 : 1 automatic free wheeling hubs	
Final drive	4.625:1	
Suspension	Semi-elliptic leaf springs all round	
Steering	Servo-assisted, very light and twitchy with no feeling Recirculating ball	
Brakes	Discs at front, drums at rear, handbrake on rear drums Servo assisted	
Tyres	205 R 16	
Turning circle	38.7 ft/11.8 metres	46.6 ft/14.2 m
Electrical	12 volt or 24 volt	
Battery	12 volt or 2x12 volt 70AH	

SWB Nissan patrol station wagon.

NISSAN 720 PICK-UP SERIES/SEV 6

Sold as the 720 series in Australia and the SEV6 in the USA and Nissan 4WD pick-up in the UK. These 4x4 pick-ups are available as standard King Cab or Dual Cab (Crew Cab), the King Cab having jump seats behind the main seats. These vehicles are based on car type suspension and comforts rather than true off-road robustness. Automatic free-wheeling hubs are standard. In Australia they come wth a limited slip rear differential as standard.

The King Cab attracted car tax in the UK, so now only the standard model is brought in, with a 4 cylinder 2.3 litre petrol engine, giving 99 bhp @ 4800 rpm.

Estate versions of these pick-ups are sold as Pathfinder in the USA and Terrano in Japan, both having coil spring rear suspension and the Terrano having a diesel engine.

Wheelbase	116.1"/2.95 metres
Engine	V6 petrol
Displacement	3.0 litre
Bore	87.1 mm
Stroke	83.1 mm
Compression ratio	9.0:1
Maximum power	140 bhp @ 4800 rpm
Maximum torque	166 lb ft @ 2400 rpm
Transmission	5 speed manual gearbox
	1st gear 4.06:1
	2nd gear 2.357:1
	3rd gear 1.490:1
	4th gear 1.000:1
	5th gear 0.862:1
	Reverse 4.125:1
Transfer box	2 ratio with low of 2.020:1 part time 4WD engageable & disengageable on the move below 25 mph
Final drive	4.375:1
Suspension	Independent front suspension with double wishbones & torsion bar. Live axle at rear on semi-elliptic leaf springs
Steering	Recirculating ball & nut Servo assisted
Brakes	Discs at front, drums at rear Servo assisted
Wheels	15"
Tyres	31 x 10.50 R 15
Turning circle	46 ft/14 metres

NISSAN 1 TON 4WD PICK-UP

UK version of the Nissan 720 series standard pick-up with 4 cylinder 2.388 litre petrol engine, 16" wheels, manual free-wheeling hubs and double skinned rear body. King cab versions attract car tax, so are not imported.

Wheelbase	116"/2.95 metres
Engine	4 cylinder petrol
Displacement	2.388 litre
Bore	89 mm
Stroke	96 mm

Maximum power	88.5 bhp @ 5200 rpm
Maximum torque	109.6 lb ft @ 3600 rpm
Transmission	5 speed manual gearbox
	1st gear 3.592:1
	2nd gear 2.246:1
	3rd gear 1.415:1
	4th gear 1.000:1
	5th gear 0.825:1
	Reverse 3.657:1
Transfer box	2 ratio with low of 2.020:1, part time 4WD, manual free-wheeling hubs
Suspension	Front independent double wishbones, torsion rod & anti-roll bar. Rear live axle on semi-elliptic leaf springs
Steering	Recirculating ball & nut
Brakes	Discs at front, drums at rear servo assisted, handbrake on rear drums
Wheels	16″
Tyres	205 R 16
Turning circle	46 ft/14 metres

NISSAN PATHFINDER/TERRANO

4 wheel drive estate, based on the 720/SEV6 pick-up series but with coil sprung rear suspension instead of leaf springs. Until recently, sold only in the USA with the 3.0 litre 140 hp V6 engine, but now being offered in Japan as the Terrano with a 2.6 litre normally aspirated 4 cylinder diesel engine. Rear suspension is now live axle, located by four trailing links and with a Panhard rod. Limited slip diffs and automatic free-wheeling hubs are optional.

The Terrano/Pathfinder was shown at the Geneva Motor Show in 1987, so it may yet come to Europe. 1988 models will have the Aisin/Warner 4 speed automatic gearbox.

NISSAN SAFARI
Refer to Nissan Patrol

NISSAN SEV6
Refer to Nissan 720 series

NISSAN TERRANO
Refer to Nissan Pathfinder

PANTHER STAMPEDE
Refer to Dong-a Korando

PEKING
Refer to Beijing BJ-212

PEUGEOT 504 (DANGEL)

Dangel 4x4 conversions of the Peugeot 504 pick-ups and estates, with Peugeot limited slip differentials front and rear and a Dangel 2 ratio transfer box to give additional low ratio. The body is also stiffened and skid plates added underneath.

PEUGEOT P4

Peugeot built versions of the Mercedes G Wagon using Peugeot 4 cylinder 2 litre petrol engine, developing 79 bhp @ 4750 rpm or Peugeot 4 cylinder 2.5 litre diesel engine developing 70 bhp @ 4500 rpm. Main transmission is also Peugeot. In use with the French and Irish armies, some should soon be on civilian sale.

PEUGEOT 6x6

Peugeot built G Wagon in 6x6 form, with each of the rearmost wheels driven by a large V-belt from the wheel in front, by large pulleys fixed to the hubs on the insides of the wheels.

PEUGEOT TALBOT EXPRESS 4X4

Dangel 4x4 conversion of the Peugeot Talbot Express vans.

PONCIN 4x4

Frenchman Giles Poncin, well known for his various 4x4 conversions of standard vehicles and specialist All Terrain Vehicles, such as the VP 2000, also has two glass fibre bodied 4x4 specials on his own design box section chassis with Citroen 2CV type independent suspension and Citroen engines. The front differential and transfer gears are built into an 8 speed gearbox. 4 wheel drive can be selected on the move and there is a differential lock on the rear axle. Engines are 0.652 litre 2 cylinder from the Citroen Visa or 1.3 litre 4 cylinder from the Citroen GSA.

PORTARO PAMPAS

The Romanian ARO, built under licence in Portugal but fitted with Daihatsu/Toyota diesel engines and transmission. Strongly built, available as hard-top, soft-top and pick-up, including long wheelbase (125") version the Campina. Manual free-wheeling hubs are standard.

	250	2800 D
Wheelbase	92.5"/2.35 metre	or 125"/3.2 metre
Engine	4 cylinder diesel	4 cylinder diesel
Displacement	2.53 litre	2.765 litre
Bore	88 mm	92 mm
Stroke	104 mm	104 mm
Compression ratio	21:1	
Maximum power	75 bhp @ 3600 rpm	75 bhp @ 3600 rpm
Maximum torque	127 lb ft @ 2200 rpm	127 lb ft @ 2200 rpm
Transmission	Part time 4WD	Part time 4WD
	4 speed gearbox	5 speed gearbox
	1st gear 4.97:1	3.647:1

232

	2nd gear 2.78:1	2.136:1
	3rd gear 1.65:1	1.382:1
	4th gear 1.0:1	1.00:1
	5th gear	0.860:1
	Reverse 5.08:1	4.351:1
Transfer box	2 ratio 1:1 & 2.18:1	2 ratio 1.30:1 & 2.351:1
	Part time 4WD, FWD & low range can be engaged on the move.	
Final drive	4.7:1	3.727:1
Suspension	Independent front suspension, unequal length wishbones with helical springs. Beam axle at rear with fully-floating half-shafts and semi-elliptic leaf springs.	
Steering	Worm & bearing, servo assisted	
Brakes	Drums all round. Handbrake to rear wheels only.	
Wheels	16″	
Tyres	6.50″x16″	
Turning circle	39 ft/12 metres	
Electrical	12 volt	
Battery	120 AH	
Alternator	35 A	

Portaro Pampas.

Portaro Pampas shows its paces in a speed event.

POWRFOR
Refer to Landmaster

RANGE ROVER
18 years old and still leading the field in off-road performance and high speed, comfortable on-road cruising, though unashamedly aimed at the wealthy end of the market. Long travel coil sprung suspension and flexible high torque engine, together with a light aluminium panelled body on a heavy, strong chassis, giving a low centre of gravity, all combine to give the best off-road performance available to date. On paper the Mercedes Gelandewagon should be better, but its weight, less flexible engine, shorter travel springs and stiffer controls work against it.

In 1986 the Range Rover finally got a diesel engine. It was aimed more at up-market performance than flexible low down torque for off-road use, but it was plenty good enough. The immediate response was an increase of 30% in export sales. (In many countries of course diesel is less than half the price of petrol). This Italian VM Turbo diesel powered Range Rover was driven around the MIRA track by a group of amateur drivers for 24 hours, covering 2444 miles at speeds of over 100 mph, breaking 27 National and Endurance records.

Recent refinements include a new ZF4 HP22 automatic gearbox for the V8, in which 1st gear can be manually locked in, to provide engine braking for steep descents, and dual-rate rear springs, to cut down the roll on cornering.

Range Rover Turbo D

Range Rover Vogue

For the up market, Vogue, electronic fuel injection for the V8, giving 165 bhp and a flexible plastic front spoiler, to improve the air flow at speed.

For 1987 the American market is now offered a left-hand drive Vogue with electronic fuel injection V8 petrol, mated to the ZF4 HP22 automatic gearbox, with air conditioning and leather seats as options. Electrically adjustable seats, electric adjust and defrost outside mirrors, cruise control and catalytic converter on the exhaust; power is down to 150 bhp @ 4750 rpm and torque to 195 lbf ft @ 2500 rpm. Compression ratio is 8.13:1, suitable for unleaded fuel. A 4.2 litre V8 planned.

For other markets the 8.13 compression ratio carburettor V8 petrol engine, produces 132 bhp @ 5000 rpm and 185 lb ft @ 2500 rpm.

For the American market a slip-in, pin-held, towing ball is available, this is illegal in the UK but would be very useful on the front of any vehicle for positioning trailers in fields etc. whilst being quickly removable for highway use.

Wheelbase	100"/2.54 metres		
Engines	V8 Electronic Injection	V8 Carburettor	VM 4cyl Turbo Diesel
Displacement	3.528 litre	3.528 litre	2.393 litre
Bore	88.9 mm	88.9 mm	92 mm
Stroke	71.1 mm	71.1 mm	90 mm
Compression ratio	9.35:1	9.35:1	21.5:1
Maximum power	165 bhp @ 4750 rpm	127 bhp @ 4000 rpm	113 bhp @ 4200 rpm
Maximum torque	207 lb ft @ 2500 rpm	194 lb ft @ 2500 rpm	183 lb @ 2400 rpm
Transmission	5 speed manual		
	Petrol	Diesel	Automatic
1st gear	3.3214:1	3.6923:1	(1) 2.4795:1
2nd gear	2.1316:1	2.1316:1	(2) 1.4795:1
3rd gear	1.3966:1	1.3966:1	(3) 1.0:1
4th gear	1.00:1	1.00:1	(4) 0.7281:1
5th gear	0.7703:1	0.7703:1	
Reverse	3.4286:1	3.4286:1	2.0875:1
Transfer box	2 ratio 1.222:1 and 3.321:1 permanent 4WD with lockable centre differential.		
Final drive	3.54:1		
Suspension	Live axles on long travel coil springs, dual-rate at rear, radius arms with Panhard rod at front, trailing links and central A frame at rear. Boge-Hydromat self-levelling strut at rear.		
Steering	Recirculating ball, servo-assisted		
Brakes	Discs all round, servo-assisted		
Wheels	6.00 or 7.00x16		
Tyres	XM+S 205 R16		
Turning circle	38 ft/11.6 metres		
Electrical	12 volt		
Battery	95 AH (twin 12 volt batteries on the diesel)		
Alternator	80 AH		

RENAULT TRM 1200/SAVIEM TP3/RENAULT SM8

Popular French 4 × 4 for ambulance, fire fighting or light recovery uses and ex-French Army for Overlanders. Wheelbase 2.64 metres/104", Renault 712 4 cylinder diesel engine developing 72 hp @ 3200 rpm, 4 forward speed 1 reverse manual gearbox with 2 speed transfer box and 9.00" × 16" tyres. Payload 1200 kg/2600 lb, 24 volt electrical system.

Renault SM8 in the Sahara.

REYNOLDS BOUGHTON RB 44

5 tonne GVW 4x4 with 130", 145" or 156" wheelbase, standard ladder type chassis design with rigid axles and semi-elliptic leaf spring suspension, available with Ford 3 litre V6 and Bedford 3.52 litre petrol engines, or Ford 3.5 litre or Perkins 4,236 diesel engines. Manual or automatic gearbox, full time four wheel drive, single ratio transfer box with lockable differential or part time four wheel drive with 2 ratio transfer box. The RB 4x4 can also be fitted with a power trailer. Latest models are fitted with Perkins Phaser 110T diesel.

RTV

5 cwt payload Rough Terrain Vehicle, built from BL Mini car parts, with the whole machine twisting about its own longitudinal axis, spreading the load more equally among the four wheels. The tyres are high flotation Terra tyres. The 1.0 litre mini engine and automatic transmission are under the floor, driving the front wheels directly and the rear wheels by a shaft running through the bearing, on which the two halves of the vehicle articulate.

Wheelbase	64.5"/1.64 metre
Engine	BL 0.998 litre mini engine
Maximum power	40 bhp @ 5000 rpm
Maximum torque	50 lb ft @ 2500 rpm
Transmission	AP 4 speed automatic with manual override
Steering	Rack & pinion

Reynolds Boughton RB44.

RTV

SANTANA SJ410 SPORT
Refer to Suzuki

SAURER
Swiss made light 4x4 with fibre glass/polyester bodywork on a steel chassis. Wheelbases are 91″/2.3 metres and 113″/2.87 metres. Engine is a Volvo 4 cylinder 2.3 litre petrol with a Volvo 4 speed gearbox. Wheels are 16″ and both axles have automatic locking differentials.

SINPAR
French 4x4 conversion for Renault road cars.

Steyr-Daimler-Puch Haflinger in an AWDC trial.

STEYR-DAIMLER-PUCH HAFLINGER
Austrian made tiny 1.5 metres/60″ wheelbase 4 × 4 with excellent performance using a 2 cylinder air cooled petrol engine, developing 27 bhp @ 4800 rpm. Four forward speed one reverse manual gearbox but no transfer box, independent suspension all round, 12″ wheels and a 12 volt electrical system and ½ tonne/1100 lb payload. Now superseded by the Pinzgauer.

STEYR-DAIMLER-PUCH PINZGAUER
Austrian made 4 × 4 forward control light truck with very good performance. 2.2 metre/87″ wheelbase, 4 cylinder 2.25 litre petrol engine developing 87 bhp

Steyr-Daimler-Puch Pinzgauer 2¼ litre air-cooled petrol engine 4 × 4.

Steyr-Daimler-Puch Pinzgauer 6 × 6.

@ 4000 rpm, 5 forward 1 reverse speed manual gearbox with 2 ratio transfer box; worm and roller steering and independent suspension all round with coil springs.

Turning circle	5.18 metre/17 ft
Tyres	7.50″ × 16″
Electrics	24 volt
Payload	1 tonne/2200 lb

This vehicle supersedes the Haflinger which is no longer in production. The 6 × 6 model has a payload of 1.5 tonnes/3300 lb and a turning circle of 6.14 metres/20 ft.

STONEFIELD

After a couple of false starts Stonefield are getting onto their feet again, being sympathetic to customer requirements and accepting the need for diesel engines and manual gearboxes in the civilian market. The two basic vehicles are 6x4 and 4x4 forward controls with space frame chassis and FF Developments four wheel drive system, giving 37% drive to the front axle and 63% drive to the back axle under all conditions. There is an automatic diff. lock on the rear axle and the central diff, with a manual diff. lock, optional on the front. The third axle on the 6x4 is dead.

	4x4	6x4
Wheelbase	110″/2.8 metre	120″/3.04 metre
Engines Chrysler V8 petrol or Perkins T4.40 Turbo Diesel		
Displacement	5.217 litre	4.000 litre
Bore	99.31 mm	100 mm
Stroke	84.07 mm	127 mm
Maximum power	150 bhp @ 4000 rpm	112 bhp @ 2600 rpm
Maximum torque	230 lb ft @ 2400 rpm	252 lb ft @ 1600 rpm

Stonefield 4x4

Transmission	Chrysler A727	Spicer T250
	3 speed automatic	5 speed manual
1st gear	2.45:1	5.79:1
2nd gear	1.45:1	2.83:1
3rd gear	1.00:1	1.52:1
4th gear		1.00:1
5th gear		0.85:1
Reverse	2.20:1	5.72:1

Transposer Box	2 speed with low ratio of 2.8:1 manual change. Permanent FF Developments 4WD with Morse chain and epicyclic differential, giving a split of 37% to the front axle and 63% to the rear axle.
Suspension	Semi-elliptic leaf springs
Steering	Manual recirculating ball & nut optional servo-assisted
Brakes	Servo-assisted drum brakes all round.
Tyres	900 x 16
Turning circle	4x4 – 44.3 ft/13.5 metre 6x4 53.5 ft/16.3 metre
Electrics	12 or 24 volt
Battery	68 AH
Alternator	60 A

SUBARU MV 4WD PICK-UP/BRAT

Contrary to claims by Audi, Fuji Heavy Industries' Subaru are the company that first popularised 4 wheel drive passenger cars with volume production, starting in 1974. Aimed at the doctor/vet/midwife/winter sports enthusiast, who must keep going in bad conditions, Subaru 4 wheel drives are well engineered, reliable and popular. So much so that most other vehicle manufacturing companies have been forced to bring out their own designs for this sector of the market.

From the tiny 3 cylinder Justy to the XD Turbo Coupes the cars have a range of 4 wheel drive systems from part time through permanent to automatic permanent. The latter has variable torque split between front and rear axles and is constantly controlled by a Microcomputer according to driving conditions.

The 1.8 4WD MV 570 kg pick-up, uses the same 1.8 litre flat four, horizontally opposed engine as the larger cars, part time 4WD, 4 speed gearbox, 2 ratio transfer box and all round independent suspension. Ground clearance is poor, so it is not really made for true off-road, deep ruts or soft sand conditions. The upmarket model is called the Brat.

Wheelbase	96.1″/2.44 metres
Engine	4 cylinder Flat 4 petrol horizontally opposed
Displacement	1.781 litre
Bore	92 mm
Stroke	67 mm
Compression ratio	9.2:1
Maximum power	81 bhp @ 5200 rpm
Maximum torque	97 lb ft @ 3200 rpm
Transmission	4 speed manual gearbox
	1st gear 3.636:1
	2nd gear 1.950:1

	3rd gear 1.226:1
	4th gear 0.885:1
	Reverse 3.583:1
Transfer box	2 ratio with low of 1.462:1, part time 4WD
Final drive	3.700:1
Suspension	Front independent with McPherson strut, rear independent with semi-trailing arms.
Steering	Rack & pinion
Brakes	Discs at front, drums at rear, handbrake on front wheels. Servo assisted.
Wheels	13″
Tyres	155 R x 13
Turning circle	36 ft/9.6 metres
Electrical	12 volt
Battery	50 AH
Alternator	50 A

Subaru 1600 4WD saloon.

SUBARU 700 4WD MICROVAN SAMBAR/MICROBUS DOMINGO

The 700 4WD high roof Micro van will carry $\frac{1}{2}$ ton, has a 0.665 litre 2 cylinder petrol engine producing 31 bhp @ 5000 rpm and 38 lb ft @ 3500 rpm, from a bore of 78 mm, stroke of 69.6 mm and a 9.0:1 compression ratio. This vehicle is available outside the UK as a Microbus called the Domingo.

Subaru 700 4x4 van

SUZUKI/RHINO/SAMURAI/HOLDEN DROVER

Designed initially for the poorer Third World, where they failed miserably due to poor load carrying capacity and unreliability. The little Suzuki Jimnys took off as a cult vehicle in the opulent west, creating its own niche in the market which, with typical Japanese thoroughness, Suzuki were not slow to develop. Now the vehicle is a poseur's dream, with flash paintwork and all manner of bolt-on extras, larger engines, good reliability and refined performance. Western popularity is so high that they are now manufactured by Santana in Spain, to ease the import restrictions within Europe. Suzukis have various local names, Rhino in the UK, Samurai in the USA (earlier models were called Jimny) and are imported into Australia as the Holden Drover.

Now the common place to see Suzukis is outside a pub in Chelsea, a housewife taking the kids to school or shopping, or performing admirably at an All Wheel Drive Club meet or even the Rally des Cimes, or loaded with tourists as a fun hire car on the Costa del Sol. As for the Third World, well that is a place where you will never see them nowadays.

A light vehicle with short wheelbase, big wheels and gutsy engine, it is hard to get the Suzuki badly stuck, but it will tip over easily. Main weakness is the clutch, the cable also sticks in dusty terrain. If like me you are over 6 ft tall, then avoid the pick-up, your knees will be under your chin. With such a short wheelbase you have to be careful on corrugated tracks, but then these do not exist in the west.

The original Jimnys had 0.36 litre 2 stroke engines and later 0.54 litre engines with 4 speed transmission. Early LJ models had 0.8 litre engines and 4 speed transmission. The new Spanish Santana built models have single leaf softer sprung suspension, which gives poorer handling on the road.

244

The vehicles are available as soft-top, hard-top or pick-up.

	SJ 410 V JL	Santana SJ 410 Sport
Wheelbase	79.9"/2.03 metres	
Engine	4 cylinder petrol	
Displacement	0.97 litre	
Bore	65.5 mm	
Stroke	72 mm	
Compression ratio	8.8:1	
Maximum power	45 bhp @ 5500 rpm	
Maximum torque	54 lb ft @ 3000 rpm	
Transmission	5 speed	
	1st gear 3.138:1	
	2nd gear 1.947:1	
	3rd gear 1.423:1	
	4th gear 1.00:1	
	5th gear 0.790:1	
	Reverse 3.466:1	
Transfer box	2 ratio part time 4WD, high 1.580:1, low 2.511:1	
Final drive	4.111:1	
Suspension	Live axles on semi-elliptic leaf springs. Santana model has a single leaf spring plus helper springs	
Steering	Recirculating ball & nut	
Brakes	Discs @ front, drums @ rear, servo-assisted Handbrake on transmission	
Wheels	15"	
Tyres	19 SR 15	
Turning circle	32.2 ft/9.8 metres	

SUZUKI SJ 413V JX/HOLDEN DROVER

Wheelbase	79.9"/2.03 metres
Engine	4 cylinder petrol
Displacement	1.324 litre

Suzuki Santana SJ 410

Maximum power	63 bhp @ 6000 rpm
Maximum torque	73.7 lb ft @ 3500 rpm
Transmission	5 speed gearbox
Transfer box	2 ratio, part time 4WD, high ratio 1.580:1, low ratio 2.511:1
Final drive	4.111:1
Suspension	Live axles on semi-elliptic leaf springs, anti-roll bar at front.
Steering	Recirculating ball & nut
Brakes	Discs at front, drums at rear. Servo assisted. Handbrake on transmission
Wheels	15″
Tyres	19 SR 15
Turning circle	32.2 ft/9.8 metres

TOYOTA BLIZZARD
Refer to Daihatsu Fourtrak

Toyota Pick-up 4x4

TOYOTA HILUX 4WD
Good, reliable pick-up, the best in its class, both on- and off-road. 950 kg payload. UK version still has leaf springs all round, some countries have independent front suspension, with A frames and torsion bar. Manual free-wheeling hubs are standard. King Cab and Crew Cab models are available outside of the UK.

Wheelbase	111.8″/2.84 metres	
Engines	4 cylinder petrol	4 cylinder diesel
Displacement	2.237 litre	2.446 litre
Compression ratio	8.8:1	22.3:1
Maximum power	92 bhp @ 4400 rpm	73.7 bhp @ 4000 rpm
Maximum torque	132 lb ft @ 2600 rpm	115 lb ft @ 2200 rpm
Transmission	5 speed gearbox	
	1st gear 3.928:1	
	2nd gear 2.333:1	
	3rd gear 1.451:1	
	4th gear 1.000:1	
	5th gear 0.851:1	
	Reverse 4.743:1	
Transfer box	2 ratio with low of 2.276:1 part time 4WD, free-wheeling hubs	
Final drive	4.556:1	
Suspension	Semi-elliptic leaf springs all round.	
Steering	Recirculating ball & nut, servo-assisted	
Brakes	Discs at front, drums at rear, servo-assisted.	
Tyres	250 SR 16	
Electrical	12 volt	12 volt
Battery	48 AH	2x52 AH
Alternator	40 A	55 A

TOYOTA LAND CRUISER

Toyota are the World's largest selling 4 wheel drives and have a standard of reliability by which all others are judged. Not particularly advanced in design, but built with good slugging power and dependability, especially in the hot climate of the Middle East, where other makes tend to be less reliable. Built in heavier gauge steel than usual, by Toyota's associate body company Arakawa, the Land Cruiser is the standard vehicle in Arabia, often covered in American type chrome, with the Hilux pick-up being the standard run about and taxi in many parts of the world.

Many Toyotas are fitted with an ignition switch, which is a thief's delight, they are easily prised out, after which a screwdriver or penknife will start the engine without having to cross any wires. Spares are very expensive and as with all Japanese vehicles can be hard to find, even in the UK.

Off-road performance of the Land Cruiser is great in open scrub country but poor in deep ruts, mud and soft sand, due to high weight, poor ground clearance and long overhangs. The power steering has no feeling, the seats have poor support and tend to break up off-road. Springs are much too soft off-road. The gear selection is beautifully slick, top speed is low by today's standard and the spare wheel is under the vehicle which is crazy for off-road work. The big engines are unbustable. Latest models have a one touch 4WD switch and automatic adjusting shock absorbers.

In the Middle East and some parts of Europe, there is a short wheelbase Land Cruiser II, with better performance and coil sprung front suspension.

Toyota Land Cruisers are also made in Brazil, as the Toyota Bandeirante series, using the 78 bhp Mercedes-Benz OM324 diesel engine. The Land

Cruiser FJ55V series was very popular and has now been redesigned as the FJ60, which comes in two forms. Standard with normal van type rear doors or De Lux with split horizontal tail gates. The old cart springs and 'Stovebolt' straight 6 petrol engines continue as standard.

Only the diesel FJ60 long wheelbase model is imported into the UK.

Toyota Land Cruiser FJ60

Toyota Land Cruiser II Pick-up stalls in a river in North Yemen

TOYOTA LAND CRUISER (LONG WHEELBASE) FJ60

Wheelbase	107.5"/2.73 metres	107.5"/2.73 metres
Engine	6 cylinder petrol	6 cylinder diesel
Displacement	4.23 litre	3.98 litre
Bore	94 mm	91.0 mm
Stroke	101.6 mm	102 mm
Compression ratio	7.8:1	20.7:1
Maximum power	130 bhp @ 3600 rpm	101 bhp @ 3500 rpm
Maximum torque	202 lb ft @ 18000 rpm	177.8 lb ft @ 1800 rpm
Transmission	5 speed manual or Aisin Warner 4 speed automatic in USA 1st gear 2.95:1 2nd gear 1.53:1 3rd gear 1.00:1 4th gear 0.72:1 Reverse 2.68:1	
Transfer box	2 ratio part time 4WD, low ratio of 1.96:1, free wheeling hubs as standard.	
Final drive	4.11:1	
Suspension	Live axles on semi-elliptic leaf springs front & rear. Anti sway bars front & rear.	
Steering	Recirculating ball, servo-assisted.	
Brakes	Discs at front, drums at rear, servo-assisted. Handbrake on rear drums only.	
Tyres	7.50x16	7.50x16
Turning circle	44 ft/13.4 metres	
Electrical	12 volt (diesels are 24 volt)	
Battery	70 AH	70 AH

TOYOTA LAND CRUISER (SHORT WHEELBASE) FJ40

Wheelbase	90"/2.29 m
Engine	6 cylinder
Displacement	4.2 litre
Bore	94 mm
Stroke	101.6 mm
Compression ratio	7.8:1
Maximum output	130 bhp @ 3600 rpm
Maximum torque	202 lb ft @ 1800 rpm
Transmission	Part time four wheel drive, transfer box giving ratios of 1:1 and 1.96:1, plus freewheeling hubs
Gearbox	1st gear 3.55:1 2nd gear 2.29:1 3rd gear 1.41:1 4th gear 1:1
Final drive	3.70:1
Suspension	Live axles with semi-elliptic leaf springs
Brakes	Servo assisted discs at front, drums at rear
Handbrake	On rear drums

Toyota Land Cruiser SWB soft top.

Toyota Land Cruiser SWB FJ40.

Steering	Recirculating ball
Turning circle	35 ft/10.7 metres
Tyres	H78 × 15B
Electrical	12 volt negative earth
Battery	12 volt 70 AH
Alternator	480 watt

TOYOTA SR5 PICK-UP/PRERUNNER

Available in the USA as standard, and Xtra Cab which is similar to Nissan's King Cab. The main difference between the SR5 and the equivalent UK market pick-up, is that it has independent front suspension using A-frames on torsion bars, which are set high to avoid impact damage. Rear suspension is the same live axle on semi-elliptic leaf springs and the engine is turbocharged.

For 1988 a 3.0 litre V6 petrol engine will be available producing 150 bhp and 189 lb ft of torque.

Wheelbase	112.2"/2.85 metres
Engine	4 cylinder 22 RTE petrol, turbocharged
Displacement	2.4 litre
Bore	91.9 mm
Stroke	88.9 mm
Compression ratio	7.5:1
Maximum power	135 bhp @ 4800 rpm
Maximum torque	173 lb ft @ 2800 rpm
Transmission	5 speed manual gearbox
	1st gear 4.313:1
	2nd gear 2.330:1
	3rd gear 1.436:1
	4th gear 1.000:1
	5th gear 0.838:1
	Reverse 4.220:1
Transfer box	2 ratio with low of 2.276:1, part time 4WD, manual free wheeling hubs.
Final drive	4.100:1
Suspension	Independent front with twin A arms & high track torsion bars. Rear live axle on semi-elliptic leaf springs.
Steering	Recirculating ball & nut, servo-assisted
Brakes	Discs at front, drums at rear servo-assisted Handbrake on rear drums
Wheels	7 JJx15
Tyres	P 225/75 R 15

TOYOTA 4 RUNNER

A full bodied 2 door station wagon, based on the Toyota SR5 Prerunner pick-up, with either the 2.4 litre fuel injected petrol engine (116 bhp @ 4800 rpm) mated to the 5 speed manual gearbox or the turbocharged version of the 2.4 litre engine (135 bhp @ 4800 rpm) mated to the 4 speed automatic gearbox. Front suspension is the same High track independent suspension with A frames and a high mounted torsion bar. The rear top is detachable. The vehicle has part time 4 wheel drive and automatic free-wheeling hubs. Wheels are 15″. On the road there is a tendency to roll on corners.

This vehicle is available in the USA, Japan and occasionally the Middle East.

For 1988 a 3.0 litre V6 petrol engine will be available, producing 150 bhp and 189 lb ft of torque.

UAZ/GAZ 69A

Russian built field car, later known as the UAZ 69 when production was transferred to Ulyanovsk.

A cheap no-nonsense old fashioned design which can be easily kept running by poorly trained, ill equipped 'mechanics', hence its popularity in very poor countries. Finally replaced in 1972 by the UAZ 469B but, the GAZ 69A has remained the more reliable of the two.

Wheelbase	2.3 metres (91″)
Engine	4 cylinder OHV petrol
Displacement	2.433 litre
Bore	88 mm
Stroke	100 mm
Maximum power	55 bhp @ 3600 rpm
Transmission	3 forward 1 reverse manual gearbox, part time four wheel drive
	2 speed transfer box
Suspension	Semi-elliptic leaf springs front and rear
Steering	Globoid worm with double collared cone
Turning circle	6 metres (20 ft)
Tyres	6.50″ × 16″
Brakes	Hydraulic with a mechanical handbrake on the transmission
Electrics	12 volt
Payload	500 kg (1125 lbs)

UAZ 69A.

UAZ 469B (LADA TUNDRA)

First announced in 1961 but only finally put into production in 1972.

Wheelbase	2.38 metres (94″)
Engine	4 cylinder OHV petrol
Displacement	2.45 litre
Bore and stroke	92 mm
Maximum power	75 bhp @ 4000 rpm

UAZ 469B.

Transmission	4 forward 1 reverse manual gearbox, part time four wheel drive 2 range transfer box
Suspension	Semi-elliptic leaf springs front and rear
Turning circle	6.5 metres (21 ft)
Brakes	Hydraulic with mechanical parking brake
Tyres	8.40″ × 15″
Electrics	12 volt
Payload	600 kg (1350 lbs)

UAZ 452D TREKMASTER

Russian built 1 tonne van or truck made by the Ulyanovsk Automobile Plant (YA3) on the River Volga, who also make the UAZ 469B field car with the

UAZ Trekmaster.

same engine, gearbox and axle. These vehicles are very basic and very easy to work on by the amateur mechanic who, armed with the very comprehensive maintenance handbook, would be much more knowledgeable than most of the hack mechanics I have seen working on these vehicles in Iran, Afghanistan and Africa where its most common weakness seems to be collapse of the differential. The ZMZ451 engine is a modified version of that in the Volga car. Freewheel hubs are standard but to disengage them you need to remove the hub cap and then unscrew the inside socket until a groove comes flush with the hub.

Wheelbase	90.5″
Engine	ZMZ251 4 cylinder, all aluminium, with wet liners
Displacement	2.445 litre
Bore	92 mm
Stroke	92 mm
Compression ratio	6.7:1
Maximum power	80 bhp @ 4000 rpm
Maximum torque	136 lb ft @ 2200 rpm
Transmission	Part time four wheel drive, 4 forward speed, 1 reverse speed gearbox, synchromesh on the top two gears only

with two range transfer box giving 1:1 and 1.94:1
1st gear 4.12:1
2nd gear 2.64:1
3rd gear 1.58:1
4th gear 1:1
Reverse gear 5.22:1

Final drive	5.125:1
Suspension	Split axles on semi-elliptical leaf springs
Steering	Worm and double roller
Turning circle	40 ft/12.2 metres
Brakes	Drum brakes all round, handbrake on transmission
Tyres	8.40″ × 15″

UMM   TRANSCAT/DAKARY/ALTER/AFRICAR

Updated version of the French Cournil, built by UMM (Union Metalo Machanica) in Portugal. A heavily built basic vehicle, it is sold as the Transcat in the UK and as the Alter, Dakary or Africar in Europe. The British distributors are no longer handling it, but do have spares available.

Latest models use the Peugeot XD3P 2.5 litre diesel engine and a new 4 speed gearbox. Manual free-wheeling hubs are standard.

UMM Transcat

Wheelbase	100″/2.54 metre
Engine	Peugeot Indenor 2.5 litre diesel
Transmission	4 speed ZF gearbox
Transfer box	2 ratio part time 4WD low ratio is 2.026:1
Final drive	5.38:1
Suspension	Live axles on semi-elliptic leaf springs, Dana-Spicer type 30 at front, Dana-Spicer type 44 at rear with Track-Lock
Steering	Worm and roller
Brakes	Servo-assisted drums all round, handbrake on rear wheels only
Tyres	7.00x16
Turning circle	34.5 ft/10.5 metres

Peugeot 1.971 litre petrol engine also available developing 87 bhp @ 5000 rpm and 119.5 lb ft @ 2500 rpm. An updated model, Alter II will be available in 1988 with new British distributors.

VOISIN
French 4x4 conversions for Citroen 2CV, Dyane and Ami 8 road cars.

VOLKSWAGEN ILTIS
½ tonne four wheel drive being supplied to the German Army since 1978 using the Volkswagen Passat engine. A civilian version will soon be on the market having 12 volt electrics instead of the standard military 24 volt system and a diesel option.

Differential locks are fitted to both differentials. The fuel tank is heavy plastic (good to cut down rust).

Wheelbase	79.4″ 2.02 metre
Engine	4 cylinder, steel block, aluminium head
Displacement	1.60 litre
Bore	86.4 mm
Stroke	79.5 mm
Compression ratio	8.2:1
Maximum power	75 bhp @ 5500 rpm
Maximum torque	98 lb ft @ 2800 rpm
Electrics	24 volt negative earth
Battery	2 × 12 volt 45 amp = 24 volt
Alternator	55 amp
Transmission	5 forward speed, 1 reverse gearbox, synchromesh on all forward gears, but no transfer box
	1st gear 7.60:1
	2nd gear 3.91:1
	3rd gear 2.28:1
	4th gear 1.46:1
	5th gear 1.09:1
	Reverse gear 7.32:1
Final drive ratio	5.27:1
	Differential locks are standard front and rear
Suspension	Independent all round using upper transverse leaf springs and wishbones at the bottom

	All suspension parts are interchangeable, front and rear, left and right
Steering	Rack and pinion
Brakes	Servo assisted split circuit, drums all round, handbrake on rear drums only
Tyres	5.50″ × 16″

VOLKSWAGEN TRANSPORTER/CARAVELLE SYNCRO

The best selling Transporter and Caravelle vehicles, fitted with advanced FF Developments viscous coupled permanent 4 wheel drive system, further developed by Steyr-Daimler-Puch. The viscous coupling automatically senses when one axle is moving at a different speed from the other and moves torque to the axle that can use it. Thus the vehicle can be driven straight from dry tarmac to loose surfaces without the driver having to engage 4 wheel drive. The viscous coupling also protects the drive train components, by releasing any inter-axle 'wind-up'. Front and rear differential locks are fitted as standard in the UK.

Volkswagen Transporter Syncro

The new front drive unit, fits where the fuel tank used to be, so a new plastic moulded tank has been fitted over the gearbox, in front of the rear axle. The front suspension has been strengthened. The whole body has been raised by 20 mm and a crawler gear added. Various underbody skid plates have been added; all these additions adding 140 kg to the overall weight of the vehicle.

The end result is a vehicle like the Bedford CF, having a very good loose terrain performance, the only drawback is its limited ground clearance and ideas are already around for raising the vehicle still further off the ground. A four wheel drive Transporter/Caravelle Syncro has been a dream of many travellers around the world, the only fault with this one is its very high price.

Wheelbase	96.8"/2.46 metres	96.8"/2.46 metres	
Engines	Horizontally opposed 4 cylinder petrol	In line 4 cylinder diesel	
Displacement	1.913 litre	2.109 litre	1.558 litre
Bore	94 mm	94 mm	76.5 mm
Stroke	68.9 mm	76 mm	86.4 mm
Compression ratio	8.6:1	10.5:1	23.0:1
Maximum power	78 bhp @ 4600 rpm	112 bhp @ 4800 rpm	70 bhp @ 4500 rpm
Maximum torque	104 lb ft @ 2600 rpm	128 lb ft @ 2800 rpm	102 lb ft @ 2500 rpm
Transmission	4 speed gearbox plus crawler gear which is 60% lower than 1st gear & is the same ratio as reverse. Full time 4WD with viscous coupling, centre differential, diff. locks front & rear, engageable on the move, front diff. lock buton is protected to prevent its use by mistake on a hard surface.		
Suspension	Independent all round, double wishbones, coil springs and anti roll bars at front. Diagonal arms, mini block springs & struts at rear		
Steering	Rack & pinion		
Brakes	Discs at front, drums at rear, servo-assisted.		
Tyres	185 R 14 C or 205 R 14 C		
Turning circle	35.7 ft/10.9 metres		
Electrical	12 volt		
Battery	54 AH	54 AH	63 AH
Alternator	90 A	90 A	63 A
Payload		950 KG	

VOLKSWAGEN LT40

3.5 tonne high top van put together by N.A.M. of Newton Abbot using mostly Volkswagen/MAN components. A modified rear axle is used on the front and a Volkswagen 5 speed gearbox is mated to a Chrysler New Process transfer box. Tyre size is 7.50" × 16"

VOLVO 4140 1 tonne

Very good 1 tonne with 2.3 metre/91" wheelbase 6 cylinder petrol engine developing 125 bhp @ 4250 rpm, 4 forward, 1 reverse speed manual gearbox and 2 speed transfer box. Underslung semi-elliptic leaf springs at front and overslung semi-elliptic leaf springs at rear. Available also as Hard Top (C303) and 6 × 6. Payload 1 tonne/2200 lb. Now out of production but may be produced under licence in Britain to replace the now discontinued Land Rover 1 tonne, and using the 3.5 litre V8 ex Buick Rover engine.

Volvo L3314.

Appendix II

Vehicle Accessories — Spares and Outfitting

VEHICLE MANUFACTURERS AND DISTRIBUTORS UK

Africar, The Africar Centre, Caton
Road, Lancaster

Agrover, A.T. Vehicles
Holme Bank, New Hall Hey Road,
Rawtenstall, Rossendale, Lancs

Amphi-Ranger (UK) Ltd
325 Gladbeck Way, Enfield,
Middlesex

County Tractors Ltd
Fleet, Aldershot, Hants GU13 9RW

Dacia Duster, Dacia Concessionaires
Ltd
Dilton House, Station Road,
Westbury, Wiltshire BA13 4HT

Daihatsu (UK) Ltd
Poulton Close, Dover, Kent CT17
OHP

Eagle Cars Ltd
Unit K5, The Chantry Estate,
Chantry Lane, Storrington, West
Sussex RH20 4AD

Esarco Ltd
Tidworth Road, Ludgershall, Nr
Andover, Hants SP11 9QE

Isuzu (UK) Ltd
Ryder Street, West Bromwich, West
Midlands B70 OEJ

Jeep
Howes Motors 4WD Centre, Eaton
Bray, Dunstable, Bedfordshire

Lada Cars
Satrac (GB) Ltd, Carnaby Industrial
Estate, Nr Bridlington, N.
Humberside YO15 3QX

Land Rover Ltd
Lode Lane, Solihull B92 8NW

Mercedes-Benz (UK) Ltd
Tongwell, Milton Keynes, Bucks
MK15 8BA

Mitsubishi, Pajero/Shogun:
The Colt Car Co Ltd, Watermoor,
Cirencester, Glos. GL7 1LE

Nissan (UK) Ltd
Nissan House, Worthing, Sussex
BN13 3HD

The Panther Car Co Ltd
Brooklands Industrial Park, Byfleet,
Surrey KT13 OYU

Portaro Pampas:
Pampas Country Vehicles, 2 Water
Street, Ramsey, Isle of Man

Stonefield
Knight Road, Strood, Rochester,
Kent ME2 2AT

Subaru (UK) Ltd
Ryder Street, West Bromwich, West
　Midlands B70 OEJ

Suzuki GB Cars
Gatwick Road, Crawley, West Sussex
　RH10 2XF

Toyota (GB) Ltd
The Quadrangle, Redhill, Surrey
　RH1 1PX

UMM Alter II
SMC Engineering (Bristol) Ltd, SMC
　House, Bristol Road, Hambrook,
　Bristol BS16 1RY

Volkswagen/Audi
Yeomans Drive, Blakelands, Milton
　Keynes MK14 5AN

ALL TERRAIN VEHICLES

Crayford Special Equipment Co.
　Ltd.
High Street, Westerham, Kent
Argo ATVs

Croco UK Ltd
Archerfield Estate, Nr. Gullane, East
　Lothian

Travelong Ltd
Marlborough Road Industrial
　Estate, Wooton Bassett, Swindon,
　Wilts SN4 7EH
Argo, ATVs & Poncin V.P. ATVs

SPECIALIST CONVERSIONS

Aeroparts Engineering Co. Ltd
Commercial Road, Hereford
Hydraulic PTOs and winches

Broadfields
London Range Rover Centre,
　Standard House, Cockfosters
*Distributor for Vantagefield Conversions
　including 6WD*

Brockhouse Harvey Frost & Co Ltd
PO Box 16, Dunmow Road, Bishops
　Stortford, Herts

James Cuthbertson, Ltd
ML12 6DQ, Scotland

FF Developments
Siskin Drive, Coventry, West
　Midlands CV3 4FJ
*Full time 4WD with viscous coupling
　centre differential*

Gloster Saro Ltd
Hucclecote, Gloucester GL3 4AD

Glover Webb
Hamble Lane, Hamble, Hampshire

HCB Angus
Southampton Industrial Park,
　Testwood, Southampton SO4
　3SA

Herbert Lomas Ambulances Ltd
Radnor Park Industrial Estate,
　Congleton, Cheshire CW12 4XJ

Hotspur Cars Ltd
Yn Ysygergerwn Avenue,
　Aberdulais, Neath, West
　Glamorgan SA10 8HH

JNR Motors Group
Wainwright Street, Aston,
　Birmingham 6
6 wheel Range Rover conversion

Laird (Angelsey) Ltd
Beaumaris, Gwynedd LL58 8HY

Lowdham Ltd
Tel Nottingham 664112
Peugeot 4x4 conversion in the UK

Mountain Range Ltd
Unit A, Lancaster Fields, Crewe,
   Cheshire CW1 1FE

Overfinch Ltd
Index House, Ascot, Berks
Schuler Presses Range Rover versions with
   FF Developments 4WD automatic
   gearboxes etc

Pilcher Green Ltd
Victoria Gardens, Burgess Hill, West
   Sussex RH15 9NA

Quest 80s Ltd
Abbey Farm, Holton-cum-
   Beckering, Lincolnshire LN3
   5NG

Reynolds Boughton (Scottorn
   Division)
Bell Lane, Amersham Bucks HP6
   6PE

Short Bros & Harland Ltd
PO Box 241, Airport Road, Belfast
   BT3 9DZ

Simmonites
755 Thornton Road, Thornton,
   Bradford BD13 3NW

Sinpar
Rue D'Arsonval X1, 69680 Chassie
   9, France
4x4 conversions on Renault vehicles

Special Vehicle Operations at Land
   Rover Ltd

Specialist Vehicle Conversions
Carmichael, Gregorys Mill Street,
   Worcester

Stanford Scott
Sampson House, Sampson Road
   North, Birmingham B11 1BL

Townley Cross Country Vehicles
701 Sidcup Road, Eltham, London
   SE9
L/R, R/R conversions

Mr Voisin
RN91 – Livet, 38220 Livet Viziue,
   France
4x4 conversion to Citroen 2CV, Dyane,
   Ami 8

Wadham Stringer Ltd
All branches

Wood & Pickett
Victoria Road, South Ruislip,
   Middlesex HA4 OJU

ENGINE CONVERSIONS

Andover Vehicle Services
3 Princes Close, Walworth Industrial
   Estate, Andover, Hampshire
Turbocharged BMW M21 D 24WA 6
   cylinder diesel conversion to Range
   Rover

Cross Country Vehicles
Hailey, Nr Witney, Oxon
Conversions to Peugeot 2.5 diesel

4x4 Specalists
43 Iden Road, Frindstury, Rochester
   upon Medway, Kent ME2 4PP
Fit V8 in L/R and Mitsubishi 2.4 Turbo
   Diesel engines into L/R & R/R

Gretton Motors
Nr Cheltenham, Gloucestershire
L/R Isuzu diesel engine conversions

Landi-Hartog
New Bartholomew Street,
  Birmingham B5 QS
Liquid petroleum gas engine conversion

Motor & Diesel Engineering
Station Works, Old North Road,
  Bourn, Cambridge
Diesel engine conversion for L/R, R/R &
  Jeep

W.E. Phillips Engineering
Preens Eddy, Coalport, Telford,
  Salop TF8 7JG
BMC 2.2 & 2.5 litre diesel, Perkins
  4/203 3.3 litre diesel, Rover V8 petrol

Jake Wright
Hilltop, Burley-in-Wharfdale, Ilkley
  LS29 7JW
L/R, R/R service, engine conversions etc

TURBOCHARGING

Allard Turbochargers Ltd
Unit 3, Alton Road Industrial
  Estate, Ross-on-Wye,
  Herefordshire HR9 5NB
For Land Rover & Suzuki

BBW
Oxford Road, Brackley,
  Northamptonshire NN13 5DY
For Pajero/Shogun; Daihatsu & Isuzu

TB Turbos Ltd
Turbo House, Port Royal Avenue,
  Lune Industrial Estate, Lancaster
For Land Rover & Suzuki

Turbocharger Services Ltd
West Yorkshire
Tel 0924-401066
For Land Rover, Nissan Patrol, Toyota
  Land Cruiser & Jeep

Janspeed Ltd
Castle Road, Salisbury, Wiltshire
  SP1 3SQ
For Land Rover & Range Rover

ACCESSORIES, SPECIALIST SPARES & OUTFITTING

ASG
Manchester Street, Derby DE3 3GA
Manufacturers of tailor made accessories
  for L/R & R/R

Bearmach
Bearmach House, Mandy Road,
  Cardiff CF2 4XN
Nudge bars, light guards etc

PA Blanchard & Company
Foggathorpe, Selby, Yorks
Land Rover spares, Series I spares &
  military surplus

Broadfields
Standard House, Cockfosters

Brownchurch (Components) Ltd
308-310 Hare Row, Off Cambridge
  Heath Road, London E2 9DY
L/R, R/R safari preparation

Cotswold Motor Spares (4WD) Ltd
28a Dyer St, Cirencester, Gloucester
0285 68015
Nudge bars

John Craddock Ltd
70/76 North Street, Bridgetown,
  Cannock, Staffordshire
L/R's, parts, spares, accessories, books &
  manuals. World's largest stock of L/R
  Series I parts

263

Dixon Bate
Unit 45, First Avenue, Deeside
Industrial Park, Deeside, Clwyd
CH5 2LG
Towing couplings, nudge bars, light guards

Express Alloy Products
Unit 19, Atlantic Trading Estate,
Barry, South Glamorgan CF6 6RF
Aluminium nudge bars

Fawkham Forge
Fawkham Green, Dartford, Kent
L/R spares and gearbox specialists

4x4 Products
214/218 Pasture Road, Stapleford,
Nottingham NG9 8JB
Accessories for most 4WDs

Land Rover Parts and Equipment
Ltd
International House, PO Box 333,
Bickenhill Lane, Birmingham B37
7HA
L/R, R/R parts, main distributors

ICM Equipment
Unit C, Shay Lane, Longbridge PR3
3BT
L/R, R/R parts/accessories/winches

JW Designs
2 Beach Wood Cottages, Lansdown,
Bath
Soft-top hoods for L/R

LRP
Unit 11/13, Warwick Industrial
Estate, Budbrooke Road,
Warwick CV34 5XH
L/R, R/R body parts

Ian Middlehurst
27 Osborne Road, Finsbury Park,
London N4
L/R 101" 1 tonne

Mobility Accessories
Unit 6, Trafalgar Trading Estate,
Jeffreys Road, Enfield, Middlesex
EN3 7UA
Acessories for most 4WDs

N&S Motorcare Inc
Plusfour, 8 Downs Parade, Warren
Way, Woodingdean, East Sussex
Nudge bars

Overland Vehicles and Supplies Ltd
Aysgarth Road, Waterlooville,
Hampshire PO7 7UG
Overland conversion & supplies

PRB Services
275 Tong Road, Leeds LS12 4NQ
*L/R, R/R spares, service and 101"
1 tonne Land Rovers*

PWS Nudge Bars
74 Bracken Road, Ferndown,
Wimborne, Dorset

Quaife Power Systems
Botany Industrial Estate, Sovereign
Way, Tonbridge, Kent
L/R parts & Torque Biasing Differentials

Robby Tops
Cruwys Morchard, Tiverton, Devon
GRP light truck tops

Stever Parker
Unit 72, Healey Dell, Rochdale
*Components to fit Ford 2.5 & 3.0 litre
diesel engines into L/R*

Trailblazer
61 Nottingham Road,
Loughborough, Leics LE11 1ES
Accessories for most 4WDs

Upcountry Autoproducts (UK) Ltd
Norwich Road, Halesworth, Suffolk
IP19 8HX
Accessories for most 4x4s

Wadham Stringer (Guildford) Ltd
(Express Motor Factors)
Slyfield Green Industrial Estate,
Guildford, Surrey GU1 1RX
L/R, R/R spares

Wadham Stringer (Southampton)
Ltd
The Avenue, Southampton SO9 5SB
L/R, R/R spares

Weller Wheels Ltd
Wyverne House, Longfield Road,
North Farm Industrial Estate,
Tunbridge Wells, Kent TN2 3EY
Wheel manufacturers & sales

JEEP SPARES

Howes Motors
Eaton Bray, Dunstable,
Bedfordshire
UK largest distributor

Hyde Car Centre
Manchester

Metamet
20 Daleham Mews, London NW3

Mike Stallwood
RR Services, Bethersden, Ashford,
Kent

CARRY GRILLE-FOLD DOWN, "WORKING" NUDGE BAR

M&G Trading
PO Box 7, Shaftsbury, Dorset

WINCHES

Most electric winches have a horizontal drum, except for the Sidewinder which, like a Capstan winch has a vertical drum. Instruction in the correct and safe use of winches is advisable and the half day courses by David Bowyer or Bushey Hall are recommended.

Bushey Hall
Bushey Hall Drive, Watford, Herts
WD2 2 EP
Ramsey electric winches

FW Engineering
Abbey Rise, Whitchurch Road,
Tavistock, Devon
*Formerly Fairey winches – drum &
Capstan Winches. Electric or engine
driven plus vehicle ground anchors.*

Haltrac
119/123 Sandycombe Road,
Richmond, Surrey
*Superwinch, Tensen, Sepson & Rule
electric winches*

ICM 4x4 Equipment, Unit C, Shay
Lane Industrial Estate,
Longbridge PR3 3BT
*Superwinch, Rule, Tensen, Thomas &
Sidewinder electric winches*

Ryders (Winch division)
Knowsley Road, Bootle, Liverpool
L20 4NW
*Warn electric & hydraulic winches
Maxpull manual winches*

Skidmore 4WD Ltd
60 Sandwell Street, Walsall, West
Midlands WS1 3EB
Superwinch

The Winch Warehouse
Autosteer Controls, Moorfield
 Industrial Estate, Yeadon, Leeds
 LS19 7BN
*Rule, Sepson, Pierce, Tensen &
Sidewinder electric winches*

Tirfor
Halfway, Sheffield, Yorkshire SL9
 5GZ
Manual Jockey winches

HI-LIFT JACKS

Peter Walsh
St Ann's Cottage, Clifton,
 Deddington, Oxon

Also sold by:
All Wheel Drive Club
Brownchurch
John Craddock

TIS
88 Greenhill Road, Paisley

ADJUSTABLE TOWING PLATES, UNIVERSAL TOWING COUPLINGS

Dixon Bate
Unit 45, First Avenue, Deeside
 Industrial Estate, Deeside, Clwyd
 CH5 2LG

P.J. Lea Ltd
Lavenders Brow, Churchgate,
 Stockport SK1 1YW

LOCKING DIFFERENTIALS

Road Styles
22 Westerham Avenue, London N9
 9BU

AIR CONDITIONING

Salmon Diavia at
1)Whitney Road, Daneshill
 Industrial Park, Basingstoke,
 Hampshire RG24 ONS

2)Kingston House Estate,
 Portsmouth Road, Thames
 Ditton, Surrey KT7 OSE

3)Stonehouse Commercial Centre,
 Stonehouse, Gloucestershire
 GL10 3RH

SNOWCHAINS

Brindley Chains Ltd.
Tatton Court, Kingsland Grange,
 Warrington, Cheshire

Rud Chains Ltd
1-3 Belmont Road, Whitstable, Kent
 CT5 1QJ

Snowchains Ltd
West Kingsdown Industrial Estate,
 West Kingsdown, Sevenoaks, Kent
 TN15 6EL

BUSH REMOVERS

Bushwaka
The Meads, Llechwedd, Conwy,
 Gwynedd LL32 8DX
*Bushwaka Extractor for Land Rover
spring, chassis & rod bushes*

DEMOUNTABLE CARAVAN/AMBULANCE CONVERSION

Pod Ltd
Ashlyns Hall, Berkhampstead, Herts
*Suntrekker/Pod, demountable GRP
module suitable for caravan or
ambulance use*

REFRIGERATION etc

Avtech International Ltd
Avtech House, Hithercroft Road,
 Wallingford, Oxfordshire OX10
 9RQ
Swiftchill/film cooler/heater

AIR BAG JACKS

Rob Pendleton
St Johns West, Murchington,
 Chagford, Devon TQ13 8HJ

TYRES

Anthony Pollard & Ass. Ltd
Knights Close, Ball Hill, Newbury,
 Berks RG15 ONN
Armstrong Norseman

Avon Rubber plc
Abbey Mills, Bradford-on-Avon,
 Wiltshire

Dunlop SP Tyres Ltd
Fort Dunlop, Erdlington,
 Birmingham

Michelin Tyre plc
Davy House, Lyon Road, Harrow,
 Middlesex HA1 2DQ

Pirelli
Derby Road, Burton-on-Trent DE13
 OBH

Southampton Tyres
Unit 3, Torrington Avenue, Tilehill,
 Coventry CV4 9AP
BFGoodrich

Watling Tyres
West Street, Gravesend, Kent
BF Goodrich

John (Big Wheels) Fielden
Starhouse Farm, One House,
 Stowmarket
Kelly Tyres

Chessington Tyres
Bordon Trading Estate, Bordon,
 Hampshire GU35 9HH
BFGoodrich

Sinton Tyres
Broughton Manor Farm,
 Broughton, Milton Keynes MK10
 9AA
Mickey Thompson and General Crubber

Watling Tyre Service
1 Pelham Road, Gravesend, Kent
 DA11 OHR
Firestone

OFF-ROAD TUITION

Overlander Off-Road Centre
East Foldhay, Zeal Monachorum,
  Crediton, Devon
Off road driving and recovery tuition
4x4 Bookshop
T. Stake, Ground Anchors, Vehicle
  ground anchors

Ronnie Dale Off-Road Adventure
  School
Whiteburn, Abbeystreet, Duns,
  Berwickshire TD11 3RU

Rough Terrain Training
St Anne's Cottage, Clifton
  Deddington, Oxfordshire OX5
  4PA

Sweet Woods Off-Road Centre
Cowden, Edenbridge, Kent TN8
  7JN

UK SAFARIS

Bill Jones –Northern Safaris
121 Goodshaw Lane, Goodshaw,
  Rossendale, Lancs BB4 8DJ

Also various All Wheel Drive Club
  and Rover Owners Club meets.

4x4 BOOKS

Refer to:
Overlander 4x4 Bookshop
John Craddock Ltd

OFF-ROAD ACCESSORIES USA & CANADA

Acme
1600 W. Walnut PKWY, Compton
  CA 90220
Fibre glass body parts

Advance Adapters Inc
PO Box 247, Dept 230, Paso Robles
  CA 93446
Adapters & Winches

AJ's Sales & Manufacturing
RD3, Box 284A – B111, Jersey Shore
  PA 17740
Hard tops for Jeep

Arrow Tanks
1031 Smelcross Avenue, Unit B,
  Plancentia CA 92670
Auxiliary fuel tanks

ATV Mfg Inc
11108 NW 33rd Avenue, Vancouver
  WA 98685
TX2 Winches

Aussie Bull Bars Inc
3711 Briarpark Suite 300, Houston
  TX 77042
Bull Bars

John Baker Performance Products
  Inc
4304 Alger Street, Dept F, Los
  Angeles CA 90039
Mitsubishi parts

Bilstein
11760 Sorrento Valley Road, San
  Diego CA 92121
Shock Absorbers

Brown's Toyota City
7167 Ritchie HWY, Glenburnie MD
  21061

Buzz's Off-Road Centre
3611 NE 82nd Avenue, Portland,
  OR 97220
Toyota Parts

GI Carvin Industries
316 Millar Avenue, El Cajon CA
  92020
Accessories

Central 4 Wheel Drive Inc
3248 Auburn BLVD, Sacto CA
  95821
Accessories

Dick Cepek
9201 California Avenue, South Gate
  CA 90280
*Leading off-road specialists in tyres,
accessories and camping. For catalogue
1700 Kingsview Ave., Dept 4W,
Carson, CA 90746*

Clemson 4 Wheel Center Inc
HWY 123 West, PO Box 1006,
  Clemson SC 29633
Accessories

De Dona Enterprises
Tel 914-965-4444
All customising

Desert Rat Off-Road
3545 S. Richey, Dept F 10, Tucson
  AZ 85713
Accessories

Dirty Parts
PO Box 921, Santa Monica CA
  90406
Accessories

Downey
10001 SO. Pioneer BLVD, Dept FW,
  Sant Fe Springs CA 90670
Accessories for Toyota

Drivetrain Warehouse
Divn. of Four Wheel Parts
  Wholesalers, 1900 W. 135th
  Street, Gardenia CA 90249
Axle gears & locking differentials

Dyneer
Tractec Inc, PO Box 882-FW, 1145
  Stephens Drive, Warren MI 48090
*Detroit Locker positive track lock
differential*

Fly-n-Hi
3319 W. McDowell Road, Phoenix
  AZ 85009
Accessories

4 Way Suspension
5760 Chesapeake Court, San Diego
  CA 92123
Suspension & steering parts

4WD
44488 ST.RT.14, Columbiana OH
  44408
Accessories

Mr 4 Wheeler
908 31st Ave West, Tuscalousa AL
  35401
Accessories

Four Wheel Parts Wholesaler
1900 W. 135th Street, Gardenia CA
  90249

4 West
650 E. Valley Blvd, Colton CA 92324
Accessories

Galloway's 4WD Center
HWY 52 No Box 8, New London
  NC 28127

Heckethorn Off-Road Products Inc
PO box 526, Dyersburg TW 38024
Nitrogen gas shock absorbers

Helder Mfg Inc
11043 -C HWY, 70 Marysville CA
  95901
Packmule off-road trailers

Hicks 4x4 Specialists
1321 S. Garey, Pomona CA 91766
Axle parts & locking differentials

Hoaks 4WD
813 Hellam Str, Wrightsville PA
   17368

Jonah Springs Co
11203 Rush Street, El Monte CA
   91733
Leaf springs

J.T. Industries
8157 Wing Avenue, El Cajon CA
   92020
Body lift kits

K Bar S
3753 Scripps Way, Las Vegas,
   Nevada 89103
Bronco accessories

Kentrole Inc
PO Box 3304, Youngstown, OHIO
Stainless steel Jeep accessories

Malotte
PO Box 305, Lincoln CA 95648
Fibre glass bodies

Man-a-Fre Co
5076 Chesebro Road (4W), Agoura
   CA 91301
Toyota specialists

Master Rac
15391 Electronic Lane, Huntingdon
   Beach CA 92649
Locking stainless steel security boxes

Meadowlands 4WD
946 Patterson Avenue, East
   Rutherford NJ 07073

Mercury Tube Industries
3628 San Fernando Road, Dept FW,
   Glendale CA 91204
Roll bars, Nudge bars

Meridian Off-Road
655 New Castle Road, Butler PA
   16001

Mister 4x4
1800 West 3500 So, Salt Lake City
   UT 84119

National Spring Co Inc
630 Grand Avenue, Spring Valley
   CA 92077
Springs

National Tyre & Wheel
N. River Road, PO box 407,
   Wheeling W.V.A. 26003

North West Off-Road Specialists
1999 Iowa Street, Dept FW,
Bellingham WA 98226
Assessories for Toyota

Off Road Ltd
15551 E. 6th Avenue, Aurora CO
   80013

Off-Road Unlimited
Dept 4W, 821 W. Broadway Road,
   Mesa AZ 85210
Accessories

Off Road–West Inc
3340-C Sunrise BLVD, Rancho,
   Cordova CA 95670
Suspension parts

Pro Zap
14397 Cuesta Court, Sonora CA
   95370
Winch Bumpers

Quad Off-Road Centre
3330 Clinton Street, West Seneca NY
   14224

Ramsey Winch Co
PO Box 58150, Tulsa OK 74158

Rancho Suspension
PO Box 5429, 6925 Atlantic Avenue,
   Long Beach CA 90805
Shock Absorbers

Reider Racing (Gears)
Telephone 313-281-1677
Limited slip & locking differentials

Ring & Pinion Sales Inc
22250 Schmeman, Warren MI 48089
Differential locks & gears

Rocky Mountain Off-Road
  Warehouse
211 Horn Lane, West Monroc LA
  71291
Suspension & steering

Leon Rosser Jeep
1724 1st Avenue No, PO Box 709,
  Bessemer AL 35021
Accessories

Republic Off-Road Centre
617 S. Hayden, Tempe AZ 85281

Rough Country 4 Wheel Drive
1049 S. Cobb Drive, Marietta GA
  30060

Rugged Trail Suspensions
PO Box 260, MT. Braddock PA
  15465
Nitrogen gas shock absorbers

Shell Valley Fiber Glass
RT. 1 Box 69 FWA, Platte Center NE
  68653
Fiber glass panels

Sky Jacker Suspension Warehouse
PO Box 1878, Dept 379, West
  Monroe, Louisiana 71291
Suspension kits

Smittybilt
2112 N. Lee, Dept FW, South E1
  Monte CA 91733
Roll bars & bumpers

Speciality Parts
1617 Old County Road Suite 8,
  Belmont CA 94002
Jeep parts

Specter Off-Road
21723 Plummer Street, Chatsworth
  CA 91311
Toyota parts

Strictly Suzuki
828 W. Vermont, Unit D, Anaheim
  CA 92805
Suzuki accessories

Summit Racing Equipment
580 Kennedy Road, M4W 8711,
  Akron, Ohio
Accessories

Sunrise 4 Wheel Drive
11001 Rockville Road, Indianapolis
  IN 46234
Accessories

Superwinch
Dept FW, Conn Route 52 Exit 95,
  Putnam CT 06260

Surplus CITY
11796 Sheldon Street, Sunvalley CA
  91352
Jeep parts

Tensen Winches
304 S.E. 2nd, Portland OR 97214

Trailmaster
649 E. Chicago Road, Coldwater MI
  49036
Suspension kits

Tyres International
619 E. Tallmadge Avenue, Akron,
  Ohio, 44310
Tyres & accessories

Warn Industries
13270 SE Pheasant CT, Milwauke
  OR 97222
Winches

J.C. Whitney & Co
1917-19 Archer Avenue, PO Box
  8410, Chicago IL 60680
Accessories

Whitco
4401 Mark Dabling BLVD,
  Colorado Springs CO 80907
Jeep soft tops

Winchmaster
908 31st Avenue West, Tuscalooga
  AL 35401
Winch bumpers

271

Appendix III
Four Wheel Drive Clubs

All Wheel Drive Club   David Sarsfield – Hall, Flat 6, 85 Henley Road, Caversham, Reading RG4 ODS

MEMBER CLUBS OF THE ASSOCIATION OF ROVER CLUBS LTD

Reg. Office & Hon Sec of
The Association of Rover Clubs Ltd
G.R. Day, 10 Highfield Road,
    Bagslate, Rochdale, Lancs OL11
    5RZ
Tel: (0706) 30200

Anglian Rover Owners Club Ltd
Andrew J. Flanders, 3 Mortimer
    Hill, Tring, Herts HP23 5JT
Tel: (044282) 2565

Breckland Land Rover Club Ltd
Mike Plummer, 39 Northfields,
    North Parr, Norwich, Norfolk
Tel: (0603) 57841

Cornwall & Devon Land Rover Club
Mrs Marion Rolstone, 7 The Close,
    Fairmead Mews, Saltash,
    Cornwall PL12 4SJ
Tel: (075 55) 6726

Cumbrian Land Rover Club
Peter Anstiss, 4 Bluecoat Crescent,
    Newton-with-Scales, Preston,
    Lancs PR4 3TJ
Tel: (0772) 685735

Essex Land Rover Club
Dave Bygrave, The Knoll, Bygrave
    Road, Ashwell, Nr Baldock, Herts
    SG7 5RH
Tel: (046274) 2418

Hants & Berks Rover Owners
Andy J. Smith, 29 Silverdale Road,
    Tadley, Nr Basingstoke, Hants
    RG26 6JL
Tel: (07356) 3395

Lancashire & Cheshire Rover
    Owners Club
Ian Foster, 7 Slimbridge Close,
    Redbridge Park,
Breightmet, Bolton,
Lancs BL2 5NT
Tel: (0204) 396449

Land Rover Register (1947-1951)
Mrs Sally Cooknell, Langford
    Cottage, School Lane, Ladbroke,
    Leamington Spa, Warwickshire
    CV33 OBX
Tel: (092681) 2101

The Land Rover Safari Owners Club
Andy Grew, 7 George Street,
    Wordsley, Stourbridge, West
    Midlands DY8 5YN

Land Rover Series One Club
David Bowyer, East Foldhay, Zeal
  Monachorum, Crediton, Devon
  EX17 6DH
Tel: (036 33) 666 – Business hours
  only please

Land Rover Series Two Club
Ross Floyd, 2 Brockley End
  Cottages, Cleeve, Avon BS19 4PP
Tel: (027 583) 3772

Leicestershire Land Rover Club Ltd
Christine Hardy, Fearn House, 1
  Guildford Drive, Wigston Fields,
  Leics. LE8 1HG

Lincolnshire Land Rover Club
Rick Wells, Shepherds Hut,
  Horkstow, Barton-on-Humber,
  South Humberside
Tel: (065 261) 603

Midland Rover Owners Club
Derek Spooner, Bank Cottage,
  Abbots Moreton, Worcester
  WR7 4NA   Tel: (0386) 792767

North Eastern Rover Owners Club
George Atkinson, 9 South Drive,
  Cleadon Village, Nr. Sunderland,
  Tyne & Wear SR6 7SX
Tel: (091 436) 2083

North Wales Land Rover Club
Mrs Pauline Morris, The Filling
  Station, Pentrefoelas Road,
  Bylchau, Denbigh, Clwyd, N.
  Wales LL16 5LS
Tel: (074 570) 237

Peak & Dukeries Land Rover Club
Mrs Janet Williams, 10 Eckington
  Road, Beighton, Sheffield
  S19 6EQ   Tel: (0742) 481066

Pennine Land Rover Club
Mrs Ann Whittaker, 121 Brown
  Lodge Drive,
Smithy Bridge, Littleborough, Lancs
  OL15 OET
Tel: (0706) 78475

Range Rover Register
Chris Tomley, Cwm Cocken,
  Bettius, Newtown, Powys SY16
  3LQ
Tel: (0686) 87430

Red Rose Land Rover Club
John Waltho, 8 Glenmore, Clayton-
  le-Woods, Chorley, Lancs PR6
  7TA
Tel: (0772) 37157

Scottish Land Rover Owners Club
Kenneth Deas, 10 Silverburn Drive,
  Peniculic, Midlothian EH26 9AQ
Tel: (0968) 76103

Somerset & Wiltshire Rover Owners
  Club
Michael Hall, Nightingale Farm,
  Broome, Swindon, Wiltshire SN3
  1NA
Tel: (0793) 34372

Southern Rover Owners Club
Geoff Edwards, 3 Eton Close,
  Walderslade, Chatham, Kent
  ME5 9AT
Tel: (0634) 684530

Staffordshire & Shropshire Land
  Rover Club
Dennis L. Jones, 3 Manorford
  Avenue, West Bromwich, West
  Midlands B71 3QJ
Tel: (021 583) 5892

The Wye & Welsh Rover Owners
  Club
P. Thomas, 1 Bracelands Drive,
  Christchurch, Coleford, Glos
Tel: (0594) 33289

Yorkshire Rover Owners Club
Mrs Sue Whiteley, 10 Thorncliffe,
  Kirkburton, Huddersfield HD8
  OUG
Tel: (0484) 603564

ASSOCIATION OF ROVER CLUBS OVERSEAS

Liaison Officer (UK contact for
Overseas Rover Clubs)
Bill King, 223 Chartridge Lane,
Chesham, Bucks HP5 2SF
Tel: (0494) 783809

OTHER FOUR WHEEL DRIVE CLUBS

BRITISH ISLES
The Austin Gipsy Register, Mike
  Gilbert, 8 Thoresby Court, Stem
  Lane, New Milton, Hants BH25
  5UJ
Tel: (0425) 618793

Buchan Off-Road Drivers Club
Eddie McConochie, 15 Slains
  Crescent, Cruden Bay, Peterhead,
  Aberdeenshire
Tel: (0779) 813200

The Deeside Four Wheel Drive Club
Lorraine Allan, c/o Banchory
  Lodge Hotel, Banchory,
  Kincardineshire AB3 3HS
Tel: (03302) 2625

The East Devon Land Rover Club
Sue Nancekivell, Willow Lodge,
  Behemsbury, Devon
Tel: (040484) 434

Midland Off-Road Club
Charles Deverill, 101 Westley Road,
  Acocks Green, Birmingham B27
  7UW

The Military Vehicle Conservation
  Group
Nigel Godfrey, 8 Selbourne Close,
  Blackwater, Camberley, Surrey
Tel: (0252) 870215

Northern Off Road Club
Margaret Marlow, 2 Moor View,
  Bingley Road, Menston, Nr
  Ilkley, W. Yorks LS29 6BD

Short Course Off-Road Racing
Andrew Cooke, SCORR, 10 Rawling
  Road, Bearwood, Warley, West
  Midlands B67 5AA
Tel: 021 558 9135

Southern Counties Off-Roaders
Penny Baker, 21 Broadhurst
  Avenue, Ensbury Park,
  Bournemouth, Dorset BH10 6JW
Tel: (0202) 514111

The Subaru Owners Club
Steve Eardley, Club Subaru, Subaru
  (UK) Ltd, Ryder Street, West
  Bromwich, W. Midlands B70 0EJ
Tel: 021 557 6200

Suffolk 4 Wheel Drive Club
Fred Cutler, Welwyn, Twites Corner,
  Gt. Saxham, Bury St Edmunds,
  Suffolk
Tel: (0284) 810167

The Suzuki Rhino Club
Ian Catford, Suzuki Club, Suzuki
  GB (Cars) Ltd, 46-62 Gatwick
  Road, Crawley West Sussex
  RH10 2XF   Tel: (0293) 518000

THE REST OF EUROPE
Le Hors Macadam Club
116 Rue des Praires, 62100 Calais,
  France

Club 4x4 Cote D'Azur
4 Avenue Ste- Marguerite, 06000
  Nice, France

IDF 4x4 Club
44 Rue de la Convention, 75015
  Paris, France

Club Auto Verte (Green Car)
52 Rue Guynemer, 94200
  Courbevoie, Inquiries: P.
  Zaniroli
Tel: 333.03.94 Office

Scandinavian Off-Roaders
  (Denmark)
Postbox 523, DK-2200,
  Kopenhavn, Denmark

Norwegian Land-Rover Club
Erik Winther-Sørensen,
  Anerudskogen 95, N 1370, Asker,
  Norway

Scandinavian Off-Roaders (Sweden)
Sverige Industrivagen 23, S-433-61
  Partille, Sweden

Danish Land Rover Club
Trjelsdalvej 14, Marup, 4340,
  Tollose, Denmark

German Land Rover Club
c/o Walter Eggers, Harburger
  Scholbstrasse 36A, 2100
  Hamburg, West Germany

Swiss Rover Owners Club
URS Halter, Kirchstrass 4, 9532
  Recken Bach, Switzerland

USA

Adventure Trip Guide
Adventure Guides Inc, 36 E. 57th
  Street NY 10022

Land-Rover Owners Association
  USA
Steve Hill, P.O. Box 162201
  Sacramento CA 95816

National Four Wheel Drive Assn.
PO Box 386, Rosemead CA 91770

West Coast Land Rover Owners
  Group
7440 Amarillo Road, Dublin,
  California 94566

CANADA

Association of Land Rover Owners
  in Canada
1-95 Fourth Avenue, Ottawa,
  Ontario K1S 2L1 Canada

Index

Index

279